Take Your Wings and Fly

A Journey Through a Private Pilot's Licence

First Edition 2013

Cover design by John Wright

ISBN 978-0-9567187-5-4

Airport maps are not meant for real life navigational purposes.

© **Jason Smart**

British Library Cataloguing-in-Publication Data

A catalogue record for this book is available from the British Library.

Published by Destinworld Publishing Ltd.

www.destinworld.com

For Angela

Contents

Foreword

This tale is for anyone interested in learning to fly. It is also for anyone simply curious to know what is involved in becoming a pilot. However, it is *not* a training manual for prospective students and neither is it a textbook detailing the technical aspects of learning to fly.

What it does offer, I hope, is an insight into the personal achievements that training to be a pilot makes possible. Learning to fly isn't fun and frolics all the way. It's sometimes painful, both mentally and physically. Indeed, after some lessons I felt so exhausted that I wished I'd never started in the first place. However, there was also the jubilation and exhilaration, and those feelings greatly outweighed the negatives. For instance, the first solo flight was something truly amazing. The fact most people will never do anything like it made it even more special.

Learning to fly *is* a mighty challenge, but it is also an achievable challenge. In fact, after reading about my progress you might think, 'if he can do it, then there's hope for us all' and you would be right.

I've written the book in a similar style to a diary. This is intentional. You will find an account of every day I had a flying lesson, even if I didn't actually take to the air. This was one way of getting across my frustration with the British weather. Cold fronts, drizzle and haze are, in my opinion, the greatest hurdles to overcome when doing a UK flying course; they will scupper you at every turn.

Towards the end of the book, you'll come across my *My 8-Point Plan of Action for a Pre-PPL Pilot*. This is a rough guide of steps to take before taxiing along the runway to becoming a Private Pilot's Licence (PPL) pilot. And then, at the very back, you'll find a simple glossary of aviation acronyms. Acronyms are a way of life in aviation and, unfortunately, there is no way of avoiding them.

Enjoy.

Jason Smart

Beginnings

'Are you sure this thing can fly?'

–Jason Smart (Prospective PPL Student)

I'd always wondered what it would be like to fly in a small aircraft, so there I was at the airfield about to go up in a microlight for the first time in my life. Lining up for take-off, I was apprehensive. I wondered how long it would take before my fear of heights would leave me a weeping and gibbering mess. Not long I reckoned.

"Roy," I asked the pilot sitting in front of me. "Where's my parachute?"

"Parachute!" he laughed over the intercom thing. "Don't be daft! A parachute would be useless. You'd be in a field before it even opened."

The gibbering had begun.

Fascination

I'd been fascinated with aeroplanes from a young age and it all started with my first flight in a real plane.

I was 10 and my family were flying to Australia because of my Dad's job. The rush of adrenalin as the engines screamed out just before take-off was phenomenal. As we rocketed down the runway, I thought it couldn't get any better. Flying had hooked me from that moment.

I drew aeroplanes, read about them, and looked skywards whenever I heard the drone of one overhead. Then came the joy of Airfix model kits. By my early teens I knew I wanted to be a pilot; I just didn't know how I was going to achieve this goal.

Then things changed: aged 15, thoughts of becoming a pilot started slipping from my mind. I had a new and much more exciting hobby to think about — being in a rock band was all that mattered now. Girls love rock stars and rock stars play guitars. Thus I became embroiled in the world of amateur rock 'n' roll. This fixation lasted for years, until we recorded a CD that nobody ever bought. And then I went to university.

During my degree in civil engineering, thoughts of aviation rarely crossed my mind and, three years later, with a newly minted degree in my hands, I considered my options. Flying didn't even enter the equation. Electing to leave the gritty side of engineering alone, I did a further qualification enabling me to teach primary school children. Twelve months later, I was a fully qualified educator. And there I remained for the next few years.

Then something strange happened. In my thirties, thoughts that had remained dormant suddenly flickered back into life. I once again wanted to be a pilot but there was one thing bothering me about learning to fly: I was scared of heights. I couldn't look over the side of a bridge without feeling slightly nauseous. Hell would freeze over before I'd even contemplate doing a bungee jump or going up in a hot air balloon. I even had difficulty climbing a ladder. How would I cope being cooped up inside a small aircraft?

Microlight Flight of Terror

I didn't have long to wait to find out. Roy Barber, a friend from the local pub, had recently gained his licence to fly a microlight. He asked if I wanted to go up in it to get some firsthand experience of flying in a small aircraft. I foolishly agreed to this folly. So on a gloriously sunny and windless day in February Roy and I drove over to Barton Aerodrome near Manchester. At the airfield, Roy led us into a hangar, pointing at the machine that would be taking us into the sky.

It was tiny. I couldn't believe its miniscule size. The main section, which resembled a toboggan with a propeller attached to the back, had a fabric wing hoisted above and a set of wheels dangling below. When I peered inside the front of the toboggan I couldn't see any control column or yoke. I asked Roy how it could be steered in the air.

"See this here?" he said, pointing to a horizontal metal bar that dangled below the wing. "This steers it. Watch." He pushed the metal bar backwards and forwards. The wing thing moved as he did so. "I'll show you how it works when we go up. You can have a go if you like."

Death Grip

After donning some impressive-looking overalls, he handed me a headset and told me to put a crash helmet on over it. Next Roy passed me some heavy-duty gloves to protect my hands from the cold temperatures up in the air.

I looked nervously at my seating arrangements for the flight and noticed to my dismay that there were no comfy cushions or even a reclining seat. I couldn't locate the button that would summon a pretty flight attendant, and I was positive there would be no in-flight entertainment. In fact, the seating consisted only of two small seats — one behind the other. Even worse, I grimly noticed, was that there were no sides to speak of. I might as well be strapped to a flying go-kart.

Nonetheless, I had to be brave and so manfully climbed into the craft, managing to hide my tears and nervous twitch. Roy strapped me in with a single safety belt and then squeezed into his forward position. I felt about as safe as a man wearing a metal suit standing on a skyscraper during a lightning storm. After making sure we could hear each other via the headsets, Roy started the engine.

Feeling vibrations all around, I placed my hands onto the small metal edge that ran around the side of the microlight: the only thing separating me from the elements outside. A few seconds later, we were off, trundling along the grass. My death grip tightened.

Up We Go

Once we'd lined up for departure, Roy spoke to somebody on the radio and then told me to hang on tightly. With the throttle pushed to maximum, off we sped.

As we bumped along the uneven surface of the grass strip I increased my grip on the metal edge even further. Less than 10 seconds later we were airborne and I opened my eyes for the first time and peered down over the abyss by my side. This proved to be a mistake. I was immediately scared witless. Clinging on for dear life, I began a fresh bout of gibbering.

At 500 ft or so I felt an awful stab of vertigo. With the wind rushing noisily past my face, I focussed my gaze on the back of Roy's helmet but it was no good, I felt like I was going to pass out.

"How are you doing back there?" asked Roy.

Coming clean, I told Roy I was scared stiff. I had visions of me toppling over the side at any moment.

"I see. Do you want to go back?"

"Yes please."

After turning around, which involved a terrifying bank that made me wish I was blind, Roy spoke to someone on the radio again and we headed back towards Barton. On final approach, I shut my eyes and gritted my chattering teeth. A minute later we were down, taxiing back to the parking area.

Froth

Once I'd stopped shaking and frothing at the mouth, I began to think that learning to fly in a small aircraft was not such a good idea after all. If I was this scared going up in a slow-moving microlight, imagine what it would be like in a faster Cessna 152.

"How was it?" a voice said.

I turned to see another microlight friend of Roy's. He and I had been chatting before I'd set off on the nightmare journey. He looked concerned.

"It was okay," I said, then grinned. "Actually, it was hellish. I've never been so scared in all my life."

He laughed. "So does that mean no flying lessons?"

I shrugged. "I'll have to think about it."

And that's what I did. A few weeks later, after a bit of rest and recovery, I made up my mind. I rang Barton Aerodrome asking about the availability of trial flights (or 'introductory flights' as they are sometimes called) in a Cessna. I just hoped that being inside an aeroplane, rather than strapped onto it, would mean the difference between fear and enjoyment.

"We've got a spare slot next Wednesday," said a cheerful man on the other end of the phone. "How does that sound?"

"That sounds... great." My stomach coiled in apprehension.

When I enquired about appropriate clothing or footwear to wear, I was instructed to don something comfortable and casual. He added that I wouldn't need flying goggles but if I wanted to wax my moustache out at the ends, then that would be fine. I hung up, wondering what I'd just done.

Trial Flight

On a lovely spring day I headed over to Barton Aerodrome for a one-hour flight in a small Cessna. When I arrived I entered a busy room full of people hanging around. I sheepishly introduced myself at the desk and a man handed me a form to fill out.

"Your instructor will be here shortly," the man said. "Just have a seat and he'll shout out your name when he arrives."

I sat down and surveyed my surroundings. I noticed lots of charts and maps on the walls. I didn't understand what they represented, so instead looked at my fellow companions. To me, none seemed nervous at all. Even a woman of about 70, sitting nearby, seemed full of rapture and joy. I wondered if I was the only one feeling nervous. It certainly seemed that way to me.

Photo © Sue Hill

Just then a burly man in his early thirties entered the room. In his hands he carried an aviation chart and a couple of headsets. With his leather jacket and handsome features he appeared to be a throwback from World War II. I secretly hoped he wasn't my instructor.

"Mrs Haverstock!" he announced with a theatrical flourish. "Come on down!"

Quick as a flash, the sprightly-limbed pensioner jumped up and introduced herself. Thirty seconds later the pilot led her outside much to everyone's amusement. It was at that point that I began harbouring thoughts of cancelling my flight. I seemed to be the only one not smiling. Before I could take any action, another instructor entered the room and shouted my name. I gingerly got up. He passed me a headset and told me to follow him outside. I did so like a man condemned.

Cessna 152s are Small

As we wandered towards the Cessna 152, a small two-seater aircraft, Jake told me he was a part-time instructor who worked at a nearby prison. Because he loved flying so much he'd gained his commercial licence enabling him to instruct others. When he told me about some memorable flying trips he'd been on, my nerves began to settle somewhat.

"We'll have to fuel it up," he said, after looking in some holes on top of the wings. "The last guy must have cruised in on vapour." He then proceeded to cough and splutter in the manner of an aeroplane losing its engine due to fuel exhaustion. Before I could make my escape, Jake asked me to help push the aircraft to some nearby pumps. As I did I was surprised to find that the plane was very light. In fact, it seemed positively flimsy.

After fuelling up, Jake told me to climb into the left side of the plane and put on my headset. This wasn't as easy as it sounded. Contorting myself into a painful position, I put a shoe on a footplate underneath the wing strut and somehow managed to clamber into the cramped cockpit without snapping anything. Finally, I sat back, taking stock of my situation. There I was, sitting inside a tiny plane, about to go up in the air to make an important decision. At the end of the flight, I'd have to decide whether learning to fly was something I could actually do.

While waiting for Jake to finish checking things outside, I stared at the various instruments on the panel ahead of me. I could immediately recognise most of the obvious ones such as the *altimeter* and *airspeed indicator*, which were just like the ones on my flight simulator. I also recognised the *attitude indicator* (or *artificial horizon*) and *heading indicator*. But other instruments and dials were less familiar to me, such as the radio panel — which looked like nothing I'd seen before.

Eventually Jake climbed into the right-hand side of the cockpit and began faffing with his seat belt. We were both pressed shoulder to shoulder and knee to knee. I couldn't believe how cramped it was. My legs were bent upwards in a space less than half that of the average family car.

Jake then briefed me on the use of the safety and emergency equipment carried, which amounted to a shoulder and waist harness and a strategically placed fire extinguisher. Next, he told me he'd be doing the necessary internal checks before getting us airborne. Then the engine started.

I couldn't believe the racket and vibrations. It felt like the plane was about to fall to bits. Jake reached over and plugged my headset in which made things a lot quieter.

"Can you hear me okay?" he asked as he fiddled with some switches on the radio panel.

"Loud and clear," I answered, wanting to impress him with my knowledge of aviation lingo. Jake nodded and prodded a few more knobs and buttons. I wondered what they all did. Just then, he said something incomprehensible over the radio and we started moving across the grass.

When we were ready for take-off I looked at the grass runway ahead — the very same one I'd taken off from in the microlight flight of terror. It looked ominous and green. Next to me, Jake was saying something over the radio and then we were off. I felt a similar rush of adrenalin as when taking off in an airliner — back pressed into my seat — and within seconds we were airborne. I tentatively looked out of the side window.

It looked amazing. I could see houses and roads getting smaller and smaller and I felt great. It was so different from the microlight. It felt safe for one thing. As we climbed higher I relaxed and breathed easily. Maybe I can do this, I thought.

Your Control!

Once we were clear of Manchester Airport's low-lying Class A airspace, Jake handed control over to me. He told me to put my left hand onto the yoke to keep the plane steady. "Try to keep the altitude at 2,500 ft," he said. "And keep on this heading if you can."

I nodded unable to believe I was controlling a plane. My eyes flickered to the altimeter in a futile attempt to stay on 2,500 ft but it was impossible. We were going up and down like a rollercoaster. Jake took over and levelled us back off at 2,500 ft. It took him only a few seconds.

I looked at him incredulously. "How did you do that so easily?"

Jake smiled. "It just takes practice."

He handed me back the controls and told me to look outside. "Try to keep us straight and level by using the horizon."

We were flying over patchwork fields of many colours and in the distance was the sea.

"Now I want you to turn to a heading of 280°," Jake said.

I looked at the heading indicator and began a turn. It was nothing like driving a car I quickly realised, because as soon as the turn began we started to drop.

"Don't worry," prompted Jake. "Just pull back on the yoke a little bit."

I did just that as the compass arc swivelled around. When it was at about 280° I tried to straighten us up but ended up going right past where I was supposed to be heading. I quickly steered back the other way and eventually managed to get us pointing more or less the right way.

"Not bad," said the instructor. "For a first attempt."

I asked Jake if he could demonstrate some steep turns for me. I'd read somewhere that they could be quite nerve-racking — a *real* test of my mettle. He agreed and quickly banked the aircraft 45° to the left. Almost immediately I could feel the pull of the turn and cautiously peered though the side window, expecting my panic to return, but it didn't: I was still having fun!

Landing

When it was time to head back to Barton, Jake allowed me to have another go at flying but then took over as we approached the airfield. "Can you see the airfield yet?" he asked a few minutes later.

I looked up and down as well as from side to side, but couldn't see any sign of an airport anywhere. Jake laughed and told me to look directly ahead. And of course, there it was, in front, merging in with the surrounding landscape.

With the grass runway looming up on our right-hand side, Jake started talking again over the radio. "Golf-India Mike is downwind for zero niner right."

What that meant I had no idea and so I simply watched and waited with trepidation. Then Jake pulled out a knob located on the cockpit panel and we began to go down. I saw him reach towards another lever and heard a whirring noise coming from somewhere behind us. "That's just the flaps going down, Jason. They help to reduce airspeed."

As we slowed down and got lower still, it seemed that my stomach was still 100 ft above us, so I gripped my chair as the instructor began saying strange things aloud to himself.

"Teas and Peas okay. Mix full. Heat off."

I wondered what he was referring to but having no clue I merely watched and waited as the runway got closer and closer.

"Golf-India Mike is finals for zero niner right," the instructor uttered over the radio.

There was a garbled response from Barton Tower. I couldn't understand a word of it. Luckily, Jake did though. "Wilco," he answered, using the radio communications phrase *wilco* for "will comply".

A few minutes later he made a soft landing on the grass runway and I felt a wave of euphoria wash over me. I had loved the flight we'd just taken. I reckoned I could actually learn to fly. As we taxied back to park the plane, I asked Jake if he thought I had what it took to be a flying student.

He told me that he couldn't see any reason why not, adding I'd done very well. After shaking his hand I thanked him and went home in a triumphant mood. I could now go ahead and do a Private Pilot's Licence (PPL). But before that there were I few things I needed to do. The first was the medical.

The Aviation Medical

After some research, I found out that to fly solo, I'd need to have either a Class 1 or Class 2 medical certificate. I'd need a Class 1 if I wanted to become a commercial pilot (and this is the medical examination all airline pilots have to pass regularly). The Class 2 medical is for private pilots and is less stringent and cheaper than the Class 1. Also, I could visit a relatively local aviation doctor to be examined. I booked my place and went for it.

At that time I was a smoker and also liked a few beers, so I was worried I might fail the medical. In addition, I'd convinced myself that my eyesight was poor. Although I didn't wear glasses, I felt as if I had been straining them of late. Pondering these worrying notions I set off.

Upon arrival, I found myself not to be at a medical establishment but a residential house. Confused, I rang the bell and very quickly a white-haired gentleman greeted me. He introduced himself and led me into his home.

"I've got one room converted into a medical office," he told me as we climbed some stairs. "And this shouldn't take more than an hour."

After I'd filled out a questionnaire the medical began. All sorts of things were tested and probed — including my hearing, eyesight, reflexes, sense of balance, lung capacity and blood pressure. The good doctor then checked my height and weight, and took samples of my blood and urine. He also made me look through a book full of different coloured dots to establish whether I am colour-blind. I'm not.

Another strange test involved shutting my eyes, putting a finger into my ear and *then* standing on one leg! I honestly believed it had to be a joke, but he *actually* wanted me to do it. It was to ascertain that my inner ear was in good working order (the inner ear provides a sense of balance.) Later, I had to lie down and remove nearly all my clothes. Was it the dreaded beer belly investigation? Thankfully no, it was to check my spine and feet.

The doctor also attached a lot of wires and pads all over my chest and connected them to a contraption nearby. It was an ECG machine, which produced a zigzag graph of the condition of my heart. When the printing had finished, the doctor picked it up.

"Okay, that's everything," he said, studying the reading. "All I've got to do now is send these results off to hospital, but as far as I can tell, they look fine. You're a healthy specimen."

I had provisionally passed my medical! After I'd paid my bill of £160, I went home feeling elated.

A few weeks later, an envelope arrived from the Civil Aviation Authority (CAA) containing my Class 2 medical details. The ECG readings *had* been fine. With the certificate in my hand, I'd passed another hurdle on my way to becoming a pilot. The next decision was when to start my training.

Study, Study, Study

With no spare cash available I decided to defer my training for a year. In the meantime I would give up smoking and begin studying. With seven exams to pass there would be plenty of reading to do. Luckily I didn't have to buy any of the study books because Roy had done the same exams for his microlight training and offered to lend them to me. The series covered the following subjects:

Flight Training *(How to fly the plane.)*
Air Law & Meteorology *(How to not end up in court and about the weather)*
Navigation *(How to know where you're going, and more importantly, how to get there!)*
The Aeroplane Technical *(How the aircraft works. My least favourite!)*
Human Factors *(How the body and mind work — the easiest!)*
Communications/Radiotelephony *(Learning how to speak gobbledygook)*

There was another piece of equipment I bought that would help me with my navigation studying. It was a flight computer (often called a whiz wheel), which was basically a circular slide rule. It had two sides: a wind side (to work out wind speed and headings) and a calculation side (to work out time and distance problems). I could have bought an electronic version but I'd read somewhere that instructors usually preferred the metal slide rule versions. And anyway, my aluminium one would never need any batteries.

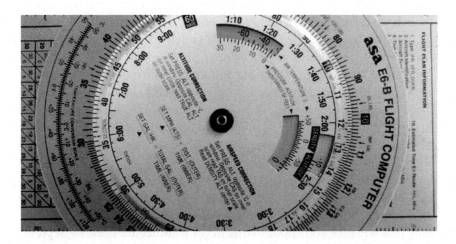

I also bought a 1:500,000 aviation chart of Northern England and Ireland and soon become enthralled with everything on it. Airspace boundaries, tall masts, danger areas and much more besides would captivate me every time I looked at it. Just by buying the chart, I actually felt as if I'd stepped onto the road to becoming a pilot. But the next decision was perhaps the biggest one of all: where to do my training.

Choosing a Flying School

A few months after my medical, I looked at a number of flying schools within travelling distance from my hometown of Bradford, West Yorkshire. There were a few available but I eventually narrowed them down to just one, mainly because it was only 20 minutes away from my house.

Leeds Bradford Airport, a mid-sized regional airport, caters for both light aircraft and commercial traffic. It has a flying school based there, which I decided to visit. It would give me a chance to suss the place out properly.

Upon arrival I met an instructor. He seemed nice enough and told me the school's training aircraft consisted mainly of Cessna 152s — the same type of plane I'd flown during my trial flight. He took me out to the airport to see them.

As we wandered around one, the instructor explained some of the course details and mentioned that Leeds was a good airport to train in if I was harbouring any thoughts of becoming a commercial pilot.

"Leeds is great for the radio," he explained. "You'll be speaking with Air Traffic Control and airline pilots from day one. It will set you in good stead for any future training you might do."

At home I decided that Leeds would be a good choice. I grew excited that I'd made a decision about where to learn to fly. Striking while the iron was hot, I rang the flying school and booked myself a place on their 45-hour Private Pilot's Licence course. They seemed delighted that I'd chosen them.

"So that's all arranged then," said Dylan Dowd, the Operations Manager of the flying school. "You're booked in for two lessons every day during your six-week holiday. Only your weekends will be free. Hopefully that will give you enough time to get your licence done by September, assuming the weather plays ball. In the meantime do some studying and we'll see you in a couple of months."

I put the phone down and gulped. It was official: I was going to have flying lessons! My mind reeled at the possibilities of this. I might even be able to call myself a pilot in as little as four months! That somehow didn't seem possible.

A day later, I got hold of a multi-band radio that could in the right conditions pick up radio chatter between Leeds air traffic controllers and the various pilots flying in the area. Every so often I'd listen in to their conversations in utter confusion, wondering what they were on about.

In the meantime, I continued teaching my class of ten-year-olds, all the time thinking of my impending first lesson at the controls of an aeroplane.

Battle with the Weather

'This July has had the most rain since records began!'

-TV Weather Reporter

Day 1. Monday 22 July

The alarm went off at 9 am. As I pulled the curtains apart my heart fell with a thump. It was overcast and windy. Topping that, it was raining. Peering dejectedly into the murk I heard the wind. It sounded like a typhoon in its early stages of development. Things did not bode well for my first flying lesson.

Closing the curtains, I went downstairs and felt the first stirrings of anger. This was an emotion I was to become very familiar with over the coming months.

I rang the flying school and Dylan Dowd answered. He agreed with my predictions about the weather, telling me he doubted any flying would be going on. But he did suggest I head over to the airport so I could meet the instructors.

I surveyed the home of the flying school again. It was a large cabin about a mile away from the airport with a lot of old bangers parked outside. Later I would learn that these cars belong to the flying instructors, the only set of wheels they could afford on the pittance they are paid.

Entering the cabin I said hello to Dylan who then introduced me to an instructor called John Denson. John's father was the owner of the flying school.

John was about 25 and had a ponytail that made him look like a student. Sitting down, he told me about the peculiarities of the weather around Leeds Bradford Airport.

"We're basically on a big hill and get some interesting wind patterns which will mean you'll get a lot of practice doing crosswind landings."

Ignoring how scary that sounded, I asked the instructor whether students ever became tired with lessons. It was something I was worried about.

John thought for a moment. "Not very often. But if they do it's usually in the circuit bashing stage of the course. That's probably where most frustration can occur."

I nodded. Circuit bashing is where a student pilot learns how to land. They take off, circle the runway and land, then repeat the whole process over and over again.

After about 20 minutes of chatting, John listened to the latest weather report to see if there was a chance of flying but it had turned worse if anything. I said my goodbyes and left in slightly downhearted spirits. Thank God I had lots of weeks remaining to get my PPL done.

When I arrived back home, I found a text message on my phone from a friend asking how my first lesson had gone. I replied, telling him about the poor weather. His next message was rather cruel. It read: "At least the skies will be safe for another day."

TOTAL (HOURS) = 0.0

Day 2. Tuesday 23 July

As predicted, the weather was even worse: strong wind, a bit of drizzle and a splash of heavy rain for good measure. Dylan said I could go over and do some studying if I wished but I declined. Instead I remained at home to remove my four stripes and aviator sunglasses.

TOTAL (HOURS) = 0.0

Day 3. Wednesday 24 July

I opened the curtains to see sunshine! I turned on the multi-band radio and tuned it to Leeds Bradford ATIS. ATIS stands for Automatic Terminal Information Service, and is a continually updated voice recording of the local weather around an airport. As well as this, it gives data about the runway in use and other important pieces of information. It said:

> *"Leeds Bradford Information. Time 08:35. Runway in use 32. Surface wind 300 at 8 knots, varying 270-340. Visibility 20 km. Scattered 1,100. Temperature +12. Dew point +11, QNH 1014. Information Tango."*

"Hmm," I said rubbing my chin. "Very interesting." So the runway for landing and take-off was runway 32. And at this juncture I think it is important that I explain a little thing about runways.

All runways have a number based on their approximate magnetic heading. Runway 32 meant the runway alignment was on a heading of 320°. Its opposite end was runway 14, which denoted an approximate heading of 140°, which, as you would expect, was the reciprocal (opposite) heading of 320°.

Back to the ATIS report. The wind speed was 8 knots in a general direction of 300° but could vary between 270° and 340°. Not really a problem for runway 32. Visibility was good (anything over 10 km was regarded as good) but there was scattered cloud at only 1,100 ft, which was a bit marginal for PPL flying. The temperature and dew point were only 1° apart, which explained the low cloud base because basically, when air temperature cools to the dew point temperature, cloud will form. Air temperature drops by about 2°C every 1,000 ft upwards, so the air around Leeds Airport didn't have to rise very far to cool to its dew point and form that annoying cloud.

QNH 1014 meant that the air pressure was 1014 millibars, which was important for setting altimeters in the cockpit. A pilot would turn a little knob on the altimeter so that 1014 was set. *Information Tango* was what a pilot would have to say back to ATC to acknowledge that they had listened to the latest ATIS. The next ATIS would be *Information Uniform,* and so on. Anyway, I rang Dylan who said the weather seemed just about okay, despite the low cloud base.

I was ecstatic. I had a quick slice of toast and collected my things. As soon as I stepped outside though I felt some drops of rain on my head. I looked up at the clouds. They were dark and foreboding, mocking me by their presence.

I decided to give Dylan a quick ring just to make sure it was still worth my while heading over to the airport.

"Hang on," he said. "I'll just check."

A few seconds later he returned with bad news. The cloud base had lowered making it a no go. "But come over anyway," he said. "You can chat to an instructor about things. Besides, the weather might clear up while you're here."

I told him I'd be there in 20 minutes.

Once there I met another instructor, a big Yorkshireman in his mid-thirties named Geoff McPhail. He had only recently become a flying instructor.

"How you doing?" he said as he pumped my hand. "I've heard you want to be a pilot, eh?"

"Yeah," I smiled, gesturing towards the window. "But with this weather, I might as well not bother."

Geoff nodded knowingly. "The great British weather. You'll just have to get used to it."

I followed Geoff through a door into a smaller room that was set out with rows of tables and a large whiteboard at the front. It was the ground school study room. Sitting at a desk, I listened as Geoff went over some basic aircraft theory using a snazzy wooden aeroplane with little moving parts. Afterwards, he asked if I wanted to go out and see the aircraft again. I nodded enthusiastically.

Getting to them involved a quick drive over to the airport, so we each donned a fluorescent high visibility vest which, rather predictably, I put on all wrong. When we stepped outside, a sudden gust of wind caught it, and it flapped so much it tangled around my arm. Geoff ignored this obvious sign of ineptitude and led me to his car.

Two minutes later, Geoff flashed his security pass and the guard allowed us to enter the general aviation section of the airport. Geoff led me to one of the school's training aircraft, a Cessna 152, and told me to be very careful when approaching an aircraft with a propeller. If I ever happened to be walking near a propeller that suddenly started up then I could kiss goodbye to an important part of my body.

Geoff showed me the normal checks I'd be required to make before every flight. Known as the walkaround, it had its own set of checklists.

Earlier, I'd bought a book of checklists for the princely sum of £6 and in it there were checklists for every aspect of flying a Cessna 152, including some alarming ones entitled: *Engine Failure During Take-Off Run, Emergency Landing without Engine Power, Ditching, Landing with a Flat Main Tyre* and a nice one called *Wing Fire*.

I watched Geoff as he completed the walkaround, and noticed him looking at the sky once again.

"It's no good," he told me. "It's still overcast and drizzly. There's no point in wasting your money."

I drove home in an unhappy mood.

At 2 pm, I rang Dylan, who said that flying looked quite likely at 3 pm. After putting the phone down, I hastily collected my goggles and scarf and set off back to the flying school in the hope I'd finally get into the air. The weather, perhaps predictably, dashed my hopes.

Geoff McPhail told me it was just about flyable. "I've just been up with another student," he said. "But we were thrown a bit. And the clouds were low so we had to fly in the turbulent air close to the ground."

He looked out the cabin window for a second. "I'd take you up if you'd had a few lessons. But you'll only feel sick right now. It would be a waste of your money."

I said goodbye and headed home. And thus came to the end of Day 3. The closest I'd got to being airborne was going over a speed bump a little too fast on the way back from the airport.

TOTAL (HOURS) = 0.0

Day 4. Thursday 25 July

"Leeds Bradford Information. Winds: 250° at 12

> *knots. Showers in the vicinity! Visibility: 11 km. Scattered cloud at 1,100 ft. Broken cloud at 1,400 ft..."*

I might as well have done my PPL in Iceland; it was probably glorious over there. Grinding my teeth, I rang Dylan, who cancelled my lesson. I put the phone down and immediately felt angry and hard done by. It was July for God's sake!

Almost a whole week of holidays wasted because of the British weather. I was starting to wish that I'd gone to Florida, or at least somewhere guaranteed to have decent weather. I felt like going in the back garden and cursing the clouds. I was not happy in the slightest. What was going on with the weather?

TOTAL (HOURS) = 0.0

Day 5. Friday 26 July

It was sunny. There were a few wispy clouds. From my window it *looked* like a nice summer's day. But it didn't *sound* like a nice summer's day. The latest ATIS report told me the wind was blowing at a whopping 26 knots.

On the phone, Dylan agreed the winds were wild and no good for flying. The afternoon lesson was a no-go as well, with high winds spoiling any chance of a flight.

And so to the end of Week One and I hadn't even done a *single* hour in the air. As I sat and brooded upon this misfortune, it seemed to me that I'd chosen to begin my PPL at the worst possible moment in British weather's history.

And just as a final thought to end this bleak chapter, I remember years ago hearing a certain novelty song in the charts and deriding it considerably. But now, I can empathise with that poor green bird, Orville, and especially the poignant first verse. (For anyone lucky enough not to have heard the song in question, Orville was a ventriloquist's dummy, who with his partner in crime, somehow had managed to score a hit single in the UK charts. The first line of the song described Orville's wish to be able to fly, even though he knew he would never be able to. This lyric now brings a tear to my eye.)

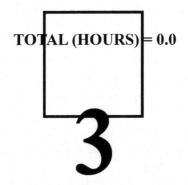

3

The Battle Continues

'Curse you, evil clouds.'

–Jason Smart (PPL Student)

Day 6. Monday 29 July

Lesson 1: *Primary & Secondary Effects of the Controls/Simple Turns/ Taxiing*

After a weekend of perfectly flyable weather I fully expected to wake up to see a return of poor weather. But I was wrong. It was sunny, there were only a few clouds and there was hardly any wind. I listened to ATIS with baited breath!

"Leeds Bradford Information. Winds variable at 2 knots! CAVOK. Temperature: +19. Dew point: +15…"

CAVOK, pronounced 'Cav-okay', means the **C**eiling and **V**isibility is **ok**ay, which basically meant that the visibility was in excess of 10 km, with little or no low cloud.

When I arrived at the flying school, my instructor for the day was a New Zealander named James Jarvis. He was a tall, dark-haired man in his mid-thirties. As we shook hands, I thought he looked like a professional pilot — what with his white shirt and black tie, together with some sunglasses poking out from his shirt pocket. A few gold stripes on his shoulder and he could have been an airline pilot.

"G'day mate!" he said. "I know you've had a bit of hassle with the weather last week, but today we'll get you up in one of the little bug-smashers!"

"Bugsmashers?"

"Yeah. That's what we used to call Cessna 152s back in New Zealand when I flew for the coastguard."

James told me that he and his girlfriend had moved to the UK about a year ago because he had been due to get a job with a well-known British airline. However, in the end that chance had fallen through and so he'd decided to take up instructing until the aviation industry picked up.

After a quick cup of tea, James took me into the little room used for ground school to explain how the airspace around Leeds Bradford Airport worked.

"It's controlled airspace," he told me. "This means that all pilots have to follow instructions from Air Traffic Control. The *zone* is the airspace around the airport and there are five places to enter or exit the zone. Each of these places is highly noticeable from the air and on today's flight we'll exit the zone to the north via Menwith, a group of white domes that look like giant golf balls."

Handing me a spare headset (which I'd borrow for the rest of my training) James and I drove out to the aircraft.

Once there, I saw lots of other pilots and students and noticed I was missing one piece of vital kit — aviator sunglasses. Everyone had them on, including James. He told me they were not *that* vital, but could be useful to avoid the glare from the sun if flying for a long time. Anyway, as we reached our aircraft for the day — a Cessna 152 with the registration G-BSDO, James demonstrated the pre-flight checks.

"I always start by having a general look over the aircraft," he said as we surveyed the Cessna from a distance of about 15 ft. "And what I'm looking for is anything obvious I need to sort out first."

"Like what?" I asked.

"Well, I'd want to get rid of any tie-down ropes or chocks. I always remove these first so I won't forget about them later on."

With this, James walked over to the front of the aircraft and pulled out a chock that someone had put in front of the nose-wheel.

"The next thing is to look inside the cockpit. Check the master switch is off and that the magnetos are off. You wouldn't want to be walking around a plane if they were on. The engine could spring to life — with a part of you getting chopped up in it."

"Does that happen often?"

"Not if you check the cockpit first."

"I see."

We walked to the left-hand door of the aircraft, and James opened it. Reaching inside, he removed a strange looking device that had been holding the yoke in place. He informed me it was a control lock, used to keep the elevators and ailerons still when the plane was not in use. He put it in a pouch behind the seat.

James then pressed down on a large red switch, which he explained was the master switch. "We need this on to get some power to the flaps."

Next, he pulled on a lever and I could hear a whirring noise coming from the back of the wings. "I'm watching the flaps on both sides to make sure they are going down symmetrically,"

I nodded, trying to remember everything. I said, "James, when will I have to do all these checks?"

"This afternoon, mate! She's all yours then! But don't worry; I'll be doing my own checks afterwards for the first few lessons."

"Yes, but what about after that?"

"It'll be down to you, Mr Smart."

"But what if I forget something?"

James looked serious. "Make sure you don't."

"I see."

James turned the master switch off and closed the cockpit door.

I followed James to the side of the little Cessna.

"Right then Jason, I always start the external checks on the left-hand side of the aircraft, but other instructors might start somewhere else. My old instructor back in New Zealand taught me to begin on the left, so that's what I do. So it's how I teach my students."

I followed James to a position just behind the left-hand door and watched as he ran his hand along the fuselage making his way to the back of the aircraft. "I'm looking for popped rivets and dents. Anything out of the ordinary really."

He then went behind the small wings at the back (which I later found out were not wings) and knelt down to lift the elevator, which was the flap thing on the rear portion. At the same time, he examined the link-ages and cables attached to it. Satisfied that everything was okay he stood up and moved the rudder from side to side.

"See these cables here," James said, pointing at some thick-looking pieces of metal connected to the rudder. "Always check they're connected properly."

I looked and saw that they were indeed connected. "What would happen if they snapped?"

"You'd have no rudder control, mate. You'd have to fly the plane without it."

"Is that easy?"

"It depends."

"I see."

Next, James reached up and gave some aerials a good twanging before moving onto the right-hand side of the aircraft. He bent down again and checked the right elevator, making sure a bolt attached to another little movable section called the *trim tab* was secure. He explained that I would find out about the trim tab on a later lesson.

James stood up and began to make his way up the right-hand side of the aircraft. As he moved along, he ran his hand along the fuselage, once again checking for anything unusual or out of the ordinary. After a few seconds he arrived at the wing. He gave the flaps a good hard wobble, and then looked underneath the wing to inspect the flaps further.

"Always give them a good shake before a flight. And always check the linkages." He pointed to a screw-like object, which he proceeded to give a good twiddle. "Make sure this is tight and secure."

With me following like a confused lapdog, James moved along the wing until he reached the aileron.

"Move it up and down like this. And while you're doing that, look inside the cockpit to check the yoke is moving from side to side. If it's not, then you have a major problem."

He then peered at the underside of the aileron and carefully raised it. "You've got to be careful here, Jason," warned James. "When you lift the aileron to check for these (which turned out to be small weights) don't get your fingers trapped in the gap."

By bending down I could see what James was referring to. As he raised the aileron, sunlight shone through a small slit that separated the aileron from the wing. This slit was just wide enough to accommodate a person's fingers. With a dramatic pause for effect, James released the aileron and we watched as it swung — guillotine like — back into its position.

"Ouch." I said.

"Yup," replied James.

Later in my training, I found out about another risk involved in checking the ailerons — a much more common occurrence than getting your fingers abruptly shortened. Whenever it rained, water would collect on the aileron, so whenever I did this check myself, crouching down to inspect the aileron, I'd get a thorough soaking of freezing cold water as I lifted it. Some of it would even go in my mouth. If I was lucky, there'd be a fly in it.

James walked to the end of the wing and gave the navigation light a bit of a prod, before moving to the front of the wing, running his hand along its leading edge.

"There's a dent!" I said, spotting a slight indentation at the front.

"Oh that's nothing to worry about, mate. I'm looking for big dents. Big dents or bends where bends shouldn't be. I'm also looking along the top and bottom of the wing, making sure none of the rivets have popped out of place."

At this point, James checked the wing strut by giving it a sharp tug. Then he bent down to inspect the wheels.

"Now I'm not an engineer or anything, so all I'm looking for are obvious things like leaks and flat tyres. I'm also looking for cuts or anything out of the ordinary."

He gave the tyre a kick and tugged on a white metal bar that connected the tyre to the fuselage. Satisfied everything was in order there, James moved to the nose of the aircraft.

Opening a small compartment located on the side of the nose, he told me he was checking the oil. I watched as he unscrewed a yellow cap and removed the dipstick.

"The engine oil should be between 5 and 6. If it's below, you *must* put some oil in. The worst thing that can happen is low oil when flying. The engine might blow, and you'd have to find a field quick."

Gripping my high-visibility jacket, I said, "Have you ever had an engine failure?"

James shook his head. "Not yet. Touch wood."

At the very front of the aircraft, James gave the propeller a good old tug. He also ran his hand along the length of it, to check there weren't any nicks or small dents. Next, he bent down and checked the front nose wheel — once again checking for tyre inflation and any leaks in the immediate vicinity of it.

I followed as James walked along the other side of the nose to check the left-hand wing. "What's that pointy thing there?" I asked, referring to a strange-looking metallic object dangling below the wing.

"That's the pitot tube. You check that the opening is free of obstructions. It needs to have air blowing into it. That's how some of the cockpit instruments work. Air goes into the tube and pressure is converted into airspeed and altitude."

"So what happens if it gets blocked up — say with ice?" I inquired.

"In the cockpit, there's a pitot heat switch. In winter you'd give the tube some heat to get rid of any ice. But it's important to do a visual check first. And not only that, check the static vent as well." James ran his fingers over a small circular piece of metal on the side of the nose.

After he'd checked the left undercarriage, he told me he was going to inspect the windows and doors. He got a cloth and rubbed the front window until it looked a bit more presentable, then he shut the door making sure it stayed securely shut. I watched, wondering how on earth I'd remember everything.

"Now it's time for the fuel checks," announced James. "Open the door and reach behind the seats. Get me a fuel drainer and wing tank dipstick."

"What do they look like?" came back my not unreasonable request.

James reached past me to retrieve the articles in question himself. He passed me a strange-looking plastic tube about 15 cm in length. "That's the fuel drainer. We'll use it in a minute. But this thing I've got here (a clear plastic tube with a scale along its length) is the dipstick. You stick it in the fuel tanks like this. Watch."

James put his foot onto a small metal plate located on the wing strut, and by using a strategically placed handgrip, he hoisted himself up into a position overlooking the wings. I watched him as he unscrewed a cap and put the dipstick in.

"Make sure you put the end of your finger over the top of the dipstick before you pull it out. If you don't, you won't get any fuel to stay in it. This fuel tank's fine — 8 gallons. Plenty."

He repeated the performance on the other side and declared the fuel quantity to be sufficient for our purposes.

"Now I'm going to check the fuel quality." He gestured for the fuel drainer.

I watched carefully as James crouched below the left-hand wing just behind the cockpit door. With the fuel drainer in his hand, he pushed it up onto a small valve-type object. Some fuel flowed onto the drainer.

At about three quarters full, he removed it and walked out from underneath the wing. He held his sample aloft and then held it under his nose. "Here — smell this. And note the colour too."

The colour was light blue, and the smell was like petrol.

James said, "This looks okay. Check the fuel's clear though. Also closely check for sediment or globules. If you ever see something, get it checked out. Simple as that."

He then flung the contents onto the ground away from the aircraft. We both stood there a moment staring at the small puddle.

"Another good way of checking the sample is to do what I've just done. Aviation fuel will evaporate much quicker than water. That puddle will be gone in a minute." And he was right, out there in the sun, the fuel evaporated in next to no time.

With the external checks complete, we both turned around as the roar of a jet engine silenced everything around. It was a Ryanair 737 landing from Dublin. After watching it taxi towards the terminal we climbed aboard the aircraft and strapped ourselves in. Lesson number one was about to begin.

James started the engine then contacted Leeds Tower. What the controller and James talked about was a mystery but I did notice James writing things down, such as altitude clearances and QNH pressure settings. I sat as still as possible, trying to take it all in.

After a bit more confusing chat, James taxied to the runway and lined up. It seemed to stretch for miles compared to the grass strip at Barton. As we waited for clearance, I was a little nervous, but this soon disappeared as James pushed the throttle to maximum and released the brakes.

We shot off down the runway like a rocket and very quickly became airborne. About 10 seconds later, James spotted a flock of birds in our path and swung around them narrowly avoiding a messy situation. "Leeds gets a lot of birds," James said as he continued with the climb. "Always keep an eye out for them."

Very soon, Air Traffic Control (ATC) told us to contact Leeds Approach. The *Approach* controller was in charge of any aircraft departing or approaching Leeds Bradford airspace. The *Tower* controller was in charge of aircraft near the airport. Imagine two concentric circles surrounding an airport. The inner and smaller circle is the domain of Tower Controller. The outer circle — both wider and higher in altitude than the first — is where the Approach Controller is in charge.

Anyway, James twiddled a dial and spoke more gibberish to someone who came back with even more claptrap. Ignoring it all, I looked outside. We were over green countryside and farmers' fields. A minute later I could see some golf-ball-like structures, which meant we were nearing Menwith. James said something over the radio and we flew over them.

"We've just left the Leeds zone," said James. "That's all there is to it."

When we got to 2,000 ft, James levelled off the aircraft, removed his hands from the controls and folded his arms. He turned and looked at me obviously awaiting some kind of response. All I could do was make my Adam's apple bob up and down a bit quicker than usual.

What was he doing? Was the plane was flying by itself? *Was I at the mercy of some crazed lunatic?* But before I could begin to scream, James explained that a Cessna 152 was a very stable aircraft and on a calm day it was very easy to fly.

After placing his hand back on yoke, he demonstrated how to go up and down by using it to control the elevators. Then it was my turn. It seemed very straightforward — especially with my experiences on the flight simulator at home.

Next, I was given the chance to practise a simple turn, but James told me that before a turn was actually initiated, something known as a *clearing turn* must be done first. If I was intending to do a turn to the left for example, then I first must bank a little to the left and then the right, lifting each wing in turn, checking for any conflicting traffic lurking in the blind spots. James demonstrated this for me, then handed control over to me. I banked the aircraft.

"My control," said James a second later. "Hold the yoke like this."

I looked and saw that he was holding it lightly, not in the ham-fisted death-grip way I'd been doing.

"And watch your altitude. In a turn, you don't want to lose too much. A bit of back pressure on the yoke next time."

"How much altitude did I lose?"

"300 ft."

"Is that good?"

"No."

Because I was concentrating so intensely on flying the plane, every now and again, just to give me a bit of a breather, James would take control. When he did this I got the chance to look down at the ground.

It was marvellous looking down at the farms and country roads below us. Also, the number of private outdoor swimming pools astonished me. Did the people who own them not realise that they were living in England?

Later, when flying over the town of Harrogate, James pointed out where he lived, before showing me a good landmark in the centre of town. It was a large building that towered above everything else. I tried to take a mental photograph of it for later in my training.

Next we moved onto climbing and descending, but time was running out, and after only a few demonstrations of these manoeuvres we had to head back to the airport. As we neared the white domes of Menwith, James received a set of complicated landing instructions from ATC, which he seemed to understand. After replying back, he told me to steer a course for the airport. When it was in sight, James took over and made a perfect landing.

As we taxied back to park the aircraft I was given a chance to steer the aircraft using the rudder pedals. I remembered from my trial flight how difficult this was, but I made a much better attempt in this lesson, even managing to go around a bend. I'd love to brag I was controlling the aircraft at an impressively fast taxiing speed, but we were probably only doing about 2 knots.

At a particularly sharp bend in the taxiway, James noticed me attempting to use the yoke as a steering wheel. He told me it was a completely futile gesture. He added that virtually every new student did what I'd just done. James took control and parked the aircraft. I'd completed my first hour of training.

Lesson 2: *Preparation for Flight/Straight & Level Flight/ Turns/The Art of Trimming/Recovery from Strange Attitudes (Introduction)/Taxiing*

The afternoon lesson went ahead too. James Jarvis once again showed me how to do the before start checks — especially being vigilant about checking the fuel quantity and condition. The aircraft was low on fuel so was filled up, and eventually we climbed in and started the engines.

After take-off we left the zone to the north-west via Harrogate. The lesson was all about straight and level flying.

James told me to fly at selected altitudes, which seemed quite easy in the calm conditions. He then introduced me to the rudder as a means of keeping the aircraft in balance. An aircraft in balance will be smooth and stable in its flight path. This 'balancing' is achieved by looking at the *balance-ball coordinator* instrument in the cockpit.

It is basically a spirit level, and I had to try to keep the ball in the middle of the instrument by using the rudder pedals. This was hard to do. Concentrating on turning the yoke, looking at the horizon, glancing at the balance-ball coordinator and *then* adding a bit of rudder (but being careful not to add too much) was condition overload for me. I wondered how people ever got used to doing so many things at once.

Next James taught me about the trim wheel. If you wish, you may skip this and the next few paragraphs. We're talking a bit of theory now. But for those of you who are still here — listen carefully!

At the back of a Cessna 152 there is something called a *horizontal stabiliser* (this is what most people think are the back wings of the aircraft). Attached to it, on rear hinges, are movable control surfaces called *elevators*. These elevators control the pitch of an aeroplane (i.e. the up and down movement) and they are controlled from the cockpit by the yoke. Got everything so far?

Okay then, one of these elevators also has its own smaller movable surface called the *trim tab*, which is controlled from the cockpit by a strange-looking device called the *trim wheel*. This wheel is located between both yokes on the bottom portion of the cockpit panel, and is moved by a pilot's hand. Pilots use it to relieve themselves from the sometimes-difficult job of 'hands flying' the aircraft all the time. For example in a climb, a pilot would have to pull back on the yoke to keep the aircraft pointing upwards, which can sometimes get tiring, especially during a prolonged climb. The trim wheel relieves this pressure.

More often though, an aircraft is trimmed for straight and level flight, and James showed me how to do it. It looked simple and quick but when

I had a go myself, I couldn't really judge if I had set enough trim or not.

After a while of practising straight and level flying and trying to get to grips with the trim wheel, James informed me that he was going to manoeuvre the aircraft into a strange *attitude*. Attitude is the position that an aircraft is relative to the airflow and not to be confused with the similarly spelt altitude. He steeply banked and descended the aircraft, and then told me to recover it back to straight and level.

I grabbed the yoke and pulled us up. The plane moved with me and then I turned slightly to get us straight. I looked at James, wondering what he thought.

"Not bad," he said. "How about this one?"

And so we did another one, and another one after that. Afterwards, according to James, I'd recovered from them all quite well. He did add though, rather modestly, that my good progress was the direct result of superior instructing on his part.

As the lesson drew to a close, James told me to maintain a certain altitude and heading as we flew over the strange golf balls at Menwith. When we had permission from ATC to re-enter the zone I flew a course for the airport. James said that he'd manoeuvre and land the aircraft, but I had to lightly hold the yoke so I could feel what he was doing throughout.

He also said he would fly low along much of the length of the runway for two reasons. One, I was to get a mental image of what the runway looked like while coming in to land, and two, James said it was great fun!

It *was* great fun and once down, I got some more practice with steering the aircraft using the rudder pedals.

We parked up and James said that I'd done very well. I told him about my doubts over the use of trim, and he did agree that I was using it a bit tentatively, but with practice, he said, it would turn out okay.

I'd really enjoyed both of my sorties and I couldn't wait for more lessons. James had been professional and friendly throughout. I went home feeling satisfied with the way things had gone.

TOTAL (HOURS) = 2.1

Day 7. Tuesday 30 July

I woke up to the not very distant sound of thunder accompanied by lashings of torrential rain. I wasn't holding out much hope of flying. ATIS confirmed this:

"Leeds Bradford Information. Winds variable at 3 knots. Fog. Thunderstorms in the vicinity. Visibility 600 m, cumulonimbus 800 ft, broken 1,000 ft. Temperature +17. Dew point +17…"

Cumulonimbus clouds are thunderclouds. They produce strong up and down currents that can cause severe stress to an aircraft. They can also produce a phenomenon known as *wind shear.*

Wind shear is especially dangerous when coming in to land. Imagine approaching the landing but suddenly just before touchdown, a violent shove jolts the aircraft towards the runway. That is wind shear. It is invisible but has caused many aircraft crashes, including those of large airliners. Flying near thunderstorms is a recipe for disaster and so Dylan cancelled my morning lesson.

James Jarvis rang me at home and told me something interesting though. Because the weather had been so poor he'd taken some students over to the Tower to meet the air traffic controllers who worked there.

"While we were chatting to them," James told me. "A bolt of lightning hit the *NDB* beacon!"

I made suitable sounds of shock at hearing this. "What happened to it?"

"It stopped working so the controllers had to implement emergency procedures. It was all very exciting though!"

NDB stands for **Non-Directional Beacon.** These beacons are located all over the world sending out radio signals that the cockpit **ADF** can receive. Of course, **NDBs** are nowhere near as accurate as **VORs**, which in turn, are not as accurate as **ILSs.** But all of these work better if you know the **QNH** or **QFE,** or are perhaps requesting a **QDM.** In addition, sometimes **ATC** might want to know the **POB** for an **ETA** at your chosen **FBO** with its **DME** equipment.

These acronyms and many, many more will confuse you in the initial stages of flying.

TOTAL (HOURS) = 2.1

Day 8. Wednesday 31 July

The last day of July, and guess what? No flying because of the weather. The weather was so bad it actually made the national news. Floods had caused massive landslides and road closures. Every time I glanced out of the window, all I could see was rain and drizzle. According to the weather forecasters, the bad weather would last until the weekend. Another wasted week.

TOTAL (HOURS) = 2.1

Day 9. Thursday 1 August

Same as yesterday. Fog, rain and thunder, and lots of it.

TOTAL (HOURS) = 2.1

Day 10. Friday 2 August

No let up in the weather. When will it ever end?

TOTAL (HOURS) = 2.1

The Training Begins

'What does this knob thing do again?

–Jason Smart (PPL Student)

Day 11. Monday 5 August

Lesson 3: *Climbing/Medium Turns*

The start of week three brought freak weather over Yorkshire. By freak weather, I mean flyable weather. I went over to the flying school for my third lesson: climbing and descending.

James made me do the walkaround on my own today. I used my checklists. Afterwards he checked the fuel and oil himself followed by his own walkaround before we both climbed inside. This was where I had my first trauma.

After donning the headset, I tried to move the receiver part closer to my mouth but as I did so a section snapped off. Hastily trying to repair the damage before James noticed my vandalism I fiddled around with it but sensed him staring at me. The snapped bit was dangling from my hand. James shook his head.

He tried to fix it, but couldn't. "If you need to speak," James finally said. "Hold that bit to your mouth."

I nodded and turned to the front.

While I sat in shame, James contacted Leeds Tower. With that done, he asked me to read the 'after start' and 'before take-off' checklists. I held the snapped bit to my mouth and read off the items from the list. Finally, we started taxiing; with me once again steering using the rudder pedals.

During take-off, James asked me to lightly hold the yoke and rest my feet on the pedals while James flew the aircraft. We gained speed and I could feel the controls moving around as James manipulated them. Once up in the air, I noticed the wind was surprisingly high and the visibility quite poor. We headed for Harrogate.

I rehearsed a bit of straight and level flying again before practising some climbing. With this, I could apply the throttle and change the attitude with no bother, but trimming the aircraft was still proving to be a problem. James said I was doing okay, but it was more by luck than any judgement on my part. After only a short while, the clouds were too low to practise any more climbing so we moved on to turning.

"When you first go into the turn," said James. "Try to get a picture of what the horizon looks like compared to the dashboard. Then try to keep that angle constant throughout the turn. That way you won't have to keep chasing the altimeter."

I nodded and began the turn. James's tip turned out to be a good one because after an initial drop in altitude I managed to keep it fairly steady.

"Good," said James. "Now it's time for some 30° turns. Give me control."

James showed me the method for doing steep turns and then let me have a go. These were much harder than a normal turn because I needed to pull back on the yoke quite a bit to maintain the altitude, as well as applying some rudder to keep the turn coordinated. I managed to do one relatively well but then James then showed me who the master was by doing a stomach churning 60° turn while keeping the altitude perfectly constant.

He looked at me and grinned. "I love doing that."

Back near the airport James flew the approach but began explaining each manoeuvre he was doing. For instance, when we joined the circuit to land and ATC gave us instructions to contact them *downwind* for runway 32, he told me what this meant.

Downwind was when we were flying parallel to the runway but on the reciprocal heading to the landing direction. Downwind is also the part of the circuit where we were flying with the wind behind us (usually) and thus explained its name. When we got there, James made his call and then turned onto *base*, which is perpendicular to the runway. A short while later he made his last turn onto *final,* which meant the runway was in front of us.

As he did all of these turns he said checklists aloud to himself and fine-tuned various controls as we got lower and lower. And in between all this he spoke to ATC and seemed to juggle all the jobs with complete ease. With the runway almost below us, I thought that there was an awful lot to do while landing, and began to wonder if I'd bitten off more than I could chew doing a PPL.

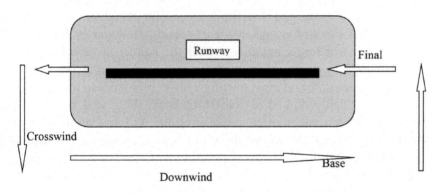

Fig (1) Diagram showing a typical left-hand circuit.

Lesson 4: *Climbing and Descending/Use of Carb Heat/Braking*

"I've fixed the headset," said James.

I looked at him and nodded.

"Just be careful with it from now on, you cack-handed git."

For the afternoon lesson, James told me the visibility had increased and the cloud base had risen. That meant we could practise climbing and descending properly.

Over Harrogate I practised some climbs. This was straightforward because all I had to do was pull back on the yoke and add some power. I was also getting more confident with using the trim wheel. I was turning it much more vigorously now, rather than just a fraction of an inch like before.

"You are doing okay with this," said James. "But you need to be less hesitant with the rudder pedals. It's strange actually, because every other beginner student I've had has been heavy with them."

Next we practised descending, which sounded easy. In fact, all I thought I'd have to do was point the nose of the aircraft downwards and that would be that. (It was possible to do it that way, but it wouldn't have been a controlled descent.) What I had to do was pull out the *carb heat* knob, reduce the throttle to 1700 rpm, put the aircraft in a nose-down attitude and then trim like I knew how to trim. And while all that was going on I had to simultaneously scan the flight and engine instruments *and* also look outside, and then think about a bit of rudder.

All of that should have taken a few seconds. However each time we descended, I was forgetting about either the rudder or carb heat, and couldn't seem to cope with everything going on. Getting the rpm to 1700 was impossible and I was starting to lose confidence in my abilities.

James suddenly replied to something from ATC, and I realised I hadn't even been aware of anyone calling us. As I had another go at descending, I began to worry about not having enough spare mental capacity to do all of the things required to fly an aircraft. I needed another hand for one thing. Another set of eyes would not have gone amiss either. And finally, I needed a pair of gigantic satellite-type ears tuned to the radio because ATC was just a blur of background noise that I simply couldn't understand.

Carb heat, by the way, stands for 'carburettor heat'. Whenever power is reduced (e.g. in a descent) the carburettor must have some heat otherwise ice may build up and block parts of it up. This is done by pulling the knob out. If no heat gets to the carburettor and ice does form, the engine could begin to run very roughly or even stop altogether, which would be a BAD thing.

When we were back straight and level, I asked James how much spare mental capacity he had while flying.

"What do you mean?"

I decided to give him a theoretical scenario. "Do you think you could make a ham and salad sandwich while doing all this?"

James looked at me like I was an imbecile. "You're asking me whether I could fly a plane and make a sandwich at the same time?"

"Yes."

James laughed. "Easy! Maybe not while I was actually landing, but just flying around would be no problem. Bring some bread next lesson and I'll show you."

When it was time to head back, James told me to fly the aircraft into the *right downwind* position of the circuit. He did the radio calls while I flew the aircraft until we were flying parallel to the runway, with it on our right-hand side.

Down on the runway, just about to line up for take-off, was a KLM Fokker-100 jet airliner, so ATC told us to orbit left. This meant that instead of turning right onto *base*, I had to do a 360° turn to the left that would give the Fokker time to take off.

James told me that when doing an orbit I would need to locate an obvious landmark around which to circle. He pointed out a large farmhouse, and then a section of woodland, which were both suitable for the task. I began my orbit.

It was around this time that I began to wonder if James intended me to fly the aircraft all the way to the runway. Surely, this wasn't going to be my first landing? I hadn't even taken off yet! But before I could ponder this, ATC told us to report *final*.

James told me to reduce power for a descent and while I battled with the controls, James dealt with the trim wheel. I'd forgotten all about the damned thing. After a hellishly short time, James told me to turn to the right.

I looked outside and could see the runway coming up.

"Good," said James. "Now see if you can line up with the runway centreline. Just gentle movements. I'll do the flaps."

By my reckoning we were about 200 ft away from touchdown and I was nervous! James then said, "my control," which meant I had to take my hands and feet off everything. I stopped palpitating and watched as James made a perfect landing.

Once off the runway I steered with rudder, which I could now do competently — but it was all about to go wrong. The problem was with applying the brakes.

In the average car there is only one brake pedal, and when it is pressed the car will slow down in a relatively straight line. Not so in an aeroplane! For one thing, I had two brake pedals to contend with and both were on top of the rudder pedals.

James told me to press them and come to a stop. I felt it would be no problem for the Master of the Skies, but we swivelled sharply to the left, which resulted in the aircraft pointing 90° to where I wanted it. James couldn't manage to suppress a guffaw but straightened up the aircraft for me. I had another go with the same result. James suggested that I should apply a slight touch of rudder while braking, which helped slightly but not fully.

I had one final go, but still couldn't get the aircraft to stop in the direction we had been going. James told me not to worry and expertly turned the plane on a pinhead to park it.

We did the shutdown checks and removed our headsets before finally exiting the aircraft. James said he was pleased with my progress and asked how I was feeling about things.

I said, "I just can't believe the amount of things I have to do. Even with something as simple as descending I was coming apart at the seams."

"No you weren't," said James. "You did really well. I was quite impressed actually."

"What about my braking just now? You weren't impressed with that. I heard you laughing."

James nodded, smiling. "Yeah that was funny. But don't worry about braking, mate. You'll get more practice next lesson."

I nodded, hoping that none of the camcorder-wielding plane spotters had filmed me spinning in such a laughable manner. I had no wish to see myself appear on one of those TV programmes dedicated to home-movie mishaps.

I was also very thankful that my training aircraft didn't have one of those impossible to miss *LEARNER* signs that are so common on driving school cars. Imagine having one of those on top of your aircraft?

TOTAL (HOURS) = 4.6

Day 12. Tuesday 6 August

Lesson 5: _Descending with Flaps_

Another relatively good day, so I went over to Leeds for my fifth lesson. Before we climbed into our aircraft James decided to show me around a large hangar that was nearby. Inside there were a couple of executive jets, a lot of twin-engined business aircraft and a few helicopters.

I asked James whether he'd ever flown in a helicopter and he told me he had — having lessons up to the first solo stage before giving it all up. When I asked him why, he told me that it had been too expensive (an hour of helicopter flying is more than twice the cost of a normal fixed-wing plane).

James also pointed out a twin-engined aircraft that belonged to the flying school. "A while back," he said. "A couple of airline pilots had an embarrassing experience in it. As they were carrying out their pre-take-off checks, one of them pulled the wrong lever. The front nose-wheel retracted! The nose ended up on the concrete going nowhere fast. Luckily it happened off the runway."

I shook my head. "How much did that cost to fix?"

"About 25,000 quid!"

With the ground and internal checks done, James and I taxied to the runway for take-off. Once above 1,000 ft it became obvious that the visibility was poor. Even though it looked sunny from the ground, in the air it was a different matter.

This proved to be a problem for two reasons. Practising descending was impossible because we couldn't climb to a suitable altitude in which to start the descents (the higher we got, the worse the visibility got). Secondly, ATC kept warning us about other aircraft operating in the general area but we couldn't see them because of the murky conditions. This understandably perturbed James a lot.

As a relevant aside, I'm going to use this opportunity to describe some of the difficulties when trying to spot other aircraft from the air — even in good visibility. We all know it's easy to spot an aircraft when standing on the ground, because when a person hears a plane they will often look upwards scanning the sky. After a moment or two, the observer will locate the aircraft, because it's silhouetted against the sky.

It is a different matter when in the air. It's extremely hard to spot aircraft flying at lower altitudes. They merge in with the landscape below. On numerous occasions, when James asked if I could see aircraft he'd already spotted, I would have great difficulty. I couldn't even spot the things when James was pointing right at them. It was all quite worrying.

James, obviously aware the lesson was going to be potentially wasted, moved on to something new. He taught me about descending with *flaps*. Luckily we didn't need to climb as high for this. James demonstrated one such descent for me.

After starting the descent, he lowered the flap lever to the first notch. This made the flaps on the rear of the wings go down by 10°, which in turn caused the nose of the aircraft to rise, and the speed to subsequently drop. To maintain the descent *and* keep the required speed, James needed to lower the nose slightly.

In a Cessna 152, there are three flap settings, and each one causes a progressive raising of the nose with a subsequent drop in airspeed. Forward pressure on the yoke, together with a bit of trim counteracts this. When the flaps are fully down, it is possible to travel at a relatively slow speed. This is a desirable outcome, because when the nose is low, the pilot will have a really good view of what's in front. I needed to learn all of this because this was how I would be descending the aircraft when I came in for a normal landing later in my training.

James asked me to descend the aircraft while he controlled the flap lever. He added, "You'll feel quite a bit of force trying to push against you when I do this, so add pressure to the yoke and then trim. When you get the aircraft stabilised, I'll drop another notch of flap. Ready?"

I started my descent and heard the whirr of the flaps going down behind me. Immediately I could feel the aircraft wanting to climb and wondered what to do.

"Push down on the yoke!" reminded James. "And add some trim!"

I pushed down on the yoke and trimmed.

"What about the rudder?" James said. "And you forgot about carb heat!"

It all seemed a bit too much in such a short time span. I dreaded to think what would have happened if I was suddenly required to speak to ATC as well as fly. I think I'd have gone into mental overload, ending up totally blank.

Before I'd started my PPL, I, probably like many other flight simulator users, secretly harboured a belief that in the event of an airborne emergency — such as instructor incapacitation for example, I'd calmly take over the controls and land to great applause and mass admiration. I now knew this was a foolish thought. If James *had* suddenly keeled over in the cockpit, I'd have probably keeled over in sympathy, while weeping and foaming at the mouth.

We had one more go at a descent but I was in mental overload, and James seemed to sense that.

"Let's head back. You've had enough."

Once parked up I felt downhearted. I felt I'd struggled with some of the basics today. In fact at one point, when James had told me to reduce power, he must have watched incredulously as I attempted to push the throttle lever right in for full power! I couldn't explain why I had done that.

Last week someone asked me if learning to fly was hard, and I'd said smugly that it was quite easy. If I saw that person now, I'd tell them it is one of the hardest things I've ever done. And what worries me most is all I've been doing are the easy bits. God have mercy on us all.

Lesson 6: *Climbing and Descending Turns/Using the Radio*

Before the second flight of the day, I talked to James about my self-doubts.

"Look, Jason," he said. "You're doing really well. Better than average, actually. All students have doubts, which is normal, so don't worry. If you're doing badly mate, I'll let you know."

We went out to the aircraft.

James asked me to check the fuel while he went to the toilet. I'd never done this before by myself and immediately became concerned. I knew that I'd have to clamber up each side of the aircraft to hoist myself into a position on the wing where I could dip the dipstick in the tank.

I had visions of me tipping the aircraft up with my weight, or worse still, collapsing onto the wing and hanging over the edge like some deranged bat-like creature. Luckily, none of those things happened and I checked the tanks successfully and climbed down. James returned and we were soon strapped inside. Then James grinned. It was not a nice grin.

Earlier in the day he'd suggested I buy a kneeboard, which was basically a clipboard with a Velcro strap attached that wrapped around my knee. I could clip paper to it and write important pieces of information that ATC gave.

"Are you ready for your first radio message?" asked James, still grinning. He knew I was scared of speaking over the airwaves. My heart took a disturbing lurch. "Cos today's the day. No excuses this time."

First he showed me how to switch on the radios and how to check if I'd dialled in the correct frequency. Then he tuned to ATIS and told me to write down what the message said. Next he dictated a message for me to write down.

"Say it to me first," he said when I'd written it down.

I did so and James nodded, pleased.

He told me he was going to wait for a gap in the chat between ATC and various other pilots, and then he'd give me a signal. Upon this signal I was to press and hold down a small red button on the yoke and read out my message.

I gulped and stared at the red button. I cannot describe the apprehension I was feeling at that moment. James was about to make me to speak in the midst of all those other pilots. And they'd all have to listen to *me*! Aviation radios used only a single channel frequency which meant only one person at a time could speak. I was convinced I'd get so nervous and flustered that I'd make a complete mess of it. Imagine if I pressed the button and then froze, or said something ridiculous like, "Er… er… hello… nice weather we're having… Over…" I'd never live it down. All of these silly thoughts rushed through my mind as James gave the signal. I pressed the button and gave my first ever radio call:

"Leeds Tower, Golf-Bravo Sierra Delta Oscar. At Multiflight West with X-ray. 1018. Checks complete. Request taxi."

I'd managed to say it without a single mistake. I'd done it. I'd actually spoken to those voices on the radio!

Very quickly, a reply came back and James took over while my blood pressure returned to something approaching normality.

It's time for some ground school. This time about pressure settings. In the radio message I'd just given, I'd told ATC that the QNH was 1018.

On a little knob near the altimeter, I'd set the pressure to 1018 already. But unbelievably, a pilot could use three different pressure settings on any given day.

QNH is the pressure setting of mean sea level. With QNH set, the altimeter shows how far above sea level the aircraft is presently at. Because I'd already set the QNH, my altitude read 670 ft, the airport's height above sea level.

QFE is another pressure setting, mainly used for circuits and landings. When set, the altimeter shows elevation above the active runway. For example, while on the ground at Leeds, if QFE was set, the altimeter would read 0 ft.

FLIGHT LEVEL is the third pressure setting. Most aircraft flying above a certain altitude use this (which in the UK is about 3,000 ft — because above this, terrain is no longer a factor). Based upon a standard atmospheric pressure of 1013 mb (or 29.92 inches of mercury in the USA) pilots use the Flight Level pressure setting to reduce the risk of mid-air collision.

To put this another way, imagine two aircraft merrily flying along, one with QNH (altitude) set, the other with QFE (height) set. There could be a chance of these aircraft flying at the same altitude — even though their respective altimeters might show a difference of hundreds of feet. With 1013 (Flight Level) set, this uncertainty disappears. Most jet airliners cruise between FL26 – FL35, where the *FL* stands for Flight Level, and the numbers denotes thousands of feet. Put simply, FL29 means 29,000 ft on 1013mb.

Once up in the sky, the weather was much better than earlier and I could actually see the horizon. We practised climbing and descending, and then combining these with turns and using the flaps.

James was letting me fly the aircraft more and more by this stage, only taking over to manoeuvre us into a better position occasionally. For the first time, I actually felt as if I was in control of the aircraft — rather than the other way around.

Sometimes he'd take control of the aircraft and climb us to a higher altitude. When he did this quickly, my stomach ended up 500 ft below resulting in me making sounds of anguish. Upon hearing these pitiful whimpers James would mercilessly plunge the aircraft down again, before bringing it back up even more sharply. He claimed (rather dubiously I suspected) that these mad manoeuvres were to get me used to various feelings I'd encounter during my training later on.

After that, we headed back to the airport and I flew the aircraft to just 200 ft above the runway when James took over. Before we parked, I had another quick go at using the toe brakes, which went slightly more successfully than the previous day.

I went home in a good mood. Perhaps I would eventually make it to being a pilot after all.

TOTAL (HOURS) = 6.9

Day 13. Wednesday 7 August

Lesson 7: *Slow Flight/Taking off*

The weather didn't look too good, with grey skies and poor visibility, but James suggested that I might still go over so he could teach me about circuits.

The circuit at Leeds Bradford Airport could either be a left- or a right-hand circuit, James told me, and ATC would advise a pilot which it was to be. "Circuit height is 1,000 ft above runway, and there's a lot to do throughout. Hopefully I'll get to show you when the weather clears."

Just then the cabin door opened and an airline captain walked in. James immediately got up and shook his hand. They were friends.

He was another New Zealander called Craig Jennings, who worked for BMI, flying Embraer jets. He knew James well because he'd been one of his instructors back in New Zealand. When James went off to make some coffee, I asked Craig what James had been like as a student.

"Oh, he'd toe the line most of the time, but would occasionally cause trouble."

"Really? James caused trouble?"

"Yeah. But I'd give him a good whipping. That always sorted the bugger out." Craig scratched his head. "Sometimes, through, he used to cause problems with the hope of getting a good whipping. I could never understand that boy at times."

While we chatted the weather improved slightly so James and I headed out to the aircraft. We said goodbye to Craig, who wished me good luck.

Photo © Neil Smith

Once lined up on the runway, James told me I'd be doing the full take-off roll. With my feet pressed down on the brakes, I pushed the throttle to maximum, then released the toe brakes. We were off!

"Keep it straight with a bit of rudder, mate. And get that aileron pointing into the wind!" instructed James beside me.

I steered using the nose wheel and rudder as we hurtled down the runway. Soon I gently pulled back on the yoke and at 55 knots raised the nose even more, enabling us to leave the runway. I'd done my first unaided take-off!

Over Harrogate we practised slow flight. This involved reducing the power to a minimum and then raising the nose and trimming for stable flight. Slow flight was sometimes a useful method of flying. For instance, a pilot would want to fly slowly if he was getting too close to an aircraft in front.

After 30 minutes or so, we headed back to the airport for hopefully some circuit practice but ATC dashed our hopes by informing us there were training aircraft already in the circuit, as well as airliners approaching to land. Instead we landed and taxied off the runway.

James decided to give me more practice with the dreaded brakes. He told me to advance the throttle lever and to *gently* press on the toe brakes. This advice seemed to help a lot. Prior to this, I'd always used a lot of pressure with disastrous results. This time the aircraft stopped and was still pointing in the same direction! I did it again and it worked a treat! I was in a very good mood when we parked up and vacated the plane.

James had another student booked in but suggested that I return to the flying school to revise *Air Law* in preparation for doing the test that day. He also gave me some notes to read over before disappearing with his student.

Taking his advice, I ate a sandwich and revised *Air Law* (the exam I'd need to pass before going solo). I'd done a lot of studying already so presumed I wouldn't have any great difficulty in achieving the 75% pass mark required. After a while spent in quiet revision, the test began.

I was quite nervous about doing the exam. I hadn't done a formal exam in years and as I opened the paper and read the first question I started to panic. I didn't know the answer to it or the next four questions! It was a nightmare come true.

Get a grip, I told myself as I quickly turned the page. *Slow down and read the questions carefully.*

I tried to calm down as I read question 6 and realised I knew the answer. I also knew the answers to questions 7 and 8 and so turned back to read question 1 again. In my new state of calm, I found I could eliminate one of the three possible answers straight away. So now it was just a toss-up between the two remaining. Going through all 40 questions in this methodical way, I finished the exam after 30 minutes of the 60 allowed and handed my paper over to the flight examiner who told me he'd mark it there and then.

I passed with 88%!

I was elated, so while I waited for James to return I decided to sit another exam: *Human Performance and Limitations*. This subject covers various medical and psychological matters, and is the easiest for most people. I simply went into the room and did it. No panic this time. I ended up passing with 95%.

Lesson 8: *Circuit Bashing #1*

It had been a very productive day and then Dylan received a phone call from James, over at the airport telling me to meet him there. When I arrived, he told me he'd received permission from ATC to practise circuits. We checked the aircraft and taxied over to the runway. Once again, I took the controls for take-off.

"Keep it straight with rudder. And get that yoke pointed into the wind," James reminded me again as I released the brakes. "And pull up slightly now, you want to take the weight off the nose wheel. Okay... that's it! Keep it going! Good, now pull up a bit more. C'mon, pull back on the yoke, mate. We're at take-off speed."

With gritted teeth, I pulled back on the yoke even more and the aircraft gently lifted off from the runway.

"That's it. Well done! But don't pull back too much. That's right, let the nose drop slightly. We need to build up speed."

At about 500 ft James took over, demonstrating the whole circuit, including radio calls. From start to finish, he told me, the circuit would last between 7 and 12 minutes and there would be a lot to do. James came in to land but instead of coming to a stop on the runway he increased power and we climbed again for another circuit. It was my turn.

"It's a left-hand circuit," said James. "So when we get to about 500 ft, begin your turn to the left."

I looked at the altimeter, saw we were there already, and so began my turn, making sure I was still pulling back on the yoke so we continued to climb to 1,000 ft.

"Good," said James. "Now look outside for a reference point that you can use. I often use that mast on the hill straight ahead. Whenever I am doing a left-hand circuit, that's what I head for. Anyway, it's time to turn downwind."

Bloody hell, I thought. I'd only been up in the air for a few minutes and already I felt overloaded. Reference points, altitude checks, turning in time and Air Traffic Control, how was I supposed to do it all?

"Turn right a touch," said James. "And watch your height. Get down to 1,000 ft." I looked at the altimeter and saw that we were 200 ft above where we should have been. I hadn't even noticed. I turned and wondered if I should have a heart attack there and then or save it for later.

"When we're downwind there are two things you need to do," said James. "The first is to make a radio call. I want you to do that now."

Almost immediately I felt a twinge of panic making an unwelcome return. Pressing the button I said. "Golf-Delta Oscar is... downwind... left. Runway... ah... three-two. Touch and go."

The man in the Tower acknowledged this and told me tell him when I was ready to turn base.

"Okay," said James. "The next thing we have to do is the *before land-*

ing checks. I call it the bumfh checklist."

"Bumfh?"

"Yeah. B-U-M-F-H."

B stands for brakes, checking they are off. **U** stands for undercarriage, making sure it is down. A Cessna 152 has a fixed undercarriage, so this particular checklist item seemed absurd to me. James patiently explained that if I ever went onto further training, flying aircraft with retractable undercarriage, then I would already have this checklist ingrained in my mind. Fair enough.

M is for the mixture control and checking it is fully rich (i.e. pressed all the way in and locked.) The mixture control is another in-and-out-type knob located next to the throttle. When pushed in all the way, the carburettor would receive a rich mixture of fuel. If the mixture control was pulled all of the way out, then the fuel flow would stop and so would the engine.

F is to remind a pilot about fuel and flaps. Finally, **H** is to check whether all of the hatches and harnesses are secure.

"Look over your left shoulder," said James. "Notice where the runway is? This is a good place to turn base. Tell ATC."

I pressed the little red button and said, "Golf-Delta Oscar is… ah… ready… for erm…" I looked at James for help.

"For base!" he reminded.

"For base," I said, my heart was beating ten to the dozen.

Miraculously, the controller knew what I meant and gave the next instruction. "Golf-Delta Oscar is cleared to land. Number one on traffic. Report final for three-two."

James replied to that while I began a descent at 70 knots and started dropping the flaps in anticipation of turning final.

With the slightly gusty conditions outside I found it hard to keep the aircraft stable and asked James whether he thought everything was okay. He told me I was doing well and that it was time to turn final. I did this and then about a minute away from touchdown, James took over and landed for another a touch and go.

I did four circuits that afternoon, and James was happy with my performance during them all.

"You're progressing well," he told me. "Mainly down to the masterful instructing you're getting."

I went home happy again.

TOTAL (HOURS) = 8.7

Day 14. Thursday 8 August

<u>Lesson 9: *Stalls*</u>

Yet another flying day!

James told me the lesson was going to be about stalls. Stalling in an aircraft was a completely different thing to stalling in a car. Usually the engine was still running. An aircraft stall happened when there was no lift gained from the wings and it dropped like a rock.

James demonstrated a basic stall after climbing to 4,000 ft. First he maintained straight and level flight. Then he reduced the throttle to idle and pulled back on the yoke to maintain the height. Eventually, he had to pull back with a lot of pressure and it seemed the yoke was pulled right back at his chest. The speed slipped away alarmingly until the wings could no longer support any lift and then they stalled. We dropped forwards.

This was not as drastic as it sounded. As soon as the stall occurred and the nose tipped forward James lowered the nose further and added full power. When the airspeed increased to normal, he reduced the power and brought the nose back up. He'd regained control in about two seconds.

I had a go but keeping the wings level when approaching the stall was not very easy. Inevitably, one wing or the other would drop first and I'd 'recover' the aircraft before it had actually stalled. I had another two goes and luckily did much better, proving I could safely recover from this type of stall. Or so I hoped.

When we were flying straight and level again, James mentioned something. "Every now and again, just to keep you on your toes, I'm going to pull the power off. You won't get any warning. But I'll expect you to recover within three seconds. Okay?"

I nodded.

James then demonstrated some other types of stalls, such as stalls in a turn and stalls in the landing configuration (i.e. with flaps down) but decided I'd done enough stalling for one day. So instead, he showed me an area of the Leeds Bradford zone I'd not yet been to: Dewsbury, the southerly entry/exit point of the zone.

To me, Dewsbury just looked like any of the other built-up areas beneath us. I wondered how it would be possible to distinguish it from everywhere else, because where Leeds ended and Dewsbury began, I had no clue. James, of course, had the answer.

"It's got a water tower. Can you see it over there?"

Peering out, I could just make out a tiny white speck in the distance. But it was hardly recognisable as anything at all, let alone a water tower. I told James this.

"A lot of people say that. But there's another landmark. See that red building with a white roof down there?" I nodded. It was much easier to see. "It's a B&Q Superstore. When you see that, you know you're over Dewsbury."

While heading back to the airport, James boosted my confidence somewhat. He told me that if I'd been doing my training at a little aerodrome as opposed to an international airport, I'd have gone solo after about 12 hours. He said it would take longer at Leeds because of two main reasons.

One was that ATC didn't allow much time for vital circuit practice, and secondly, quite a lot of flying time disappeared while waiting for commercial aircraft to do their business. For example, earlier that day, ATC had kept us waiting at the hold for almost 10 minutes before allowing us to enter the runway. And remember, flight time started as soon as we switched the engine on.

Once down on the runway, I practised braking again, and then James gave me another of his *top tips of the day*. He told me that when I was about to brake I should keep the heels of my feet resting on the floor and just squeeze the brakes with my toes. Prior to this advice, I'd removed my feet from the rudder pedals completely, and then smacked them down upon the brakes. This had caused my heavy braking.

James's tip was a good one, almost as good as his previous one: that if his voice got higher and faster, then I was probably not doing what he'd asked. Or even — and this was my personal favourite — that it was usually a good idea to keep your eyes open when landing.

Lesson 10: *Circuit Bashing #2*

ATC quickly cleared us to line up and hold, and then cleared us for take-off. James had full control of the aircraft for another demonstration of the circuit. He told me that on each progressive circuit, I'd have to do more and more while he did less and less. When James landed after his demonstration, I took full control for the take-off.

I flew the first circuit, concentrating on where I was making my turns, and making sure I had a reference point on the horizon to head for. James handled the radio, while I focussed on flying accurately.

On the second go, just when I thought James was busy looking out of the window, he pointed at the airspeed indicator. "Watch your air-speed!"

I increased throttle to get back up to 70 knots.

On my third approach, James told me I was going to take the aircraft all of the way to the ground. He added that he'd control the throttle for me. It was to be my first ever landing.

As I flew closer and closer, James told me what to do and where to go. As we flew over the runway threshold, he told me to raise the nose slightly while he reduced the power to idle. I then went on to make the most perfect landing in the entire history of aviation.

Except of course I didn't. I raised the nose far too much, and we ended up ballooning down the length of the runway. Ballooning describes a landing which involves the aircraft rising up and down in the air before touching down. These balloons resemble a series of invisible small hills.

As we neared the ground again, James told me to hold the nose up and let the plane sink to the ground in a stall-like situation. I tried to do this but bounced hard and James took over to avert the ensuing disaster.

Back up in the circuit, James told me not to worry. "It'll snap into place eventually."

Or else I'll snap the plane in half, I thought.

On the next approach I had to handle all of the controls (i.e. flap, carb heat, throttle, yoke and rudder). James told me to look at the far end of the runway, and to make small corrections if I veered off course. Just above the runway I pulled back slightly and reduced power. This time, only a small balloon occurred before we started to settle downwards. James helped to control the yoke and a second later the main wheels touched down on the concrete. I had no time to reflect though, it was full power for yet another go.

This continued for quite a few more circuits, until James felt I was doing sufficiently well. "On the next lesson," said James. "We'll have to get you on the radio more."

That was my greatest worry. Every time I pressed the red button, I could feel my pulse racing. I was becoming more worried over this aspect of flying than anything else. James was aware of my fear and thought it was perhaps partly his fault. He felt he should have introduced the radio calls sooner, or perhaps more often in the lessons so far.

I wondered how I'd cope with flying and speaking. To me, they couldn't work in tandem.

TOTAL (HOURS) = 11.1

Day 15. Friday 9 August

The weather was awful today with no chance of any flying. I wasn't too disheartened though; I'd done a lot of flying in the week. Also, I was quite pleased to be having a break from it all.

So instead of heading over to the airport, I did a bit more studying, rehearsing the radio calls I'd inevitably have to make next lesson. Little did I know how hard this was going to be.

TOTAL (HOURS) = 11.1

Progress and Worry

'Keep the nose up, you silly idiot!'

-James Jarvis (Flying Instructor)

Day 16. Monday 12 August

Lesson 11: *Aborted Circuit Bashing*

Yesterday, James rang saying he was having today off. For that reason, he'd arranged for me to go up with another instructor. That instructor turned out to be Tony Denson, the owner and chief pilot of the flying school.

The weather was good with only a little wind trying to spoil things and, while I waited for Tony to arrive, I began chatting to another PPL student called Dave Hanson. He was further into the course than me, at the solo circuit stage. Once the elusive first solo was out of the way, a student must notch up four hours of solo flying in the circuit, and that's what Dave was doing.

"How've you found speaking on the radio?" I asked.

Dave shrugged. "Alright. It's other things I'm worried about. Like the exams. I don't have the time to study. Last week I failed meteorology by 5%." He shook his head in disgust.

After making suitable sounds of commiseration, I said, "Well I sound like an idiot over the radio. I just can't get to grips with it. I don't know what's wrong with me."

Just then, Dave's instructor arrived. They both shook hands and headed for the door. On his way out, Dave turned back to me. "Good luck with the radio. If that's all you're worried about then count your lucky stars."

I nodded, smiling.

Ten minutes later Tony Denson arrived. Tony is also a flight examiner. Though I didn't know it at the time, he'd turn out to be the examiner of my skills test. He was a small man in his early fifties, and after chatting to him for a minute or so, I decided he was an amicable enough chap. Once we had the keys to the aircraft, Tony informed me that ATC had turned down his request for a student to do some circuit work.

"But don't worry, I've got a little trick up my sleeve," said Tony. "We'll leave the zone via Eccup Reservoir and ask for re-entry a couple of minutes later. ATC might let us in for circuits then. This, I found out, was a common ruse used by instructors. James ended up doing it a few times too.

We headed over to the airport.

From the outset, it became very clear that I would be required to make many more radio calls than I'd previously done. After doing the initial call to ATC I waited for the reply.

"Golf-Delta Oscar, taxi and hold, Foxtrot Three," said the man in the Tower.

Usually, at this point, James would read back these new instructions for me, but Tony was clearly waiting for me to do it. Pulse building rapidly, I pressed the button and tried my best.

"Taxi to Foxtrot Three."

Tony pressed the button himself and added our call sign. *Damn*, I thought. He must think me a fool.

At the hold, we had to wait for over 20 minutes before we got our next clearance. And when it finally came, it made me realise just how much I still needed to learn:

"Golf-Delta Oscar," said the controller. "You're cleared to leave the zone via Eccup. VFR. Not above 2,000ft. Squawk 2655."

VFR stood for visual flight rules and meant that I had to fly visually as opposed to using the instruments. I wrote bits of this down and somehow managed to read it back to the controller but had no chance to collect my thoughts before the next instruction came.

"Golf-Delta Oscar, after the landing Dash-8, you're cleared to enter and cross runway three-two. Hold short Alpha-Two for further instructions."

He might as well have asked me to hold short on Mars. I didn't have the faintest clue about where to go or what to say back. I spotted the Dash-8 easily enough (a large turboprop that had just landed) and could see it turning off runway 32 onto a taxiway. But I wasn't sure what I was supposed to do. I started panicking. With static hissing in my ears, I pressed the button, then released it. Finally, I turned to Tony, shaking my head.

Tony told me what to say in reply to ATC, and after what seemed like an eternity, I finally got the reply back to the controller. Next, Tony told me to follow the Dash-8, which I did.

Upon reaching the Alpha-Two holding point, I reduced the power and held the brakes. I had a minute to take stock of things. Breathing deeply, I brought myself under control. Tony seemed unaware of my anguish, simply staring out the side window, so I forced myself to concentrate. With pen poised over kneeboard, I waited for the next instruction.

A minute later, after the Dash-8 had safely parked and the BMI jet taken off, ATC gave me instructions to continue to the Bravo Hold. I did this and eventually took off.

Feeling overloaded I headed for Eccup Reservoir, another of the exit-entry points. Throughout the climb, I was required to fly the aircraft and to make radio calls. I was not feeling very confident. I suppose this was because I was with another instructor and the comfort zone that had been present with James had gone.

We circled around Eccup Reservoir and headed straight back for the airport. Unfortunately ATC seemed wise to our ruse and wouldn't allow us any circuit practice. We had to land. After parking up, I thanked Tony, asking him how I'd done.

"Fine. You sounded okay over the radio. General handling's good. Your circuit work could do with tightening up though. Have you been over to Sandtoft?"

I shook my head. Sandtoft was a small airfield about 20 minutes' flying time away. Going there had not even come up in conversation with James Jarvis.

"Maybe you should go there, then. Do circuits at your leisure. You'll have no commercial traffic to bother you."

I nodded, thinking that this sounded like quite a good idea. Besides, it would be interesting to visit a different place for once. I made a mental note to ask James about it on my next lesson.

Just before I left, Tony apologised for the initial wait we'd endured at the start of the flight. He told me that he'd log my flight time as less than it actually was so I wouldn't have to pay for the whole wait. This, understandably, cheered me up because for every minute the engine had been on it had cost me £1.50.

TOTAL (HOURS) = 11.5

Day 17. Tuesday 13 August

Lesson 12: *Instrument Flying*

"James," I said. Can I have a word?" We were in the briefing room of the flying school. It was 8.50 am, an early start for my 12th lesson.

"Course you can, mate." He took a quick slurp from his coffee.

"I want to you listen to how *I* think I'm doing,"

James nodded, putting his cup down. "Okay…"

I told James I was happy with flying in the air. I told him I was pleased with the way I could turn, climb and descend. And I was fairly comfortable with using the trim wheel.

"I'm also happy steering on the ground using the pedals — as long as the turn's not too tight," I said. "And I'm reasonably happy taking off." I paused. "But I can't land for toffee. And braking…? Last week I thought I was okay. But now, I'm not sure. But my biggest worry is the—"

"Radio…?" James interjected.

I nodded, telling him I was developing a phobia about using it. "Whenever I press that button, everything goes out of the window. I might as well have my eyes shut when I speak to ATC. I can't think about anything else full stop."

James tried to calm my worries by saying it was a natural fear, and that all students go through similar periods of radio anxiety.

"Look," he said. "When I first became a policeman in New Zealand, I felt exactly the same on the radio. You'll eventually get used to it. All you need is more practice."

Yes, you did read that correctly. Before James became a commercial pilot, he'd been a policeman in New Zealand. But not only that, he was also a qualified lawyer!

I took a sip of my own coffee, unconvinced at what James had said.

"Cheer up," said James. "Like I said before, if I thought you were doing badly, I'd tell you. But you're not, so let's go out and have a nice flight."

We got up and left the cabin.

At the aircraft I asked James about the possibility of doing circuits at Sandtoft. He shook his head, saying he was loath to go there for three reasons.

First, it would involve a 20-minute flight, which in itself would waste a lot of instruction time. Second, we might set off only to find the weather poor at Sandtoft. Third, he told me, he'd only take a student to Sandtoft if the student's landings were not improving and needed some extra practice. "And yours are fine," he added.

Dylan had already tried to book us in for some circuit practice, but ATC weren't having any of it. Instead, James said we'd do a lesson normally done after the first solo: instrument flying.

Above Harrogate, James told me to put the foggles on: plastic glasses with a frosted top half. Once donned, I couldn't see outside. James told me to scan the instruments, to maintain straight and level flight.

I found it relatively easy. I'd done a lot of instrument flying on my flight simulator. Seeing how comfortable I was with this, James made me practise some turns, climbs and descents, just using instruments. I found these okay as well. In fact, I was enjoying myself.

James told me why basic instrument flying was included in the PPL syllabus. It was a safety measure in case a pilot found himself in cloud and couldn't see anything outside. Using instruments, the pilot would turn the aircraft through 180° and fly back out of the cloud into hopefully good conditions.

James gave me a dramatic simulation of what it was like flying into cloud. After removing the foggles, James told me to fly straight and level. "Now close your eyes," he said.

With my sense of sight out of action, all I could rely upon was my sense of balance.

"Do a turn to the left. Not too steep." I did as requested, eyes tightly shut.

"Now go back to straight and level."

I straightened the aircraft out with my eyes still shut. After 10 seconds or so, James asked me how I thought we were doing.

"Fine," I said. "Straight and level, I think."

"Open your eyes."

We were in a turning descent! Another minute and we'd be crashing. I couldn't believe it. My senses had fooled me into thinking we'd been flying straight and level.

James explained a serious side to the demonstration. Apparently, in some well-documented general aviation fatalities, novice PPL pilots had lost control of their aircraft because they'd flown into cloud by mistake. Instead of trusting their eyesight and using the instruments, a few unlucky pilots had believed their instruments to be malfunctioning. They'd ignored them. All went on to lose control of their aircraft and ultimately crashed. In studies, the average life expectancy of a non-instrument pilot entering thick cloud was about 75 seconds. Gulp!

Lesson 13: *Circuit Bashing #3*

I must write about something that happened the previous day. It started with a cup of tea.

While waiting in the cabin for one of my lessons, I decided to make myself a nice cuppa and went to the fridge to get some milk. When I opened the door, I saw something strange. It was cans of lager. Lots of them, packed from top to bottom — even lined up in the panels on the door. The only other item in there was a lonely bottle of milk squeezed tightly between two cans of Carlsberg Special Brew! I began wondering about the drinking habits of certain instructors.

Today when I walked into the cabin, there was an even more alarming sight. On the table where James was sitting rested a crate of beer.

Noticing the direction of my gaze, James tapped it, uttering, "Ah Jason, do you fancy a brew before we go up?"

Before you start to think that flying schools are the domain of sops and alcoholics, there turned out to be a good reason for the alcohol. James told me that when a student had passed a certain milestone (e.g. going solo) then that student was required to bring booze into the school as their way of saying thanks. In these instances, two people had just passed their commercial pilots' licences (CPL). And by the way, James was only joking about having a drink before we went up — we cracked them open at 2,000 ft.

Joke!

The Tower Lords had finally granted us some precious circuit time. However, the wind was very gusty, throwing our little Cessna around quite a bit. After a while, though, I discovered something interesting.

At the very start of my flying lessons, every little gust of wind had given me cause for concern. Often I was worried that our tiny Cessna would break up or even topple over. But now these gusts weren't worrying me in the slightest. I thought it amazing how my body had become so used to these strange sensations.

However, landing was proving to be tricky. As I came in for each approach, I thought I was doing well just maintaining the rough heading of the runway. The lower I got, the more the gusts would catch one wing or the other. At the last moment, James had to save every landing.

The flare, I was discovering, was the hardest portion of the landing to master. It was when the aircraft was just about to touch down and I had to raise the nose so the main wheels touched down first. The problem was judging when to begin the flare.

Another problem was veering off course during take-off. Just to put you in the picture, I'll attempt to go through the sequence of events leading up to my mistake. Okay — here goes:

Upon touchdown, I had to increase the throttle to full power, steer with the pedals, pull back slightly on the yoke (to keep the nose wheel off the ground) and then, when take-off speed had been reached, I had to pull back gently on the yoke to enable the aircraft to leave the ground. Thankfully, James would retract the flaps for me.

All of this happened in the space of perhaps two or three seconds, and at speeds of around 60 mph. So when James told me to pick a reference point on the horizon to steer towards, I had no spare mental capacity left to do this. I simply headed for what I thought was straight on.

More positively, though, I was finally getting used to the flap control and adjusting the power during the approach. Somehow I was making improvements.

After half an hour of circuits, I experienced the by now familiar common occurrence of a radio-induced mental blackout. These fugues would normally occur on the downwind section.

"Tell them you're left downwind 32 for a touch and go," James prompted.

Flummoxed, I said, "Tell them I'm left what?"

"Say: Golf-Delta Oscar is left downwind for 32. Touch and go."

I composed my mind for a moment, before asking James to give a final verification. "So I say Golf-Delta Oscar is downwind for 32 for a touch and go? Is that right?"

"Yes! Get on with it; we'll be ready for base soon."

After taking a deep breath, I pressed the little red button on my yoke. "Leeds Tower…err…G-DO is…"

I released the button.

"…*Dammit!* What do I say to him? I've forgotten!"

"For God's sake, mate. Tell the poor sod you're downwind for a touch and go!"

"Leeds Tower, I'm downwind to touch… er… 32." I finally told the poor sod.

Miraculously, we did seven circuits that afternoon, with me making more and more of my own decisions each time. My landings were slowly starting to improve, and we were now not landing on the runway like a missile had shot us down. The only downside was the radio work. It was really worrying me.

Just before we parked, James made me practise yet more braking. I even managed to spin around in a tight circle. Even I could see some improvement there.

As a final bit of instruction, James showed me how to fill in my pilot logbook, giving me a couple of tips. He told me to use the same pen colour throughout the logbook, and also to use neat handwriting. This would, according to James, make my logbook look professional should I decide to do the commercial licences at a later stage.

TOTAL (HOURS) = 13.8

Day 18. Wednesday 14 August

Lesson 14: *Circuit Bashing #4*

With lighter winds, I was looking forward to a good bout of circuit bashing but first there was something I needed to sort out. I asked James if he'd do the walkaround for me because I was worried I was missing bits out. He agreed and thankfully he only spotted a few minor things, so we got in and began. We were soon in the air.

"Okay then, Jason." he said as I turned downwind for the second time. "You can fly the circuit reasonably well now. I don't have any real issues with that. But we need to tighten up on your landings. They're still not..."

"—Any good?" I prompted.

"Yeah..."

"Does that mean we're going to Sandtoft for remedial landing practice?"

James laughed. "Not yet."

I'd always known landing would be one of the hardest things to master when learning to fly, but I didn't think I would be this bad at it. Just then though, James gestured for me to be quiet for a moment. He was looking out of his side window. "We'll have to make this the last one, mate."

I shrugged, wondering why.

"And I'll have to do the landing. This main wheel looks really scuffed. It needs to be checked out."

After an impressively soft and gentle landing we taxied to a standstill and checked the tyre. James told me he hadn't seen anything like it before. We stared at the abrasions and scuffmarks. "I can't think how it got like that."

I could. My landings had been so bad I'd nearly blown a tyre. It was the obvious explanation.

James noticed my expression and shook his head. "You've not caused them. They're in the wrong place for that. It's something else. Maybe a bit of debris on the runway. They'll have to be checked out."

I went to get something to eat.

Lesson 15: *Circuit Bashing #5*

When I returned, James told me the scuffmarks had turned out to be a bit of tar picked up on the runway. He'd rubbed the tyre with his finger when I'd gone and it had come off. He sent me off to the aircraft to do the checks. "I'll meet you there in 10 minutes."

Out at the airport, even though I knew how to do the checks, and to the casual, or even experienced observer, I probably looked quite professional doing them, I still felt somewhat strange hanging around an aeroplane by myself. It wouldn't have surprised me to hear a voice shouting through a loudspeaker: *"YOU THERE! IMPOSTER! MOVE AWAY FROM THAT AIRCRAFT IMMEDIATELY!"*

Up we went for more circuit practice. James continued to land the aircraft while I steered using the rudder pedals. Eventually, I could just about manage it. I was also getting happier with the radio calls and no longer going into mental blackout as soon as I spoke. Just partial black-out.

It was windy in the circuit and James kept going on about me drifting off course, or wavering from the required airspeed. He mentioned my poor height keeping on a number of occasions too. After the sixth or seventh telling off, I began to get worried. Perhaps I was regressing. I decided to broach the subject when we'd landed.

"Am I getting worse?"

"What?" said James, climbing out of the door. "Worse? No. You're better than ever."

"So why are you telling me off so much?"

James explained. "Basically, when you first started lessons, I didn't pick up on each and every error because I wanted to build up your confidence. But now that you are fairly confident in the air, I'm pulling you up on all of your mistakes. It's for your own good."

I nodded. It made sense. And something to back it up was the fact that James's voice didn't get as high and agitated as it used to. Well, it still did, but not as often. This proved I was getting better.

TOTAL (HOURS) = 15.5

Day 19. Thursday 15 August

Lesson 16: *Circuit Bashing #6*

The weather was good. Up we went into the circuit. After a few landings, James told me I would be doing the landing completely unaided.

My approach was good, considering the crosswind, but my landing was disastrous. In the flare, James took control at the last second to avoid a nasty liaison with the runway. We went around again.

On the next go, everything was fine until just over the runway threshold. I still couldn't judge how much to pull back on the yoke. Also just to add to my woes I found it hard keeping the aircraft straight.

"C'mon… more right rudder!" James shouted. "And more back pressure on the yoke!" And then we'd bumped down with a crunch. Up we went once more.

Yesterday, I read the average student took between 12-15 hours to go solo. I was now at 16 hours and felt ages away from even considering going up by myself. I couldn't even land. After we'd parked up, I questioned James about it, deciding to broach the subject tactfully and diplomatically.

"So am I shit at landing or what?"

James laughed, telling me I was doing very well and just needed more practice, preferably in calmer conditions. He also told me to get out of the habit of thinking I was doing badly all the time. He called me — and I quote, "a worry wart". I immediately began to worry about what he meant by this.

But he was quite right. I shouldn't have been dwelling on statistics or 'the average pilot', I should have been concentrating on being a safe pilot, especially around a busy controlled airport.

"And don't forget," James said. "You're dealing with full Air Traffic Control here. Students at smaller airfields don't have to contend with what you do. That's partly why it's taking longer for you. Especially with your radio phobia."

I nodded. What James meant was that quieter airfields, where no commercial traffic existed, there was no ATC. There were still qualified people operating the radio in some cases though, but there was a key difference between Air Traffic Controllers and these other people: instructions.

ATC give instructions and clearances that a pilot has to comply with. They are highly qualified individuals (it takes two years for an ATC to complete their training) and are in charge of the airspace around an airport. At smaller airfields, the people operating the radios do not give any instructions; they can only offer information. There are fewer rules and regulations to comply with, and therefore it is less challenging for a pilot to speak to them.

In the UK there is a three-tier hierarchy of people manning the radios. The most qualified are Air Traffic Controllers (ATC). Below them in this hierarchy are Flight Information Officers (FIS). They are licensed and regulated by the Civil Aviation Authority (CAA), though not to the same extent as Air Traffic Controllers. Finally there are Air/Ground Radio Operators (A/G). These people are not regulated or licensed by the CAA, and will hold only a basic qualification in radiotelephony.

I went out for a few drinks with some friends tonight, telling them about my poor landing skills. Instead of getting the sympathy I needed, all I received were laughs and derision. To make matters worse, they gleefully informed me that when I was on my lesson the following day, they'd be there, watching my pathetic attempts, perhaps taking photos.

One of these heartless friends even asked me whether Leeds Bradford Airport had a siren. But before I had time to answer, he started wailing, doing a commendable impression of an air-raid siren. After he'd done that for a few seconds, he then did an impression of someone shouting into a loudspeaker *"ATTENTION! ATTENTION! JASON SMART IS IN THE ZONE! CLEAR ALL RUNWAYS AND FOR GOD'S SAKE, STAY INSIDE THE BUILDING!"* Then the wailing commenced again, closely followed by the sounds of an aeroplane crash landing.

TOTAL (HOURS) = 16.6

Day 20. Friday 16 August

Lesson 17: *Circuit Bashing #7/Emergency Procedures in the Circuit*

The day before my birthday was perfect for flying with clear skies and light wind. I went for my lesson in a good mood. The lesson was at 6 pm meaning James had stayed late to do it, not wanting to disrupt the momentum we'd been building of late.

After checks, we lined up and waited for our clearance to enter the active runway. And then the problems started.

We ended up waiting 35 minutes before ATC allowed us to go, which meant James got annoyed and I got anxious. Thirty-five minutes of doing nothing was costing me about £50. If we hadn't both been so edgy, our vantage point would have been an excellent place to watch airliners take-off and land.

"Right, mate," said James when our clearance finally came. When we land, I'll do the rudder pedals. You do everything else."

I nodded, took off and flew up into the downwind portion of the circuit. I was happy with James's arrangement, and was looking forward to landing in the calm conditions.

On the approach, James talked me through each stage again, but as we crossed the threshold, I pulled up too much (which resulted in the dreaded balloon landing) and then didn't pull up enough (which caused James's voice to get high and rather agitated).

We went around again for another go. This time things went marginally better because I was starting to judge when to begin to pull the yoke back. I still couldn't quite grasp by how much, though. However, I was also getting to the stage where I could think relatively clearly, rather than everything happening in a blur of confused activity.

James was also content to let me fly the circuit as I wished, and had a rather novel approach of proving this to me. Whenever I asked him whether I should turn downwind, he'd just shrug his shoulders and mutter, "Dunno," while looking out of his side window. This was his way of making *me* make the decisions. If I ever did anything wrong, he'd tell me straight away, but as long as I was doing okay, he'd let me carry on and say nothing.

After a couple more circuits, James decided to demonstrate a few of the emergency procedures associated with the circuit again. First up was a flapless landing. This simulated a situation where there was a problem lowering the flaps. On base, instead of dropping them as usual, they stayed put. This meant I had to set the power extremely low or we'd be too fast on approach. On final, we seemed to be much lower than usual, and James explained this.

"It's because you're used to the flaps being down. When they're still up, the nose is higher. This approach is fine for a flapless landing. Keep on going."

We got down successfully and went back around again.

Next was a power-off landing. This simulated an engine failure. With the throttle pulled to idle, the nose had to be lowered drastically until it seemed to me we were heading vertically down. Under James's guidance, we got down in one piece though. But there was no time for celebration. It was up for more.

On the next circuit, as I was levelling off after turning downwind, I began to relax. I knew I had a bit of time before I had to make the radio call and do the checks. I lazily looked outside, admiring the view.

Without warning, James suddenly pulled the power right off.

"ENGINE FAILURE! What are you going to do now?"

The simple answer was nothing. I didn't know what to do. Bewildered, I flew on regardless. A second later, James took over, pushing the nose down, allowing the aircraft to build up speed.

He said, "When you have an engine failure, immediately lower the nose to maintain airspeed. Don't let the aircraft stall."

I nodded, shaken.

"What you did was feeble. In fact, it was worse than feeble. You did nothing."

"I know. Sorry."

James turned to me, smiling. "Don't worry about it. Just be ready next time. Don't let me catch you out again. This could save your life one day."

After touchdown, James said I was nearly there with my landings. It would only take a few more circuits to get them sorted out.

Thanking him for staying late, I headed home after another week of lessons. In the end, my friends hadn't turned up. And though I didn't know it at the time, my first solo was only six days away.

TOTAL (HOURS) = 17.3

The First Solo!

'I did it! I can really fly!'

—Jason Smart (PPL Student)

Day 21. Monday 19 August

Lesson 18: *Circuit Bashing #8*

Absolutely glorious weather, so off I went for an early morning lesson at the flying school. While waiting for James to arrive I began talking to a couple of pilots having a break from their training. One was in his mid-twenties, the other in his early thirties, and both were in the middle of their Instrument Ratings.

They'd only recently completed their Commercial Pilot's Licences (CPL) and were now getting all the ratings enabling them to become airline pilots.

I asked them how much harder the CPL was in comparison to the PPL. Both told me it was quite similar apart from the fact the flying needed to be more accurate. They went on to explain the training needed to become an airline pilot in the UK, as well as the approximate costs.

First, our prospective airline pilot will need to have a Class 1 Medical Certificate *(£300)*. Once passed, he or she will have to do the **PPL** *(£7,000)* followed by something called the **Night-Rating (£700)**. This five-hour training course will remove the 'day only' restriction of the PPL, and allows our pilot to fly at night. After this, the pilot will revise for the **ATPL** (Airline Transport Pilot's Licence) exams *(£2,000)*, of which there are a staggering 14 to pass. Then he or she will have to build up another 100 hours of flying experience before they can move on to the next stage of the training. Many pilots go to Florida for their hour building because the weather over there is usually very good, and more crucially, renting a plane is much cheaper than in the UK. *(100 hours of post-PPL aircraft rental in the USA (£6,000).*

Once the pilot has passed all of the ATPL exams and logged the necessary hours they will have to do the **Multi-Engine-Rating (ME)** *(£2,500)*, which takes about six hours of flight training and seven hours of ground school. It teaches the pilot how to fly an aeroplane with two engines. Unfortunately, this will not be in a Boeing 737, but will be a small twin-engined piston aircraft. Then comes the **Commercial CPL** *(£6,000)*. At 25 hours long, it means our pilot can earn money for his or her flying. Perhaps our pilot will combine these two ratings and do something called a **Multi-Engine-CPL.**

Next comes the real killer of the ratings, the dreaded **Instrument Rating (IR) (£14,000)**, which takes 45 hours to complete. It allows our hypothetical pilot to navigate solely by use of instruments (i.e. lets him or her fly in bad weather.) It also gives him the privilege of flying in Class A airspace, which is out of bounds for all other pilots. It's the hardest of all the hurdles to pass in the quest for the airlines, and even if our pilot passes it he'll have to keep the rating current by doing a re-test every year.

By the way, in the UK there are currently six classes of airspace. Class A airspace is around very busy airports such as Heathrow or Manchester. Class A is also the busy air corridors in which airliners fly (these routes are called airways). Around Leeds Bradford Airport, the airspace is categorised as being Class D. This means it is controlled airspace (controlled by ATC) and pilots can't fly into it (or out of it for that matter) without permission from the Lords of the Tower. (In the UK, there is no

Class C airspace, and Class B is other busy parts of the air, usually high altitude. Class E, F and G also exist.)

Next, in the qualifications race, a pilot needs the ***Multi-Crew Co-ordination (MCC) (£1,500)*** course, which is usually required for pilots wishing to work in a cockpit with two people. It takes 35 hours of ground school and 20 hours in a flight simulator.

After all this, our pilot will have completed about 250 hours of flying time and will have a ***Frozen ATPL (fATPL)***. This means our pilot can get a job as a co-pilot in a commercial aircraft. The licence will remain frozen until he has built up 1,500 hours of flying time (including 500 hours of multi-crew operations) and then it simply becomes an ATPL, and our pilot is now a fully-fledged first officer.

However, it's extremely rare for an airline to employ a pilot with only 250 hours of flying time (though it does happen), so our new pilot (who has spent a fortune so far) needs to build up precious hours.

There are a number of options available. He or she could hire an aircraft themselves and build up hours at their own expense. Or, since they hold a CPL, they can get a job paying them to fly. Crop dusting, banner towing and transporting parachutists are just some of the options. But these jobs are scarce. Then there is the contentious issue of paying for a type rating.

All pilots wishing to fly, say, a Boeing 737 must have a rating added onto their licence saying they are qualified to fly it. This is a called a type rating and involves simulator time, ground school and actual flight time in the relevant aircraft. In the past airlines paid for this and recouped the cost of training by deducting a new employee's salary for a while. But nowadays, many pilots are paying for these type of ratings up front with their own money. And this is thousands and thousands of pounds we're talking about here. But this, they argue, gets them to the head of the queue.

Worse still is the Pay to Fly method of getting an airline job. Not only has our pilot paid for all his or her training and licences and then stumped up for a type rating, but now they are paying an actual airline to let them fly their planes! They will pay for maybe 500 hours of line training and will hopefully be in a better position to get a job at the end of it. Some say this is the death knell for the profession, a way of prostituting pilots, but as long as there are people willing to pay for these schemes, they will continue.

Despite all this desperation for an airline job, there are still those who choose to instruct, building up their hours the old fashioned way, honing their handling skills in the process. But our poverty-stricken pilot cannot simply turn up at a flying school and expect a job. It's not that simple. Another qualification is required: the **Flight Instructor Rating (£5,000).** It takes 30 hours of flying and a whopping 125 hours of ground school. However, at least our desperate pilot can fly and be paid, as opposed to paying for the pleasure.

Unfortunately the pay for flying instructors is generally poor. When I found out how much James earned, it amazed me just how professional he was. James told me there was no excuse for poor instructing, no matter how little he earned, adding that the majority of instructors he knew were thoroughly professional in their teaching. It was only a small minority who became bitter to such an extent it affected their relationships with students.

Now, back to those two pilots I'd been chatting to. I asked them how they had paid for everything. One said he was £40,000 in debt with half of that being on two different credit cards. The other nodded sagely. "Same with me. I've re-mortgaged my house."

I asked them how they could sleep at night, without worrying about their financial plight.

"It bothered me at first," said one of the men, shrugging. "But after the first £10,000, I stopped caring."

His friend nodded. "And if I got to the age of 50 and hadn't done this, I'd know I'd regret it."

Very true words indeed.

James and I taxied to the holding point. When ATC gave me the clearance, I scribbled the key information on my kneeboard but afterwards couldn't make head nor tail of it. I pressed the communications button then released it again.

"Golf-Delta Oscar," asked the controller. "Do you copy?"

Noticing me floundering, James took over and read back the clearance while I sat helplessly. Why was I so bad on the radio?

As we were taxiing to the runway, I questioned James about what had just happened. He told me all I had to do was repeat the key parts of any message from ATC. The problem though was the variety of instructions

ATC could pass. There was no way to predict which one they'd give. Also, I hadn't written enough information on my kneeboard to help me. I looked at it again.

C 32 H A2

To James, it made perfect sense. To me, it might as well have been Ancient Hebrew. What I was supposed to read back was:

Cleared to cross runway 32. Hold short Alpha Two. Golf-Delta Oscar.

Anyway, up we went for more circuit bashing. The first landing was a bit bumpy, but with help from James we made it down. On the next go, as I made the downwind call, ATC informed me that my readability was 2. This meant they could only just about hear what I was saying (a readability of 5 meant perfectly loud and clear). This was good news for me because it meant I could concentrate on flying while James handled the cursed radio.

On the next landing, I made a very good approach, and after touching down very softly, James told me it had been the first unaided landing.

"Really?"

"Yep. Well done, mate," he said. "Let's do another."

However at that point virtually every airliner parked at Leeds decided to take off. This resulted in a series of orbits to let them all depart. Twenty minutes later, ATC cleared us to continue. I did a couple more landings before parking up.

James told me he wanted to tighten up some of my circuit work. "You're not maintaining speed accurately enough. Also, your landings are not accurate enough. It doesn't matter here at Leeds, with such a long, wide runway. But if you ever land on a small grass strip, you'll need to track the centreline better."

I nodded glumly. I thought I'd done really well.

On the drive to the cabin, I asked James a theoretical question. I asked him whether I'd be able to land if he suddenly had a heart attack. After a pregnant pause, James said, "Yep. You'd get it down okay. But the landing would be hard."

I was elated.

With a bit of time on my hands I decided to do another exam. The *Aircraft Technical* test comprised of 50 multiple-choice questions about the physics of flight, the engine, fuel, electrics and a whole lot more. Time allowed was two hours. I completed it in 20 minutes. I passed with 90%. My year of revision had paid high dividends.

Lesson 19: *Circuit Bashing #9*

The weather had deteriorated by the afternoon. Hefty crosswinds spoilt any chance of a prolonged attempt at refining my landing technique. Additionally, ATC instructed us to do orbits more than once, thus delaying things even further.

After we'd landed, James said that although my hours were quite high for someone who hadn't gone solo, I hadn't actually done that many landings.

"At a quiet airfield, you'd be banging them out," he said, shaking his head. "But here at Leeds! How many orbits have we done over the last few days?"

"Loads."

"Exactly. But on the bright side," continued James. "I reckon you're nearly there. Your take-offs are smooth. Your approaches are consistent. Even your landings are not *that* bad. Best of all is your radio work. It's finally coming together."

James was right. I'd done all the calls from start to finish today.

"In fact," continued James, "I reckon if I'd sent you solo you'd have coped on the radio no problem."

This last bit I wasn't so sure about.

TOTAL (HOURS) = 19.0

Day 22. Tuesday 20 August

Lesson 20: *Circuit Bashing #10*

To test your patience to the very limit, I'm going to reproduce a standard conversation with ATC during a typical circuit. Perhaps then you'll appreciate how far I'd progressed with radiotelephony.

Me: Leeds Tower, G-BSDO at Multiflight West with Golf, 1016. Checks complete. Ready for taxi.

ATC: G-BSDO, Information Golf Correct. QNH 1016. Taxi to holding point Foxtrot 3.

Me: To Foxtrot 3. G –BSDO. *[Now I'd trundle to the holding point and wait.]*

ATC: G-DO, are you ready for your clearance?

Me: Go ahead. G-DO.

ATC: G-DO is cleared touch and go. Runway 32. Enter and line up runway 32. QFE is 996 millibars.

Me: Enter and line up 32. QFE 996. G-DO. *[So off I'd go, and when lined up, I'd wait again.]*

ATC: G-DO is cleared for take-off. Right-hand circuit. Wind 300 at 5 knots.

Me: Cleared for take-off. Right-hand circuit. G-DO. *[I'd then take off and make my next call when downwind.]*

Me: G-DO is right downwind 32 for touch and go.

ATC: Roger G-DO. Report when ready for right base.

Me: Report when ready for base. G-DO. *[I'd continue flying downwind until ready for base.]*

Me: G-DO is ready for base.

ATC: G-DO, number one, report when final.

Me: Report when final. G-DO. *[So now I'd start a descent, eventually turning onto the runway heading.]*

Me: G-DO is final for 32.

ATC: G-DO is cleared for a touch and go with a left-hand circuit for runway 32. Surface wind 290 at 7
knots.

Me: Cleared touch and go with a left-hand circuit. G-DO. *[And now*

I'd land and do it all again!]

And these are the calls I am reasonably happy with. It's when ATC say something different that I get confused. Today, when approaching base, ATC said:

ATC: G-DO. You are number 2 to a Baron on a five-mile final. Extend downwind and turn base when advised.

So now I hope you realise my apprehension with the radio. And remember, I still have to fly the aircraft and know where I am at all times. In addition, other pilots are talking on the radio, and it's sometimes an art in itself just managing to get the call in anyway. In the circuit I remembered what James had previously mentioned — about my speed wavering antics — and so I was very careful to keep a curb on this. After the second circuit, James told me it was now no longer an issue.

My third landing of the session was pretty good. Perhaps my best yet. I asked James what he'd give it out of ten. After thinking for a second, he said, "Five."

I couldn't believe my ears. "Five? Is that all?"

"Yeah, mate. Don't feel bad. Five's good. I'd only give a nine or ten to someone with over 100 hours experience."

Grumbling to myself, I was surprised with how good the next landing was. There had only been a little veering from the centreline. I'd also got down on the piano keys (the painted markings at the start of the runway). Up we went again.

"I think the penny's dropped," said James. "I'd give that five and a half."

I think the reason for my improvement was quite simple. On each successive circuit, I could retain more and more information. I even began to have spare mental capacity in the final stages of the landing, and could therefore think clearly during the flare. In earlier lessons this was simply not possible. It was amazing how it all started to come together.

In the following section, I'm going to take you through a normal landing. If you're already a pilot, then perhaps you'd like to skip this section. For the rest of you, hang on tightly and make sure your seatbelt and shoulder harness is tight and secure. The runway is about 5 miles ahead and we're only a couple of minutes from touchdown. The approach is looking good. Here we go.

My left hand is on the yoke, my right hand on the throttle, which I pull out towards me to reduce power slightly. The runway is approaching fast and ATC have just cleared me for a touch and go landing. Glancing at the airspeed, I read back their clearance, but look straight back outside to monitor the approach visually.

I pull back the throttle a touch more — in order to fly at 70 knots — and trim for a stable approach. At 500 ft from the ground I push the carb heat knob in and drop the flaps another notch to 30°. I now have a spare second to glance at the altimeter. It's looking okay, but I can't let my eyes dawdle there; I need to look straight back outside at the approaching runway. I must keep the aircraft heading for the centreline.

I peek again at the airspeed indicator and feel a gust of wind trying to lift one of the wings. A slight turn of the yoke counteracts this. I also seem to be getting a little low so my right hand automatically pushes the throttle in a touch. We're now only 150 ft above the runway, with only seconds to go before touchdown.

After a final check of the mixture control, oil pressure and flap lever, I quickly look again at the runway in front of me. Things are looking just right! As I steal another quick glance at the airspeed indicator, I'm aware the aircraft is about to pass over the runway threshold. I bring back the power even more while simultaneously pulling back slightly on the yoke to arrest the descent. We glide over the edge.

Aiming for the runway numbers, I reduce the power to idle, pull back on the yoke, and at the same time, move my feet on the rudder pedals to straighten up before touchdown. The last thing I want to do is land at an awkward angle. Next comes the hardest part, and I must concentrate at my fullest to get it right.

At only a few feet above the runway I pull the yoke back as far as it will go. My feet are somehow managing to straighten us up and so I concentrate on the far end of the runway as we begin to settle down.

"Keep it up... keep it up... KEEP IT UP YA' POMMY BASTARD!" wails James next to me, just as the stall horn begins its cacophonous warning. And *still* I keep the yoke pulled back to my chest. We don't want to land just yet; we're still too high. But here it is, we're almost there... BUMP! We're down! I loosen my death grip on the yoke to allow the nose-wheel to gently come down. I move my hand to the flap lever, I pull on it and then push the throttle fully in for full power. And then we take off and do it all again and again and again.

During some afternoon circuits, James performed his nasty 'pulling the power off' trick. Unlike last time, I didn't freeze. I immediately pushed the nose down and added some power. I quickly recovered. James was impressed.

"Good. But what would you do if you had an engine failure just after take-off?"

I told him that I'd push the nose down and find a field in front to land in.

James nodded. "That's right. Don't ever try to turn around and land on the runway. You'll never make it."

After a few more landings, some of which were good, and some of which were rather heavy, we parked up and had a chat about things. James told me he'd seen a massive improvement in me today. "In fact, I reckon it was your best lesson yet. I almost sent you solo."

"Sorry?" My heat missed a beat.

"If you'd have done three good landings in a row, I'd have let you loose."

The fact that I'd done two in a row, followed by a poor one, meant that my elusive first solo would have to wait.

We climbed out of the aircraft just as a Dash-8 turboprop landed on runway 32. I turned to watch it taxi in, emotions running rife.

I was flattered James had so much faith in my abilities, but was worried about how I'd cope with no instructor to keep track of things for me. I'd always presumed I'd be mentally prepared to go solo — literally chomping at the bit. But I felt I wasn't ready to go it alone. What if something went wrong? What if I missed a vital call from ATC? What would happen if the engine conked out half way around the circuit? And what if I skidded off the runway during landing?

As we travelled back to the cabin, I asked James whether he thought I was *really* ready to go solo.

"Positive," he said. "You need to get this milestone under your belt so we can move onto the next part of the training."

"But what about the radio?"

James looked confused. "What about it?"

"What if I mess it up?"

"You won't. End of story."

I sat back, half excited, half deranged with fear.

Ten minutes later, as I left to go home, James reminded me that he and his girlfriend were going on a last minute holiday the following day. I'd completely forgotten. "So tomorrow, you'll fly with a friend of mine called Stuart Lodge. He'll probably send you solo." James paused, shaking his head. "I'm annoyed about this actually. He'll get all the glory. It should be me."

I shook James's hand, wishing him a good trip to Greece, pondering the prospect of my first solo.

"Oh, just one last thing," said James. "Stuart's bark is worse than his bite. Just ignore him if he starts to shout."

TOTAL (HOURS) = 20.4

Day 23. Wednesday 21 August

No flying because the flying school only had one of its Cessna 152s flying and it had already been booked by other students. The other was getting an overhaul. This annoyed me for two reasons. The first was that the weather was perfect for circuits. The wind was the other reason. Because it was so light, I'd have probably gone solo. All through the previous night, I'd mentally prepared for going up by myself and even though I knew James wouldn't be there, I still believed I could do it. But with a cancelled lesson, maybe the momentum would be lost.

TOTAL (HOURS) = 20.4

Day 24. Thursday 22 August

Lesson 21: *Circuit Bashing #11/FIRST SOLO!*

When I awoke, I was in a conflict of emotions. With a lesson booked for 11 am, I rang Dylan, who said everything looked fine. The winds were blowing straight down the runway he told me. "If you go solo, you'll have no crosswind."

On the journey to the airport my mind was in turmoil. I was thinking about the prospect of going solo and all it entailed. There would be no instructor to take over should anything go wrong. It would all be down to me. Me who has had traumas over ATC; me who has had problems with headsets; and me who has had problems getting the safety belt on! I felt on the verge of throwing up.

When I arrived at the flying school, I parked up and shook hands with my new instructor, Stuart Lodge. He was an ex-fireman in his early thirties, instructing until a job with the airlines came up. He told me he wanted to see a good circuit with some good radio calls. He expected a very good approach finished by a superb landing. I told him I'd try my best.

"Good," he said. "Or you won't be going solo."

Stuart explained that when an instructor sent a student on their first solo, then the instructor's licence legally covered the student in question. In other words, if I made a gross mistake somewhere, Stuart would be liable. "So I don't send people off who are going to fuck up."

After this hearty pep talk, Stuart sent me out to the aircraft. He remained in the cabin to fill in the paperwork.

I did the checks, and about 10 minutes later, Stuart arrived. He told me to relax because he was going to do all of the internal checks, so we could get into the circuit quickly.

"Are you nervous about going solo?" he asked, when we'd strapped ourselves in.

I nodded.

"Why? What's the worst that can happen?"

Before I had chance to answer, Stuart butted in. "I'll tell you the worst thing. You'll miss the runway and crash." He guffawed at his own mirth.

I prayed to the gods of hellfire.

Stuart then told me of another student, who, on his first solo landing, had veered off the runway, ending up on the grass verge with a collapsed nose-wheel.

"That won't happen to you, though," stated Stuart.

"Why?"

"Cos I'll kick your arse if it does."

Five minutes later, we were in the air for the first circuit. I quickly discovered Stuart had a completely different teaching manner to James. He was loud and brash for a start. He'd shout obscenities if I wavered from my assigned altitude. He'd look at me in a demented way if I started descending too fast. And on my first landing, he said, "What the heck was that? It was a load of bollocks!"

Stuart's method of instructing was a bit unnerving at first, especially since James had always been so calm and collected. But to be fair to Stuart, it was the method he always used with students — and somehow, it seemed to be working for me. He made me develop my trimming technique, especially when on final. He made me really think about the flare. And he achieved all of this by ranting and raving.

On the next circuit, he asked me what I thought of his instructing technique. Turning downwind, I said, "I think you're rather abrupt sometimes, but well intentioned."

"Do you? Well watch where you're fucking going then."

I looked at the runway to my left; we were closing in on it. I quickly straightened up.

I was doing all of the radio calls in the circuit by this point. Stuart told me if I made a good landing he'd jump out and I'd be going solo. Immediately I started worrying. Just as we were about to touch down, I veered from the runway centreline.

"*Oh my God!*" yelled Stuart. "Go around! That was shite!"

The next circuit was better, but Stuart wanted to see one more — just to make sure. I was determined to make it a good one, if only to make Stuart's incessant verbal lashings stop. With the approach looking good, Stuart made a call to ATC.

"Leeds Tower. This will be a full stop landing for Golf-Delta Oscar. I'm sending a student on his first solo."

"Copy that Golf-Delta Oscar. Cleared to land runway 32. Surface wind 300 at 4 knots."

As Stuart read back the landing clearance, I could hardly control the aircraft. *Had I just heard that right? Was I about to go up by myself?*

Amazingly, considering my state of mind, we touched down gently and Stuart told me to taxi off the active runway. As we trundled along, with Stuart in control, he turned to face me. "You ready for this?"

My heart was thumping. My palms were sweating. "Not really," I said.

"Relax," said Stuart. "You're ready. You'll love it."

I sat back, trying to control my breathing.

For the next few minutes, Stuart taxied us into a position behind two other aircraft. We were third in line for take-off.

"Right then, Jason. Don't rush your checks. And when you're happy with everything, tell ATC. They'll give you your clearance. Then just do what you've been doing for the last week or so." With that, Stuart unplugged his headset, gathered his things and said he was going for his lunch.

I sat back, flabbergasted. *Was that it? No more pep talk?*

"Oh, and when you've finished," said Stuart, suddenly remembering something. "Park in the usual spot and meet me over in the cabin."

This brought new feelings of terror because I'd never parked an aircraft by myself before. I told Stuart of this.

He shrugged. "Well it's about time you learnt isn't it!"

Before I could say anything further, Stuart slammed the door and walked off.

I was shocked. I'd always assumed that on a first solo an instructor would be waiting on the ground to offer some sort of moral support. But clearly I was wrong. I could see Stuart walking off at a brisk pace towards his parked car. I turned to the front, facing my fears.

Sitting all alone at the hold was one of the strangest feelings I'd ever experienced. I began to think about what lay ahead. Unfortunately, I had a lot of thinking time available. With two aircraft in front, and some inbound commercial traffic, time seemed to elongate disproportionably. And though I may have imagined it, I'm sure my legs started to shake. I told ATC that I'd done my checks.

As I waited, one of the aircraft in front lined up and departed. The other plane and I shuffled forward, awaiting our turn. Two minutes later, the second aircraft lined up. I was next.

Humming to relieve the pressure, I soon became convinced my headset had stopped working. I began to worry immediately. Eventually, I decided to press the button to ask for a radio check. If no reply came back then I'd obviously have to take drastic action (which at that moment in time would have amounted to fleeing the aircraft — pausing only to vomit along choice sections of the taxiway).

Just then though, ATC proved the headset was still working because

I received the following instruction:

"Golf-Delta Oscar. Cleared to enter, backtrack and line up runway three two."

I read back the clearance and taxied out. After backtracking a suitable length, I tightly turned the aircraft around and held the brakes, palpitating all the while.

"Golf-Delta Oscar. Cleared for take-off runway 32. Left-hand turn. Surface winds 310 at 5 knots."

I read back the instructions and pushed the power to maximum. This was it. The big moment had finally arrived. Make or break! I released the brakes and hurtled down the runway.

Within seconds I made a glorious take-off and found out the aircraft climbs much quicker with just me sitting in it. Before I knew it, I was turning left, climbing to 1,000 ft. I now had a bit of time to get my head around the fact I was flying an aeroplane by myself. *By myself!* It was quite a dizzying feeling seeing an empty seat next to me.

I turned downwind, made my call and did the pre-landing checks. Everything was going like clockwork. I was just about to turn base when ATC threw a spanner into the works.

"Golf-Delta Oscar, due to an inbound 757, you'll be number three in traffic. Extend downwind. Report when visual with the 757."

My mind couldn't process everything. Shaking my head in the cockpit, I pressed the button and asked ATC to repeat everything. The man in the Tower kindly obliged, but afterwards, I was still none the wiser. How far did he want me to extend downwind? And what if I didn't see the Boeing 757? Things were slipping from my control.

Perhaps sensing my despondency, the controller came back with another instruction. "Golf-Delta Oscar, if you prefer, you can orbit right until advised."

My relief was palpable. I'd done so many orbits on previous lessons that I was happy with this arrangement. I told ATC I'd take this option.

With one orbit complete, the controller gave permission for me to continue with my circuit and to report final. I was number one to land. The other two planes were already down.

Turning base, I began the descent, relaxing again. Just about to turn final though, ATC lobbed another spanner my way.

"Golf-Delta Oscar," said ATC. "Sorry about this. Due to another high-speed inbound, extend base past the runway. Then do a slow right-hand turn back onto final. You're number two in traffic."

Miraculously, I managed to understand what he meant. I acknowledged these new and totally unexpected instructions. I went past the turning for final, wondering if this was normal for a first solo. Over my right shoulder I could see a plane on final approach.

Eventually, I turned onto the runway heading, and began a steady, controlled approach. I told ATC that I was on final for runway 32 and they gave me permission to land.

I was at full concentration during my first solo landing, and when I touched down I thought it was perhaps my best landing ever.

"Golf-Delta Oscar, well done," said the controller. "And thanks for your help up there."

After turning off the runway, I taxied to the apron; expertly avoiding the wingtips of other parked planes, and managed to park the aircraft in its spot. I switched everything off and left the Cessna. When I got to my car, I collapsed into the seat, taking a large gulp of air. My pulse was slowly returning to normal, and my face was losing the red look of a man on the edge of a heart attack, but I had done it! I'd actually taken off, flown a circuit and landed a plane all on my own! I'd even coped with speaking over the radio! Even with the strange instructions I'd received. I was amazed.

When I got back to the cabin, handshakes and congratulations greeted me. Stuart told me I was a real pilot, and that the flying school wanted booze. (I told them that I would bring some in the next day).

Stuart told me to fill my logbook in, recording that I'd done 0.3 hours solo. He told me to use a red pen — the only logbook entry that would ever be in that colour. It would remind me of what I'd accomplished.

CAPTAIN		FLIGHT DETA
NAME	HOLDER'S OPERATING CAPACITY	FROM	
S. LODGE	P. U/T	LEEDS	LE(
SELF	P. I	LEEDS	LE
G. McPHAIL	P U/T	LEEDS	LE(
G. McPHAIL	P. U/T	LEEDS	LE
SELF	P. I	LEEDS	LE
P OWEI	P	LEEDS	LEf

TOTAL TIME (HOURS) = 21.7

Day 25. Friday 23 August

Lesson 22: *Circuit Bashing #12 (with Crosswinds)*

After the joy and triumph of the previous day, today turned out to be a disaster.

At the flying school I shook hands with another instructor. Not Stuart Lodge, but a Yorkshireman named Geoff McPhail (the same instructor I'd spoken to back on day three). He told me there was quite a bit of crosswind. "So today will be good practice for you. It's all well and good landing on a calm day. But what about a windy day?"

Good question. We went out to the aircraft to find out.

While flying downwind something happened that made me realise how little I knew and it had nothing to do with the wind. Out of the blue, ATC said, "Golf-Delta Oscar, due to a significant change of wind direction, I'm going to have to take you out of the 32 circuit. Instead of reporting right base for runway 32, I want you to expedite a turn to the left and report left downwind for runway 14."

Totally dumbfounded, I didn't have the faintest idea of what to say back. Trying in vain to visualise what I was supposed to do, the seconds ticked by with ATC awaiting my response. But I had none to give. Geoff took over; pressing the communications button himself.

"Wilco. Changing to the 14 circuit. Report left downwind, G-DO."

Imagine if I'd been flying solo and they had given me the same instructions? I'd have probably panicked. Thinking of the repercussions of this, my approach to runway 14 was pathetic, my landing abysmal. Geoff even had to help me out during the flare. We banged down and went around again.

At 500 ft I had to ask ATC to repeat the circuit direction because I had forgotten it. Everything seemed to be unravelling before my very eyes.

The hefty crosswind caused me a bit of hassle on the next landing flare. The result was another poor landing. Feeling miserable, we went around again, Geoff telling me not to worry.

Turning downwind on the next circuit, ATC spoke up again.

"Golf-Delta Oscar. Due to inbound circuit traffic, I'd like you to make an early base turn to join the left-hand circuit for 14. Report left downwind for runway 14."

What? I couldn't grasp what he expected me to do. At that moment in time, we were on a right-hand circuit and the controller wanted me to swap to a left-hand circuit. But how could I do that? I shook my head and looked at Geoff. I told him to take over. I let go of the controls. I'd lost confidence in myself. I told him I wanted to land. I'd had enough.

After we'd parked, Geoff told me I'd flown well, adding that my landings were not *that* bad.

"As a student," he consoled, "you'll have days of good landing, followed by days of bad ones. Eventually your experience will build up to the stage where the good landings will be more frequent."

I shrugged, in no mood for conversation.

"And you'll be off solo again in no time at all."

I unbuckled my shoulder harness. "But what if I get a strange instruction from ATC?" I said. "Like we did just then? What do I do then?"

Geoff removed his headset. "You fly the plane first and foremost.

That's your main priority. Then ask ATC to repeat what they said. If you still don't get it, get them to say it again slowly. It'll get through eventually."

I drove home in a mood just slightly above hopelessness. First solo followed by unmitigated disaster. What an emotional rollercoaster it had been. I certainly hadn't expected to be feeling so drained and worn out.

TOTAL (HOURS) = 22.7

Advanced Training

'We're not here to hold your hand anymore...'

-Clive Sheldon (Flying Instructor)

Day 26. Saturday 24 August

Lesson 23: *Circuit Bashing #13/Solo Circuits*

I'd decided that I had no choice but to break my 'no flying on a weekend' rule. With a new school term looming up, I needed to get as much flying in as possible. However, with the memory of my previous lesson fresh in my mind, I wasn't looking forward to flying in the slightest.

Geoff McPhail sent me out to the aircraft, telling me to do the checks and to start it up. This was to be the first time I'd started up an aircraft by myself, but everything went according to plan. When Geoff arrived, we took off and went for some more circuit practice.

One thing became immediately apparent. Despite the glorious weather, there was very little traffic in Leeds Airspace. For three whole circuits no other planes took off or landed. Even better was that ATC didn't give me any unexpected instructions. Because of this, my confidence started to build up again.

After the third landing, Geoff informed ATC of a crew change. It was time to fly solo again. At the hold, Geoff told me to do four circuits and to enjoy myself. He then climbed out.

I was apprehensive. After I'd done the power checks, I was up in the air before I knew it, heading downwind. When I called up ATC, they told me to do an orbit because of the incoming traffic. That was just my luck, three circuits with Geoff and not a single aeroplane for miles, but now, on my first solo circuit of the day, all the big jets decided to arrive.

I did my orbit and hummed a few tunes to myself. Then ATC told me to report final. The landing went okay, and then it was back in the air, remembering to raise the flaps in stages.

One thing I noticed during my solo circuits was that as soon as I was by myself, I was able to concentrate a lot more. Knowing there was nobody to take over if things went wrong turned out to be a great way of focussing the mind.

After the fourth landing, I taxied in, happy with my performance for the morning. I was back on track after the blip of the previous lesson.

At home, I decided to do a few circuits on my flight simulator. Flying in the virtual circuit of Leeds Bradford Airport, I simulated one of the strange requests from ATC. I pretended I'd just received instructions to change the runway circuit. By using the simulator; I found I could do this very easily. I think I know why.

Firstly, in my simulator there were no other planes anywhere (I'd switched off that option). Secondly; the virtual ATC was nothing like real life ATC. And finally, but most importantly, I knew that if something went wrong, then the pause button would take care of everything.

This is perhaps the greatest difference between flight simulators and real flight. The psychological knowledge that at home you're safe and sound. With real flying, you're up there all alone, flying around with other aircraft, talking to ATC, and dealing with a multitude of things at once. Pulling over and taking a breather is simply not an option.

However, in the defence of my flight simulator, it did give me some much needed, situational awareness of the airport. I could taxi around

Leeds Bradford Airport to my heart's content, stopping at various holding points and crossing the runway at leisure. For that I was grateful.

TOTAL (HOURS) = 24.1

Day 27. Sunday 25 August

Lesson 24: *Solo Circuits*

Weekend flying once more.

At the cabin, Geoff told me there was a 9-knot crosswind blowing at right angles to the runway, i.e. the worst possible scenario. Obviously remembering my abysmal lesson in strong winds, Geoff suggested I wait for an hour or so. The forecast said the wind would die down. I nodded and sat down.

Just then, a big Geordie bloke in his early forties walked in. It was Kevin Powell, one of the chief instructors. He mainly dealt with the commercial and instrument side of training. He saw me and said, "Why are you sat there? Golf-Delta Oscar's sat doing nowt?"

I told him about the wind.

"Don't be daft, man. The breeze is nae bother."

I looked outside and could see a few clouds racing past the window.

"Tell you what," Kevin said. "Why don't we go out for a couple of circuits? I can look at your landings and you can see what the wind is like."

I looked at Geoff, who nodded. I turned back to Kevin, thanking him for the offer.

As we lined up for a first circuit, Kevin spoke up. "I'm feeling a bit off-colour today, by the way. Dodgy curry I reckon, so I don't fancy too much flying this afternoon." He rubbed his ample girth. "So tell you what. If you do two good landings in a row, and you're happy with everything, I'll get out and leave you to it. How does that sound?"

I told him it sounded like a fine idea.

A minute later, we took off.

My first landing went very well. In fact it was my best ever, even with the crosswind. As we took off again, I asked Kevin what he thought of my skills.

He shrugged. "Nae bother man. Mind you, me standards are very low."

The next landing was just as good and Kevin told me to taxi off the runway. After lining me up at the hold for runway 32, he asked if I was happy. I told him that I was, so he jumped out leaving me to it once more.

After permission from ATC, I went back up for more solo circuits. Following the first landing I calmed down, beginning to really enjoy flying by myself. An underlying feeling of apprehension was still present but excitement seemed to have counteracted it.

An hour later, I landed and parked the aircraft. Back at the cabin, Kevin told me I could do another hour later on if I wished, even though I had no time booked. I thanked him and during the wait I decided to do another exam.

It was *Flight Performance and Planning.* I scraped a pass with 80%. Afterwards, I went back to the airport for more solo circuits.

Lesson 25: *Solo Circuits*

Earlier, I'd noticed my mouth getting dry, especially when talking to ATC, so I decided to chew gum. I'd considered taking drinks into the air but could foresee the obvious disaster in this. With my gum moistening my dry palette, I did my checks and contacted ATC.

On the first circuit I got an unexpected instruction. I didn't panic, I listened to what had been said, visualised what ATC wanted me to do and did just that. It went like clockwork.

On another circuit, I became aware of a strange habit I seemed to have been developing when flying solo: singing aloud. The more I thought about it, the more I did it. I'd sing anything, including songs I hadn't heard in years — or worse still — make my own tunes up, complete with infantile lyrics and silly accents. I had visions of me crooning these tunes with the communication button accidentally depressed, while airline pilots and air traffic controllers listened in total bewilderment.

However, my landings were getting better. I could track the runway centreline much more accurately and could even do a relatively smooth(ish) touchdown. There was one exception though. Coming in for my fourth approach, ATC told a BMI jet on the ground to wait for me to land before entering the runway.

I could see the airliner at a holding point next to the active runway. The BMI pilot told ATC they had me visual. With two airline pilots watching me, I was determined to make it my best landing yet.

I came in well and everything was looking good. I began to think that the BMI pilots would be soon on the company phone, persuading their bosses to offer me immediate employment. With a grin forming on my face, I flared the aircraft, and came sinking in fast. Panicked, I applied a blast of power and immediately ballooned, and then crashed to the ground with an eyeball-shaking jolt. It was my worst landing ever, and those two pilots had seen it all. The shame of it.

On final of the next circuit, ATC gave me another unexpected instruction.

"Golf-Delta Oscar. Due to high speed inbound commercial traffic behind you, expedite a go around. Left-hand circuit."

I immediately pushed the throttle in, raised some flap, and climbed to 1,000 ft. As I turned crosswind, I could see a Jet2 757 taxiing in. As I did this manoeuvre, I think I was humming the theme tune to *Scooby Doo*.

After another hour, I decided to land and stop for the day. While I drove home, I reflected on my day. Two hours of solo flying notched up. Nothing could stop me now. I started humming a Queen song...

TOTAL (HOURS) = 26.5

Day 28. Monday 26 August

Lesson 26: *Solo Circuits*

Before I describe my lesson, I'm going to give some advice about flying with different instructors.

All instructors have slightly different methods of teaching. Some are calm and collected, others are loud and impatient. And there are those who cover all shades of grey in between. And each of these instructors might have a slightly different way of teaching a certain thing.

For example, when flying with Kevin Powell, he'd noticed me putting down 20° of flap during the approach. He'd asked why. I told him that James had told me to do it like that. Kevin nodded, saying that as long as I knew what I was doing *and* was flying safely, then that was fine.

When flying with Stuart Lodge, just before he sent me solo, he'd also noticed me putting down 20° of flap. He said I'd done it wrong. "You should put 10° down first, and when you've stabilised the aircraft, you can lower more."

So who was right?

Both, it seems. They just had different methods of flying the approach. Be aware of this.

Radio etiquette is another source of major difference between instructors. For a radio novice like me this caused a lot of turmoil. Consider the following scenario: I've just taken off (with instructor) and Leeds Tower has instructed me to contact Leeds Approach. Changing the frequency, I collect my thoughts for a moment. The instructor notes the hesitation and tells me what to say to the new controller.

James might say, "Leeds Approach this is G-BSDO at 1,800 ft for Eccup."

Geoff could say, "Leeds Approach this is G-BSDO. Routing to Eccup at 1,800 ft."

Tony may say, "Leeds Approach, G-BSDO. On track Eccup at 1,800 ft."

Which all convey the same message. But to me, it caused needless confusion.

Arriving at the flying school, I had an incident with a part-time instructor. It started off innocently enough.

I asked the instructor whether he'd heard from James Jarvis because I wanted to know whether he'd got back from his holiday in Greece. The instructor looked up from his magazine, telling me he hadn't spoken to James since he'd gone away. He looked back down again.

Shrugging, I went into the kitchen to make myself a cup of tea. I wondered what had caused the frosty reception. Upon my return, the instructor (who I shall now fictitiously call Clive Sheldon) asked me why I wasn't happy with James.

This question obviously startled me. I told Clive I was perfectly happy with James, and asked him what he meant.

"Just something I've heard."

"Something you've heard? From who? And about what?"

Clive shrugged. "Just things." He picked up another magazine, leafing through it. End of conversation.

I also picked up a magazine, just as Geoff McPhail walked through the door. After Geoff and Clive had said hello to each other, Geoff told me to go out and pre-flight the aircraft for some solo circuits.

"Does it need any fuel?" I asked.

Before Geoff had time to answer, Clive piped up. "For God's sake. You're flying solo now. You need to find these things out yourself. We're not here to hold your hand anymore. You shouldn't have to ask about fuel."

I felt *that* small. I was just glad we were the only three people in the flying school at that time of the day. I collected my headset and high-visibility vest and left the cabin in an angry mood.

There was a nasty crosswind at the airport and, still reeling about what Clive had said, I checked the fuel and found plenty. Ten minutes later I took off on a cold and windy morning, fully expecting to have a torrid time.

Astonishingly, my first landing turned out to be my best one ever. I'd consigned the incident back in the cabin to the back of my mind. The next landing was just as good. In fact, all of my landings for the next hour were good ones. All in the worst weather yet.

However, I did notice a disturbing addition to my singing habit. Totally unnecessary head movements, possibly resembling Stevie Wonder, now accompanied my tuneless ditties. I promised myself then that I'd keep a check on this alarming development.

My final landing was to be the most exciting. ATC asked if I could accept a short final approach. There was an incoming jet, and they wanted to get me in before it landed. I told them I'd take it.

In the past, I'd seen James do this type of manoeuvre, but now it was my turn. With my pulse racing, I turned base very early, descending onto final with only seconds to spare. Stabilising the approach, I did another perfect landing and taxied off the runway.

One of the greatest feelings after flying solo comes when taxiing back to park the aircraft. As I climbed out of the Cessna, the feeling of big-headedness was immense because I knew that all the assembled spotters and students would know that I'd just flown an aeroplane by myself. It wasn't that long ago that I'd felt the very same feelings of envy. Walking towards my car, a grin spread across my face.

Lesson 27: Recovery from Unusual Attitudes/Intro to Practice Forced Landings (PFLs)

Because I only needed 12 more minutes of solo circuits to make up the required four hours, Geoff decided we could move onto some advanced training. He said I could make up the 12 minutes at a later date, perhaps when doing some solo navigation work. So in the afternoon session we left the zone for the first time in ages, heading out via Menwith. We soon arrived over farmers' fields and moorland.

First, Geoff demonstrated how to recover the aircraft from unusual attitudes. This amounted to him banking steeply and pushing the aircraft down into a dive. Quite quickly I felt my stomach take a turn for the worse.

"First pull the throttle to idle," said Geoff, doing so. "Then straighten the wings and add some rudder like this."

We were now merely heading downwards in a straight line. "Next pull up and add power." We ended up straight and level. The whole recovery had taken less than two seconds.

Then it was my turn.

Geoff manoeuvred the aircraft into a downwards roll and told me to recover. Though not quite as quick or as smooth as Geoff's demonstration, I recovered the aircraft well enough for the instructor's liking. After another go, Geoff was satisfied with my skills and told me we'd be doing a PFL.

"A what?" I said. I'd never heard of a PFL.

"A practice forced landing. It's what to do if the engine ever seizes up."

Now many people assume that when an aeroplane loses its power, it will simply fall to the ground like a brick. This assumption is incorrect. When an aircraft has no power, it merely becomes a glider. As long as the aircraft is high enough, the pilot should have enough time to locate a suitable field to land in. Indeed there are famous stories about large airliners losing power to their engines but then going on to make successful glide landings at nearby airports.

In April 2001, an Airbus A330 carrying almost 300 passengers took off from Toronto, Canada, on a flight to Lisbon, Portugal. However, somewhere over the Atlantic, the crew noticed they were rapidly losing fuel. Quickly surmising they would not reach Portugal, they immediately changed course for the Azores; a small island chain located about 1,000 miles west of the Portuguese coast. Eventually, as the fuel began to run out, both engines 'flamed out', and effectively 300 people were flying inside a gigantic glider. Somehow, though, the pilots managed to glide the aircraft down to the runway — even though they had absolutely no power for a whole 10 minutes. They came in high and fast, and though they burst a few tyres upon touchdown, everybody survived. A truly amazing story I think you'll agree.

If the engine failed at 3,000 ft in a Cessna 152, the pilot would have about four minutes to get down on the ground, which should be plenty, Geoff told me.

He demonstrated what to do upon losing the engine and pulled the power right off. Immediately, the nose dropped. Pulling up slightly, Geoff trimmed for a 70-knot glide while looking outside for a good field.

"I'm looking for a large flat one," he told me, moving his head from left and right. "And if possible, one that's slightly uphill to slow us down on the ground."

I nodded, trying to remember everything. We'd dropped about 300 ft since Geoff had pulled the power off. I looked outside to spot a field.

"I'm also looking for sheep and power lines," continued Geoff. "And in an ideal world, I'd like a field facing the wind direction. It's better to land into the wind as you know."

We slowly turned, Geoff scanning everything on the ground. At about 1,500 ft, he pointed out of his right window. "There's one. That'll do nicely. And now I've picked it, I'm going to fly downwind and try an engine restart."

For the benefit of the demonstration, Geoff pretended the engine was still knackered, and as we headed downwind to the field, he mimed pushing the communications button.

"Leeds Approach. Mayday. Mayday. Mayday. Golf-Delta Oscar with engine failure. Cessna 152, 5 miles north-west of Harrogate, descending through 1,300 ft. Two POB." (POB stands for 'persons on board').

As we turned onto final for the field, Geoff said that if it had been an *actual* forced landing then the doors would be unlatched to enable a hasty retreat after touchdown. However, we kept ours firmly secured. On short final, with enough height to easily get down, Geoff lowered all the flaps in one go, announcing we were now ready to make the landing.

At a couple of hundred feet from the ground, Geoff added full power and up we went, climbing back to 3,000 ft. Telling me to head back for the airport, Geoff said, "Tomorrow, you'll get to do it by yourself with Clive Sheldon."

"Clive?"

"Yeah. I'm having tomorrow off. I thought I'd told you."

I closed my eyes. Flying with Clive Sheldon would not be fun. I'd not spoken to him since the incident at the flying school. We undertook the journey back to Leeds more or less in radio silence.

TOTAL (HOURS) = 28.5

Day 29. Tuesday 27 August

Lesson 28: *PFLs/Intro to Map Reading*

The weather was calm when I reached the flying school. Clive hadn't yet arrived so I got chatting to Kevin Powell, the Geordie commercial instructor. I asked him whether he'd ever considered a job with the airlines, but his answer was an emphatic no.

"I'd be bored doing the same thing every day. Plus, I want to be home with my family every night. You don't get that with most airline jobs." Kevin looked pensive for moment. "Mind you, some good friends of mine are airline pilots. They love it."

Clive Sheldon soon arrived. He quickly sent me out to the airport, saying he'd be there in 10 minutes.

Trying not to think about my previous conversation with Clive, I drove over to the airport to do the checks. During my walkaround, I noticed the aircraft was low on fuel so went to find the refuelling man, who came out to fill her up. Just then, Clive arrived. "What are you doing?" he asked.

I told him about my dipstick check. "The tanks were only half-full."

"And what do you mean by *half-full?*"

I shrugged. "Only half the fuel is there."

Ignoring my flippancy, Clive asked me a different question. "How much fuel can the tanks hold, *excluding* unusable fuel?"

I admitted I didn't know.

Clive shook his head, telling me to read the books properly. Then he wandered over to the refueller. As I stowed my flight bag inside the aircraft, I could hear them laughing about something.

Once refuelling was complete, Clive began pushing the aircraft backwards. Because I was just behind the wing, I had to duck rapidly to avoid contact with the aileron. Clive apologised, and then asked if I'd done a thorough pre-flight check. I told him I had, but he decided to check the elevators and rudder himself. "I don't trust some students," he said, grinning thinly towards the refueller.

My patience finally snapped. "What's wrong with you?"

Clive looked up, confused. "What do you mean? What's wrong with me?"

"You haven't spoken a civil word since you got here." I paused, gathering my thoughts. "If you don't like me just say so. It's no skin off my nose."

Clive released the rudder. "What makes you think I don't like you?"

I reminded him about his comments about James Jarvis, as well as questioning me about putting fuel in the tanks. I said, "I don't think we should fly together, Clive. Let's just forget about this lesson. Neither of us would feel comfortable."

Clive stood up, mock innocence etched across his face. "You're being paranoid, Jason. You're imagining things. Just get in so we can have a good lesson."

After a pause, with Clive and the refuelling man watching me carefully, I climbed into the aircraft feeling extremely uncomfortable. But perhaps Clive *was* correct; maybe I *was* being stupid.

A minute later, Clive climbed in and plugged in his headset. He asked me whether I could hear him. I nodded but told him he was very quiet. Twiddling some communications knobs, he asked the same question again. I told him it was no better.

Clive began saying something else, but as he spoke, ATC gave instructions to another pilot drowning him out. When ATC finished speaking, I told Clive this and he nodded. He then told me he'd only speak if ATC were not talking. Meanwhile, I taxied to the hold.

After take-off, we left the zone via Harrogate and then, calming down slightly, I began a turn to the south-east. Suddenly Clive spoke up.

"I can't believe what you said down there." He sat back in his seat, arms folded. He looked pissed off.

My mind was in abject turmoil. My brain went into overdrive. Somehow managing to keep my composure, I told him it was obviously a misunderstanding. "I just got the wrong end of the stick," I said. "Forget it."

Clive didn't say anything for a while; he simply stared out the window. Eventually he nodded and told me we'd do some practice forced landings. I breathed easily again.

Like Geoff had done the previous day, Clive demonstrated a PFL. Then it was my turn. I found the procedure fairly straightforward, and I knew why. Psychologically, I *knew* the engine was fine and we weren't actually going to end up in a field. Additionally, I knew I had an instructor sitting next to me, even if he did hate my guts, so as a result there wasn't any real fear or urgency in what I was doing. It seemed a false scenario. Nevertheless, Clive seemed satisfied with what I'd done, so we moved onto something new: navigation.

Clive asked me to tell him where I thought we were. Glancing at the chart, then outside, I told Clive I had no idea.

Nodding, Clive pointed at a road on the chart. "That's the A1." He then gestured outside toward a tiny strip of grey. I saw it, and nodded uncertainly. It could be any road as far as I was concerned.

"And this yellow blob," continued Clive, pointing at a town on the chart, "is Wetherby." He pointed outside over the nose to the right. "There it is. The A1 curves around it."

I looked, and saw what he was referring to. I looked at the chart, and could see the same thing.

Clive told me to head east until we were over the historic town of York. I could see the Minster as well as the racecourse. They looked amazing from the air.

"Look to your left," said Clive. "See that airfield is the distance?"

Turning my head, I strained my eyes to see what he was pointing to. A few seconds later, I could just about make out an airfield in the haze. I told him I had it in sight.

"So what is it?"

I looked at the chart, and seeing only one airfield north of York, I told Clive it had to be RAF Linton-On-Ouse.

I was right.

Clive then gave me a top tip. He told me to align my chart in the direction of travel. For example, heading east, I turned my chart so that the eastern edge was facing in front of me. It made it easier to see what was coming up.

To be truthful, though, I was finding map reading difficult. I was okay with obvious features, but smaller towns were proving difficult to identify. Looking down at a town, referring to the chart and flying the aircraft as well as straining to hear Clive over ATC was proving a bit too much to do.

We soon headed back to the airport and landed. It was a hard landing.

During the lesson debriefing, Clive told me I really needed to tighten up in a number of areas, the main one being my erratic use of trim. He told me I had to use it much more positively to achieve stable flight path.

"Don't let the aircraft fly by itself. That's what you're doing at the moment." Clive paused, staring hard at me. "And I'm sorry to say this, but unless you get these basic things sorted out, you'll fail the skills test."

I didn't know what to say. I felt deflated. Mumbling a word of thanks I left the cabin, climbing into my car.

At home, I thought about my lesson with Clive Sheldon.

From the outset it had been hard work. Quite clearly there had been a clash of personalities between us. When learning to fly, a student needs to feel at ease. With Clive, I hadn't been at all comfortable, and neither, I suspect, had he. In fact, flying with Clive had bothered me so much that I considered giving up learning to fly. I'd always thought learning would be fun, and something to look forward to, but for me, the enjoyment seemed to have disappeared.

I thought long and hard about why I was doing a Private Pilot's Licence. Was I doing it for enjoyment? Was I doing it for a sense of achievement? It was perhaps a mixture of both. But unfortunately for me, Clive had managed to remove the enjoyment factor and had done a lot to erode my already shaky confidence. I wondered if it was worth carrying on if I was feeling this miserable. Was I wasting my money if I was going to fail my flight test anyway?

TOTAL (HOURS) = 29.8

Day 30. Wednesday 28 August

Lesson 29: *Basic Navigation*

I hardly slept a wink, but I had at least formulated a plan of action. I rang Dylan to ask who my instructor was to be. When he told me it was Geoff McPhail, I breathed a sigh of relief.

"Is that okay?" asked Dylan.

"Yeah, that's fine. But I must warn you; this might be my last lesson."

There was silence on the other end of the phone. Eventually Dylan asked why.

I told him about my lesson with Clive, and what he'd said to me. "So I've been dreading today. If I'd been down to fly with Clive I'd have cancelled. In fact, I was hoping for rain."

Dylan told me not to rush headlong into any rash decision. "Just come in and fly with Geoff. See how you feel after that. If you still want to drop out then that will be your decision. And don't worry about Clive. You'll never have to fly with him again."

I drove to the airport, for possibly my last flying lesson. When I arrived, Geoff McPhail took me into a little room for a chat.

"I've heard about yesterday," he told me. "Don't let Clive worry you. He says things without thinking."

"Where is he today?"

"Dunno. Probably at Sandtoft with another student. Forget about him."

Geoff told me we'd be doing a navigation trip together. He'd do all of the flying so I could relax and get to grips with map reading. I wondered if Dylan had told him to go easy on me.

After a briefing on how aeronautical charts worked, Geoff showed me how to plan a flight to the Humber Suspension Bridge via the town of Dewsbury.

First I marked the route on my chart then measured the distances of both legs. Then I worked out the headings to cater for the wind. This involved using the whiz wheel. I also calculated the approximate time it would take to travel these legs. After 20 minutes we were ready to go.

When Geoff took off I noted down the time and told him to turn on a southerly heading to get to Dewsbury. After a few minutes, I spotted the town, immediately recognising the B&Q superstore. Telling Geoff to turn east on a bearing of 093°, I just hoped my calculations would prove adequate for the task, especially since we would be skirting the northern edge of Doncaster's Class D airspace.

As we flew along, Geoff told me to look for landmarks at every opportunity in order to establish where we were and where we were going. For instance, about 10 nautical miles (nm) east of Dewsbury we passed over a motorway that I recognised as the M62. By referring to my chart I noticed that the M62 intersected the A1(M) at more or less right angles. Near this criss-cross were two yellow blobs representing Castleford and Pontefract. I looked outside and immediately spotted them.

A minute later, Geoff told me to look at the power stations up ahead. "I want you to decide whether we're going in the right direction for the bridge or not."

I referred to my chart and according to it, Ferrybridge Power Station should be up ahead, slightly to the left, exactly where it was. We were fine. I told Geoff this.

"Good," said Geoff. "But what about that little town over there?" He pointed over to the left.

Looking at my chart again, I informed Geoff it was Selby.

"How do you know?" He rolled the wings and pointed out another settlement closer by. "Is that not Selby?

I was unsure now. I looked at the town Geoff had just pointed to and referred back to my chart. Then it came to me. *Geoff's* town could not be Selby because it had no river running through it! I told Geoff the good news.

After my display of superior navigational skills, Geoff decided not to go all of the way to the Humber Bridge, but to demonstrate instead a standard overhead join at Sherburn-in-Elmet Airfield. Geoff told me there would be no ATC at Sherburn, but someone would be operating the radios to give me information. Geoff radioed them, and a well-spoken gent told us the runway in use and some wind information.

Flying over the aerodrome at 1,500 ft, Geoff turned onto the *dead-side* of the circuit, which is basically downwind, except on the opposite side and direction. He turned downwind and made a radio call to tell whoever was listening of his intentions. The person manning the radio at Sherburn didn't speak at all during the whole approach, and I thought to myself how much easier the radio work would have been if I'd done my PPL at a general aviation airfield, rather than at Leeds Bradford International Airport.

We didn't actually land at Sherburn and instead did a low approach and climb out. Geoff then asked me to estimate a heading to get us back to Eccup Reservoir for a rejoin at Leeds. Looking at my trusty chart, I told him where to head, and much to my surprise, a few minutes later, there it was, plainly visible in the distance.

Upon landing, where Geoff demonstrated an impressively soft touchdown, we taxied to the apron to park. But as we approached our intended parking space, we came to a sharp stop. About 10 people, obviously highly paid executives, were crossing the apron to board their business jet. Shaking his head, Geoff pointed out a major design flaw of the Cessna Company.

"It needs a bloody horn," he said, simulating what he'd have done *had* there been a horn present. "That'd make the buggers get a move on."

This comic banter made me realise how much I'd miss flying if I stopped. Geoff had done exactly the right thing. He'd let me build up confidence again. He'd also allowed me to relax. I knew Geoff wouldn't go berserk or start ranting if I made a mistake. And all this from a newly qualified instructor.

TOTAL (HOURS) = 30.8

Day 31. Thursday 29 August

The weather was lousy. I had a relaxing day away from the pressures of the airport.

TOTAL (HOURS) = 30.8

Day 32. Friday 30 August

The winds were horrendous, so no chance of flying. However, I was relatively pleased to be having a break from the lessons. I wanted to go back renewed with vigour and excitement. Additionally, I knew James Jarvis would be back for my next lesson. It was time to get to grips with navigation.

TOTAL (HOURS) = 30.8

Navigation

'Don't worry, it won't blow open!'

–James Jarvis (Flight Instructor)

Day 33. Monday 2 September

Lesson 30: *Dual Navigation/Engine Failure Procedure*

The weather was glorious with lovely sunny skies and light wind. I headed to the flying school to meet James Jarvis, who'd finally returned from his holiday.

When I entered the cabin, I saw Clive Sheldon standing in front of Dylan's desk reading some notes. He was the only person in the room. He regarded me for a second and then resumed his reading. Taking Clive's cue, I wandered to the back of the cabin to read some magazines of my own. A minute later Clive left without acknowledging my presence. Clive and I would continue to ignore each other every time we ran into one another. However, not long after this, Clive left the flying school. He'd secured himself a job with a regional airline, flying turbo-props.

James turned up five minutes later. "Well done on going solo with Stuart," he said, grinning. "And well done for putting up with Clive. But he's not that bad you know. In fact, he's okay."

I nodded, saying nothing.

James told me he'd really enjoyed his break because it had given him and his girlfriend a chance to discuss a few things about flying.

"If I get to 35 and still haven't got an airline job, then we'll pack up and go back to New Zealand. I just can't afford to be an instructor for much longer. That gives me just over a year to get a job."

Overhead Eccup, I flew a heading that would, according to my calculations, take us to the little town of Malton. Along the leg, James kept asking me to verify my position by using landmarks and distinguishing features.

Flying along at 90 knots, I'd worked out that we should reach Malton after 19.5 minutes. Overhead the small town, I glanced at my watch and saw I was one minute out. Not bad, I thought. Things were going remarkably well.

Next I turned towards Ripon. After 17 minutes of flying, there it was, as expected.

"Well done, said James. "But you're still not trimming properly. In fact, you haven't touched it since Malton."

I looked at the trim wheel. I rolled it a bit.

"It's a bit late now. You should be trimming after every change in attitude. It makes flying easier, mate. Use it!"

James told me that instead of heading back to the airport we'd do 20 minutes of general handling practice.

Getting me to do a gentle turn to the left, and then to the right, he suddenly pulled the power off. "We've got an engine failure!" he announced, sitting back in his seat.

Immediately, I pushed the nose of the aircraft down, trying to trim for a 70-knot glide. However I pushed down too far and the speed immediately crept up. Precious height was lost.

James took over, altering the aircraft's attitude, then handed control back to me. While this was going on, I was looking left and right, trying to spot a good field. After spotting a likely candidate, I simulated an engine restart and a Mayday call, then pointed out my chosen field to James.

"No good," James said, shaking his head. "It's too far away. We'd never make it. What about that one? The light brown one to your left?"

I spotted it, and saw it was a much better proposition. I altered course, heading for it. At 200 ft, with the field directly in front, James told me to add full power. He was satisfied for the time being.

Back at the airport I landed and taxied back to the apron. James told me he'd noticed a marked improvement in my landing, giving it a six out of ten (remember, James had not seen me land since before my first solo). He added it was a little bit on the hard side, but still a perfectly safe landing.

"Next lesson," he said, removing his headset. "We get you to speak over the radio for the whole trip."

I nodded miserably. On any trip out of the circuit, I knew I'd have to speak to different ATC units along the route. For instance, today, after we'd taken off, Leeds Tower had passed us over to Leeds Approach. When we'd left Leeds Bradford airspace, they passed us over to Linton MATZ. On the way back, the reverse had occurred. (MATZ stands for Military Air Traffic Zone, and is basically the airspace around a military aerodrome. The ATC on that frequency kept track of our aircraft, informing us of any potentially conflicting traffic.)

Additionally, various controllers had told us to "Squawk 2653" or similar four-digit number. That meant we had to tune our transponder to that particular four-digit code. The transponder is a communications device fitted to most aircraft, which enables ATC to see us on their radar. The squawk code would show up on their screen, together with a blip representing an aircraft's position and altitude.

All of this I would have to deal with by myself.

Lesson 31: *PFLs/Steep Turns/Low-Level Flying*

For my afternoon lesson, James told me we'd practise steep turns and forced landings. Climbing to 2,500 ft, James demonstrated a 45° turn to the left, and then it was my turn. Banking the aircraft to 20° I added full power before increasing the angle to 45°. We went around quickly, soon ending up back on our original heading.

James said a sign of a good steep turn was encountering our own wake turbulence on returning to the original heading. He decided to show me what he meant but as he rolled the wings to the left, I heard a metallic click. It sounded like the door latch giving way. My hands instinctively gripped the seat. As we rolled onto 45°, I heard a further click.

As I checked my belt and harness, I felt a draught of cold air seeping in through the edge of the door. I gripped my seat harder. James seemed totally unaware. What if his safety harness suddenly snapped because of the extra G-forces we were currently pulling? He'd come crashing down, barging us both into the already weakened door. Out we'd go, screaming and cursing all the way.

As James straightened up after the turn, I asked him whether he'd heard the noise.

"Oh yeah, that click thing. No worries, mate. It's just your door. It does it all the time. Don't worry, it won't blow open." He then leaned over and pulled my door securely shut. James passed control to me again and I had another couple of goes. During the third attempt, he sneakily pulled the power off again, asking me to find a field. I simulated an engine restart, the Mayday call and then pretended to do a passenger briefing. I turned to my chosen field and when it was obvious we'd make it, James added full power and up we went. Next, James said he'd demonstrate some low flying for me.

"The only time you'll ever do low flying is if you need to fly under low cloud," James said. "But you've got to be careful. At 500 ft or less, everything speeds up. And you need to keep an extra sharp look out for birds, hills and wires."

Descending low over some moorland, James flew the aircraft at what seemed like dizzying speeds. Startled sheep scurried for cover as we swept along like a fighter plane.

"I used to do this back in New Zealand when I flew for the coast-guard," said James. "And I lost count the number of times I had to do a 60° turn to get out of a gorge. He demonstrated what he meant. Looking straight ahead, James pointed to the incline of a nearby hill.

"Imagine that hill is a cliff face. We're flying inside a narrow gorge, heading straight for it. It's too high for us to go over. What would you do?"

I told him I'd begin to pray. He laughed and told me to watch and learn.

As we neared that imaginary cliff, James began the tightest and quickest steep turn I'd ever experienced. It took place so quickly that I had no time to take stock of what had actually happened. In less than two seconds, we were pointing 180° from where we'd been originally heading.

"I got really good at doing turns like that."

After this excitement, we headed back to the airport, with me making a good approach and landing. After parking, James told me I'd done really well, especially with regard to the trim wheel. Another successful lesson had ended.

TOTAL (HOURS) = 33.2

Day 34. Tuesday 3 September

Lesson 32: *Dual Navigation*

My morning lesson was cancelled because of mist. In contrast, the afternoon was fine, so I went over for a lesson with Geoff McPhail. James was not working because he was getting his car fixed.

Geoff asked me to plan a short trip to Ripon, then Market Weighton, before returning to Leeds via Eccup Reservoir. I calculated that the 87-nm journey would take 59 minutes, taking into account the 10-knot wind.

We left the zone via Menwith, heading for the market town of Ripon. As well as flying, Geoff made me do all the radio calls. We arrived over Ripon at the correct time, but were overhead the little town of Market Weighton two minutes late. Geoff told me this was acceptable for a PPL navigation test, but anything beyond three minutes would mean a fail.

On the way back to Leeds, I made an embarrassing blunder on the radio. Pressing the button, I said, "Humberside Radio. G-BSDO. Now routing on a heading of 274°."

You might be thinking that I was the master of the airwaves for such a professional radio call, but you'd be wrong. I'd called them Humberside *Radio,* when in fact; I should have addressed them as Humberside *Approach.* The people operating the control tower at Humberside Airport were Air traffic controllers and not merely radio operators.

This seemingly insignificant mistake was not lost on Geoff, who told me Humberside Radar would not be impressed with my innocent error. To make good my mistake, I pressed the button a second time. "Golf Approach, G-BSDO. On track Eccup on a new heading of 274°."

Geoff laughed even more at that. "*Golf* Approach," he said. "Who the hell are they?"

By then, I'd realised my error and was about to press the button for a third attempt when Geoff said that I didn't have to bother anymore. "I think they get the picture."

Back at Leeds Bradford Airport, I flew the aircraft onto final for runway 14. Because we were landing quite late in the day, the runway lighting made it a very impressive view. Also, I heard Dylan Dowd making his calls to ATC in the circuit. He had passed his PPL the week previously and was coming in to land after a solo flight.

As I flared, I still had too much power, which resulted in a balloon. Geoff stepped in to halt the ensuing 'hard as a brick' landing. Not the perfect end to the lesson really, but good fun nonetheless.

TOTAL (HOURS) = 34.5

Day 35. Wednesday 4 September

Lesson 33: *PFLs/Precautionary Landings*

James and I fuelled the aircraft up and left the zone to carry out some more PFLs and some precautionary landings.

While on the topic of emergencies, I read something interesting recently. It was a list of facts about air crashes based on US statistics. They listed the four most common killers of pilots in rank order.

1. **Loss of control.**

2. **Collision with terrain or water.**

3. **Collision with an object**. *(Perhaps with another aircraft, or a building.)*

4. **An encounter with poor weather**. *(This can lead to any of the above.)*

The study went on to list the most dangerous phases of flight, with regard to pilot fatalities:

1. **Doing a manoeuvre**

2. **Take-off and climb**

3. **Approach and landing**

4. **Runway incursion**

To me, landing seemed rather low in the rankings, but the study found that although landing was the most likely time for a crash, it was one of the least likely times a pilot would die, perhaps because emergency services are at hand.

The statistics also offered another pertinent set of facts. It listed the most common root cause of a fatal air crash. They are in rank order once again:

1. **Pilot error**

2. **Environment**

3. **Some sort of problem with the aircraft.**

James said that a likely cause of pilot error was panic. When a pilot was confronted with a situation that was totally unexpected (i.e. an engine failure) the worst thing they could do was panic. The pilot needed to keep focused or else they would die. James gave me a personal example of a situation that had happened to him.

He had agreed to go for a parachute jump, and because he'd never done one before, his instructors gave lots of training. He listened carefully to the emergency procedures and was heartened to find he wouldn't have to open the parachute himself, it would open automatically as soon as he jumped out of the aircraft.

So now picture yourself in a cold and draughty aircraft, perhaps thinking this is a big mistake. You observe other people looking nervously at each other, patting each other's shoulders, giving comfort in the last few minutes before the jump. Others are writing notes to loved ones and a few more are talking to themselves quietly and incoherently at the back. Suddenly, the man in charge points at you, gesturing towards the open door of the aircraft. Your legs turn to jelly, but somehow you lurch to the front, waiting your turn behind another parachutist.

Steeling yourself for the inevitable, the woman in front suddenly jumps out. With a yelp, she's gone, falling and spiralling through 12,000 ft. As her parachute opens automatically, you say a secret prayer to anyone listening. The time has come; there is no getting out of it. You prepare yourself for what hopefully will be the experience of a lifetime.

The main man gives the nod and out you go with a girlish scream. You're dropping faster than you'd ever imagined. You look upwards and see a limp knot of twisted fabric streaming above your head. *The chute is closed! Something has gone wrong!* Rapidly thinking back to the safety talk, you feel a rising torrent of panic. Before you know it, you've dropped 4,000 ft and the ground is rushing up to meet you with every passing second. This is it; you think, time to meet your maker.

I'm sure that most of you would agree that put into that situation you would panic. I know I would. I might have even blacked out before I hit the ground. Indeed, one of James's fellow parachutists *did* black out. Luckily, her parachute had opened normally, and she eventually came back to her senses in a field. But James didn't panic. He remembered the emergency procedures and pulled the ripcord of his secondary chute at about 4,000 ft from the ground. He arrived on the ground before any of his fellow parachutists even though he'd jumped out last. He'd survived that potentially fatal accident by not panicking.

After practising a couple of PFLs, we moved onto precautionary landings. This type of landing is different to a forced landing because the engine is running. In fact, there isn't anything wrong with the aircraft at all. Other factors influence a precautionary landing. James gave me a scenario.

"Imagine you're flying along, heading over some remote area when suddenly the weather closes in. It would be safer to land in a field rather than pressing on. Do you agree?"

I nodded. It made good sense.

"And because the engine's fine, there will be ample time to find a good field."

James demonstrated a precautionary landing for me. He spotted a good field and slowly flew along it at 1,000 ft. "I'm giving it a good once over," he told me.

Satisfied it looked okay; we turned around and flew down the other side of the field, once again checking for anything that could harm the aircraft. We then did the base turn and an even lower fly past. This was to make certain that the field was good for landing on. After all, with a working engine, we could always try somewhere else. After the final scrutiny, James climbed slightly and did a circuit for a landing. We didn't land, of course, but went back up so I could have a go.

Afterwards, James pointed out some characteristics of good fields for this type of landing. "Remember the seven *S*'s," he told me. "Size, shape, surface, slope, stock, sun and surrounds."

Stock refers to any livestock that might be grazing in the field, and *sun* is a reminder to think about where the sun is, because on final approach it could blind you. *Surrounds* refers to the areas close to the chosen field, and making sure there are no power lines lurking there. The other *S*'s are all self-evident.

Eventually, we flew back to the airport, and after parking the aircraft, James told me that he was pleased with my progress, adding it would soon be time for my first solo navigation trip.

I sighed. "That won't be for a while though. I'm back at school tomorrow. Only weekends for me now."

"Oh yeah, bad luck, mate. See you next Saturday, weather permitting."

I drove home, wondering how much progress I'd make with only an hour or two of lessons a week.

TOTAL (HOURS) = 35.9

Day 36. Saturday 14 September

After a week with my new class, the weekend weather turned out to be dreadful, with fog and mist throughout the whole day. I took solace in some aviation magazines I'd bought. In them I read something quite interesting. It was about the dropout rate for aviation students.

According to the article, over 75% of students did not complete their PPL for one reason or another. *Seventy-five per cent!* That figure sounded too high to be true, but the article went on to say that many dropped out straight after the first solo.

Other students dropped out for a variety of reasons. Some just couldn't afford to continue with their training, especially after finding out they had only budgeted for the minimum number of hours (which only an exceptionally skilled and lucky pilot will achieve). Others grew bored with flying once the navigation training began; flying wasn't as much fun as it used to be and was turning out to be quite difficult.

Next there were the tiny percentage who realised they did not possess the necessary skills to achieve their dream of becoming a pilot. Luckily for them though, they often came to this conclusion at the start of their flying lessons, usually within the first five hours.

Finally we come to the smallest percentage of all — those unfortunate souls who had failed their skills test and were so despondent that they never returned.

TOTAL (HOURS) = 35.9

Day 37. Sunday 15 September

Lesson 34: *Review Lesson*

Eleven days had elapsed between this and my previous lesson so James suggested I do some revision flying to hone my skills. Out I went to check the aircraft in preparation for my first flight in over a week.

As part of the external walkaround I had to check the leading edge of the wings, looking for any dents or anything unusual. The preferred method was to run the palm of my hand along the front (leading edge) of each wing visually checking for anything out of the ordinary.

This sounds easy enough — and it is — but what no one tells you, is that squashed flies coat the front section of any aircraft. There are hundreds of them. You will have to run your hand over them all. Also, because the windscreen does not escape the insect attack, you may even have to get a cloth and try to remove all the horrible red/white bits. It's especially cringeworthy when you feel a particularly juicy specimen 'pop' under the cloth.

Also, something else that no one thinks to mention before you begin training is that the fuel gauges in most PPL training aircraft are notoriously unreliable. Even when the tanks are full, the needle might show the left tank full, but the right tank half-empty. When I'd first noticed this discrepancy, I'd asked James about it. He nodded, saying that every Cessna he'd flown in had had the same problem. He added that the only time the fuel gauges would be accurate was when the aircraft ran out of fuel.

This was why a visual check of the fuel tanks was an absolute necessity before any flight. A Cessna 152 holds about 24 gallons of avgas (aviation gasoline), and in a typical flight will use roughly 5 gallons every hour. That means the aircraft has a flight endurance of around four hours. (The other 45 minutes is for emergencies — such as being forced into doing a diversion.)

I did a smooth take-off, heading over to Harrogate. James made me practise steep turns again and then pulled the power off. I handled it with ease. After successfully completing a PFL we headed back to the airport. After quite a hard landing, we parked up.

James said I'd done well. He'd fully expected me to be rusty. "And you did fine with the radio. No mistakes today!"

I went home feeling strangely buoyant. Things were going remarkably well.

TOTAL (HOURS) = 36.6

Weekend Flying — Slow Progress

'Leeds Approach. Help! I'm lost and I want to go home to my mummy.'

–Jason Smart (PPL Student)

Day 38. Sunday 22 September

Lesson 35: *Dual Navigation*

While teaching my class about the wonder of fractions, I'd often catch myself looking through the window at the calm and sunny weather outside. Worse was when I could hear the drone of an aircraft engine. Keighley (pronounced 'keethlee') was another of the entry/exit points of the zone. Every light aircraft heading west would pass over my school. It was almost too much to bear. Luckily for my sanity, the weekend would soon arrive and I could get back to my flying lessons. Or not as the case may be.

Due to the weather, my Sunday morning lesson was cancelled. It was raining and blowing a gale. But by the afternoon things had cleared up slightly, so off I went to the flying school to meet James Jarvis.

"The winds are still pretty bad, mate," he told me as he strapped himself inside the aircraft. "At 3,000 ft they're blowing at 30 knots."

I looked at the windsock. It was horizontal. I'd never seen it like that.

"It's not what I'd call PPL weather. But we need to keep your skills fresh. So I'll take off, then pass control to you. How does that sound?"

I told him it sounded fine. A few minutes later, we were off.

The wind blew us around like a kite in a storm during take-off. At the controls, James battled away, correcting for every blast of the wind. "It's certainly juicy, isn't it?" he laughed. "Makes the blood flow! Just wait till we land!"

At 2,000 ft, James passed control to me. It was the strongest wind I'd ever flown in. Steering my planned heading to get us to the power stations at Ferrybridge, I couldn't help but notice them way off to our right. The only explanation was that I'd made a mistake with my planning. I told James this.

"No, mate," he answered. "Your heading's fine. In this wind they should be way over there. We'll end up crabbing towards them. Wait and see."

And he was correct; we arrived at Ferrybridge as expected. My flight planning had been spot on. Over the power stations I made a left turn for the Humber Suspension Bridge. Halfway there, James changed the game. "We're going to do a diversion," he said. "We're pretending that something's wrong and we need to get down at the nearest airfield. Look at your chart and tell me the closest one."

I looked, quickly spotting a small airfield called Breighton to the north-west of our present position. I pointed it out to James.

"Good. Estimate a heading to get there and go for it. And don't forget about the wind."

I turned onto my estimated heading, looking for landmarks outside to check against my chart. After flying over a canal, a river and then a railway junction, I knew Breighton ought to be coming up ahead but I couldn't see it. Where was it?

James put me out of my misery. "The wind's pushed us off course. But you're actually quite near." He dipped his side of the wing and I spotted Breighton below. "Just be careful when doing a diversion in strong wind."

We headed back to Leeds.

Due to the high winds, James took over the approach on final. After a perfectly smooth landing, we taxied to park up the aircraft. James's landing made me realise how poor *my* landings actually were. With his, I'd hardly noticed the transition from being airborne to being on the ground. And it had been extremely windy. With mine, even a senseless fool was aware of touching down because I always seemed to come down with a bit of a bang, crash and a hefty wallop.

TOTAL (HOURS) = 37.8

Day 39. Saturday 28 September

Lesson 36: *Dual Navigation*

Almost a week later, and with surprisingly good weekend weather, I went over for another lesson. Over a cup of tea, James decided to give me some advice.

"About this book of yours," he said. "I like what you've done. But I reckon you need more description of *me*. You haven't even said what I look like. Make me come across as dashing and handsome, someone that the ladies would want to meet. You know what I mean."

I nodded, telling him I'd do my best.

James Jarvis is almost 5'2", balding badly, but has most of his own teeth. He walks with a lurching gait, suggesting serial stalking is a possible pastime. He often wears four shoulder stripes, especially when he knows a female student is booked in. He talks endlessly about sheep, always pointing out a good specimen from the air. He has special binoculars for this, which he claims are for spotting airfields. His favourite part of an aircraft is the wheels. He's always touching them, even rubbing them and, when he thinks no one is watching, he speaks to them.

James told me we'd fly a straightforward trip together and then I'd repeat it by myself.

"Solo?" I asked, suddenly concerned.

He looked at me and grinned. "Yes solo. We'll leave the zone at Menwith — which is due north. Then east to Harrogate. Head towards Wetherby and then south to Eccup for a rejoin, then west, back home.

Essentially a rectangle. It should take half an hour. Let's go."

After take-off, we soon reached Menwith, the strange white balls below us looking like a giant madcap sculpture. By looking through James's side window I could see Harrogate and so I turned east. Everything was going according to plan. I was speaking on the radio *and* flying the aircraft.

I turned to James and said, "This is going really well. I feel in control of things today."

"And so you should. A baboon could fly this trip."

After leaving Harrogate, I flew a south-easterly course towards Wetherby before heading to Eccup. Once there, I made a call to ATC. "Leeds Approach, Golf-Delta Oscar requires rejoin at Eccup."

"Roger Golf-Delta Oscar," replied the controller. "Cleared to enter the zone at Eccup, VFR. Not above 2,000 ft. QNH 1022. QFE 996 millibars."

I read it back, waiting for more instructions.

"Golf-Delta Oscar, join right downwind for runway 32. Contact Tower when field in sight."

After contacting the Tower and joining the circuit, I flew a good approach. Turning onto final, I reduced power, making sure I was looking towards the far end of the runway. Flaring at exactly the right height, I began to settle smoothly onto the runway. All I needed now was to straighten up using rudder. As James sat back, nodding in quiet acknowledgment, I pressed the wrong pedal, resulting in a laughable landing with much hilarity from James.

Lesson 37: *Solo Navigation*

Even so, James deemed me fit to go solo. As we parked, he gave me a briefing. He reminded me about the use of the transponder and the various modes it had.

"When you start the engine, set it to SBY (standby). When ATC give you a squawk, remember to put the four numbers in the transponder. When you're lined up on the runway, turn the dial to ALT (altitude)."

"What happens if I forget?"

James shrugged. "Probably nothing at first. But they might give you a warning if you don't switch it on by the time you've taken off. Just do it, it's easier."

I nodded, strapping the kneeboard to my knee.

James unbuckled his harness and gathered his things. As he opened the door he turned back to me. "Enjoy this, mate. Your first solo nav trip. It's another one to remember. Just don't get lost."

So there I was, all alone, about to fly on my first ever solo trip out of the Leeds zone. I was apprehensive. After checks I contacted the Tower who gave me instructions to line up on runway 32. Remembering to turn the transponder to the ALT mode, I waited for take-off permission. A minute later, I was in the air, heading for Menwith.

Climbing to 1,800 ft, the controller told me to contact Leeds Approach, who told me to contact them again when I wished to re-join the zone at Eccup later on. Overhead Menwith, I turned to Harrogate, and then a few minutes later looked for Wetherby in the distance. It wasn't difficult to spot. The bend in the M1 was a big clue.

Approaching Wetherby, I tried to locate Eccup Reservoir, which should have been on my right somewhere, but I couldn't see it. I felt the first stirrings of unease building. Turning onto a heading direct for Leeds Airport, I scanned outside, hoping to make sight of my landmark. *Where the hell was it?*

Flying with James, I'd spotted Eccup easily. But now, all alone at 2,500 ft, I had lost sight of it. I wasn't panicking yet, but I had visions of me pressing the button and uttering, "Leeds Approach. Help me, I'm lost, and I want to go home to my mummy!"

Just then, Eccup appeared like a mirage in front. And now that I'd spotted it, I was at a loss as to how I could have missed it in the first place. My pulse calmed down, allowing me to concentrate on the rejoin.

Incidentally, while on the topic of aviation problems, I was reading an article recently that stated that the three most common expressions in aviation are; *Why is it doing that? Where are we?* And my personal favourite — and one I've used time and time again, *Shit!*

I contacted Leeds Approach, who gave instructions for a rejoin, and then passed me over to Leeds Tower. After a good approach, I managed to do a decent landing, and then parked up. At the cabin, James asked how my landing went. I told him nothing had fallen off. He nodded.

I'd passed another milestone in my quest to become a fully qualified pilot. I'd actually completed a solo navigation exercise. I didn't care if a primate could do it better. I only cared that I'd done it myself.

Lesson 38: *Dual Navigation*

For the afternoon lesson, James wanted me to plan a longer navigation trip for us both to fly. It would be a straightforward flight (and one I'd actually flown before with Geoff McPhail) involving leaving the zone via Menwith and flying to Ripon, then heading off to Market Weighton before finally returning to the airport via Eccup Reservoir. About an hour round trip.

The visibility had dropped since my morning lesson, and as we headed for Ripon, this began to perturb me. It was disconcerting not being able to see very far into the distance. I couldn't verify if I was heading in the correct direction or not. If I'd been by myself, I doubted I'd have had the confidence to carry on.

Despite this, I was gratified to find we arrived overhead Ripon at the correct estimated time of arrival (ETA), and so steered for the little town of Market Weighton. Throughout this leg, I double-checked my position on the chart, while James sat beside me, allowing me to get on with it.

Overhead Market Weighton, I turned for Leeds and James decided to speak up. "When was the last time you did a FREDA check?"

FREDA is another easy-to-remember mnemonic checklist that many pilots use. It stands for **F**uel (enough of it), **R**adios (tuned to the correct frequency), **E**ngine (checking that the temperature and pressure is okay and also doing a carb heat check), **D**irection (checking whether the heading indicator is correctly aligned with the magnetic compass), and finally **A**ltitude (QNH is checked and set accordingly.) A FREDA check is done every 10 to 15 minutes — just to make sure everything is going according to plan.

I mentally berated myself. I hadn't done one since Ripon. I admitted this to James.

He nodded. "I know. Do one now."

I did so, finding the heading indicator was slightly out with the compass. I adjusted it accordingly. Thirty minutes later, I landed back at Leeds where James gave my landing a score of seven out of ten. The highest yet.

Today had been a great success for me. I'd passed the hurdle of a solo navigation trip, and for me that was a huge psychological step. I'd proved to myself that I could do it. I'd moved up another notch in my training.

TOTAL (HOURS) = 40.1

Day 40. Saturday 5 October

The weather all week had been good but I'd been stuck inside my classroom. By the weekend, a weather front had arrived, bringing dismal skies and depression.

Instead of wallowing in self-pity or perhaps constructing a weather voodoo doll, I decided to go to the flying school to sit the remaining two exams I'd not yet completed.

The first one was *Meteorology*, a 20-question multiple choice test. I found most of it straightforward except for the last question. It asked me to decipher some weather forecasts for two different aerodromes, and then decide whether I should fly the proposed flight straight away, delay it or even abandon it all together. I made a wild guess.

Next was *Navigation*. This one had 25 questions. For it, I needed my chart, pens, whiz wheel, protractor and other items associated with flight planning. I had to plan a flight across a portion of southern England and then answer questions about it.

I passed both exams with flying colours. 92% for *Navigation* and 95% for *Meteorology*. It seemed my revision technique had paid off.

TOTAL (HOURS) = 40.1

Day 41. Saturday 12 October

My voodoo weather doll is nearing completion. I just need to purchase some extra-sharp pins and then I can begin using them.

The weather was awful. Rain, mist, fog and a healthy dose of wind, making the perfect ingredients for a non-flying day.

TOTAL (HOURS) = 40.1

Day 42. Sunday 13 October

Lesson 39: Instrument Flying #2/Radio Navigation/Revision of Steep Turns/PFLs

I went to the airport for my first lesson in two weeks. When I arrived, James told me that although the weather seemed quite good, some low level fog would mean I wouldn't be doing a solo trip.

"So instead," he said. "We'll do some instrument flying revision, followed by some radio navigation."

I nodded. Radio navigation is where a pilot flies from A to B using only cockpit instruments such as the VOR. Virtually all airliners navigate using this method. I was looking forward to having a go at it myself.

In the briefing room, James told me that scattered all over the UK — and in fact the world — are navigation beacons called **VOR**s (**V**ery **H**igh **F**requency **O**mni-directional **R**adio Range Beacons). They are sometimes located at airports or could be in the middle of nowhere. Each has its own frequency that pilots dial in on the **NAV** radio. With that done, it is possible to determine an aircraft's position in relation to the VOR beacon.

Each ground beacon sends out a signal for every degree from 000 to 359 called *radials*. Some books refer to these radials as being like the spokes of a bicycle wheel, each one radiating from the centre, which in our case is the VOR beacon itself.

I'm aware this sounds confusing, and to bamboozle you further, each radial can be **TO** or **FROM** the VOR. Let's take off and see how they work.

James and I took off and left the zone via Menwith. After 20 minutes of instrument flying with the foggles on, James dialled in the frequency of a VOR beacon called Pole Hill. It was located about 20 nm south-west of Leeds Bradford Airport, and was the nearest one to us. James told me to remove the foggles.

Right," he said. "Now we've got the VOR dialled in, we need to check it's the right one."

He flicked a dial on the radio panel to *ident* and told me to listen. Over the hiss and crackle I could hear a beeping sound. I turned to James, nodding.

"The beeping is Morse Code, mate." he told me. "Every VOR has its own three-letter code. Look at the bottom of your chart and work out what the beeps are spelling."

Scanning the chart, I found the Morse code and began listening to the repeating beeps until I worked out they were spelling P-O-L. I told James this.

"Good. POL is the code for the Pole Hill VOR. We know we've dialled in the right one." He flicked it off *ident.*

He then pointed at an instrument I'd never used before. It was located to the right of the altimeter and was the **VOR instrument,** sometimes called the **Omni-Bearing Indicator (OBI).** It resembles a *heading indicator* because it has a compass arc around its circular edge. It has a little knob on the side, and a little gap in the mechanism where the word TO or FR (from) could appear. At that moment in time, it said FR. We were flying away from the VOR.

James told me we could easily establish which heading (or radial) we were on away from VOR. He demonstrated what he meant by moving the little knob until a vertical needle (more accurately known as the *Course Deviation Indicator*) started moving towards the centre of the VOR instrument. When it was exactly on the centre, James told me to look at the top of the instrument and read off the heading.

I peered closely at it. "255°," I said.

"Yep. We're on the 255 radial. But what's our actual heading?"

I looked at the heading indicator. I said, "200°."

"Right. So if we turn to 255°, we'll be flying along the VOR radial as opposed to passing through it. Turn now. Intercept the 255 radial."

I rolled the wings onto 255° and looked at the VOR instrument. The needle had moved. It was now off to the left, we were not flying along the 255 radial anymore. James had already noticed this.

He said, "This is normal. To get back on the 255 radial, you need to go left a few degrees until it comes back to the centre. When it starts to move, gently roll the wings onto 255°."

I did as suggested and the needle started swinging back to the centre. It seemed quite straightforward to do. We were flying along the 255 radial away from the VOR beacon.

"Well done. But now look at the DME (Distance Measuring Equipment) readout," said James, tapping another section of the radio panel.

"It tells us how far we are from the VOR beacon. What does it say?"

The readout said "23.5NM". I told James this.

"Exactly. So now we know precisely where we are. We're 23.5 nm from Pole Hill on a heading of 255°. Let's move on to something a bit harder."

After rotating the knob, James told me we'd intercept a specific radial. I nodded, wondering what he was on about. With the needle totally off centre, James told me to read the top again. It said 360°.

"But we're flying 255°," he reminded me. "To intercept the 360 outbound radial we need to turn onto a heading about 30-40° left of 360°. Eventually, the needle should start moving to the centre."

I turned again, turning to 320°, my brain beginning to unravel. A few minutes later, the needle slowly started moving so I turned and intercepted the radial. I had somehow done it but didn't really know how.

I asked James why VOR navigation was included in the PPL syllabus.

"If you get lost," he told me. "Dial in the nearest VOR frequency. Turn the knob until the needle gets to the centre. Check the mechanism is *from* or *to*. Read the radial at the top of the circle, then look at the VOR circle on your chart. You can work out where you are from the DME. Intercepting a specific radial is for other things. Don't worry about that for now."

I nodded, unconvinced. It seemed like a lot of mathematical jiggery-pokery to me. I looked outside, allowing my mind to refocus.

James asked me to do a steep turn. I did so, and afterwards, he said it would have been good enough to pass the skills test requirement. The smile on my face soon vanished though because James pulled the power off. It was time for another PFL. I did the checks, found a field, and arrived near it without any problem.

On the way back to the airport, something interesting happened. Flying towards Menwith for a rejoin, James pointed out some cloud straight ahead of our position. There wasn't a lot, but it was at our altitude. Obviously interested in seeing what I'd do, James sat back while I assessed the situation. Applying a touch of power, I raised the nose a few degrees in the hope of climbing over it.

James shook his head. "My control."

Applying a blast of throttle, he swerved around the clouds, heading for the clear air to the side. As he did this manoeuvre, I realised that option hadn't even entered my head.

"Look, mate," James said, handing control back to me. "Don't ever try to climb over cloud. You don't know what's behind it. There could be another plane, or a mast. Always go round the buggers."

I told him I would.

At the airport, my landing was okay. As we parked up, I finally asked James a question that had been bugging me for some time.

"What happens if I need to sneeze on final?"

James shrugged. "Just sneeze."

"What about my eyes."

"Oh, I see what you mean. Keep your eyes open."

"Right."

Lesson 40: *Aborted Dual Navigation*

For the afternoon lesson, as James and I taxied to the hold, we received a strange message from ATC. The controller told us that another instructor was on frequency wishing to speak to us. James asked the controller to patch the call through. A second later the dulcet tones of Geoff McPhail came over the radio.

"Are ya' flying solo Jason?'

I pressed the button and told him that James was with me.

"That's all right then. It's just that I've taken off and the weather's closing in. You'll be fine with James though."

James thanked him for his concern and I was secretly pleased that someone else was looking out for me.

After take-off we headed for Eccup and it quickly became obvious the weather was indeed marginal. The low-lying cloud was getting even lower as we headed outside of the Leeds zone. James decided to head to the first of our planned turning points where he would assess the weather again.

Overhead Wetherby, the weather was worse. We had to fly at barely 1,000 ft to enable us to see the ground sufficiently. Shaking his head, James decided to cut short my lesson. We headed back to the airport.

"This just proves how quickly the weather can change," he said.

I nodded in agreement, dropping the plane down to 750 ft. As we traversed at low levels, James began to get worried about the reaction of angry householders below. Flying so close to their roofs might make them step out to get our registration. He took control and pushed the power for full steam ahead.

Other training aircraft were also getting into similar problems and all were now heading back to the airport. Fifteen minutes later, we were back on the ground, happy to be there.

At the cabin, James asked me a theoretical question. "What would you have done if you were solo in that murky weather?"

I thought for a moment, then told him I would probably have done a precautionary landing in a field.

James nodded thoughtfully. "Yeah, that's always an option. But it shouldn't necessarily be your first choice. What about nearby airfields? Wetherby wasn't in the middle of nowhere was it? RAF Leeming was close by."

"Would they let me land there?"

"In an emergency, yes."

He told me that in poor conditions any airport would allow a pilot to land. "So if you ever find yourself in a serious situation with the weather, use careful judgement. Look at your chart. See what's around. Don't just go for the first thing that pops into your head."

TOTAL (HOURS) = 41.7

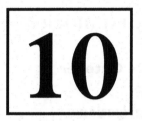

More Navigation... and Shame

'I am the flying fool, and I am in your zone!'

–Jason Smart (PPL Student)

Day 43. Monday 21 October

Today marked the start of my weeklong October half term holidays. Lessons had been booked for every day of the week. I awoke to the dismal sight of fog, rain and wind. Lesson cancelled.

TOTAL (HOURS) = 41.7

Day 44. Tuesday 22 October

Same as yesterday, if not worse. Fog all day long. Marvellous.

TOTAL (HOURS) = 41.7

Day 45. Wednesday 23 October

I looked out of the window to see a beautifully sunny day with only a few wispy clouds. However the winds were horrendous, gusting up to 40 knots. Lesson was cancelled.

After a quick calculation of the amount of lessons annulled due to bad weather, I totted up 18. That equates to 41%. Excellent.

TOTAL (HOURS) = 41.7

Day 46. Thursday 24 October

Lesson 41: *Dual Navigation*

It was a surprisingly nice day with only slightly gusty winds trying to spoil things. At the flying school James decided that we'd do a flight together and then I could go and do one myself.

Overhead Eccup, Leeds Tower passed us off to Leeds Approach. A few minutes later, they in turn passed us off to Linton Military ATC.

"Linton Zone, this is G-BSDO. Requesting Basic Service," said James, giving the standard initial call to a new ATC unit.

"G-BSDO, Linton Zone. Squawk 7343 and pass your message."

Pass your Message! What a simple request!

James then reeled off lots of information about our aircraft type, where we were, where we were going, our altitude and then read back the squawk code. I began to get worried because I'd have to deal with the same request myself when flying solo later in the day.

After flying to Ripon, we turned for the little village of Pateley Bridge. All through this flight, James was checking on my basic flying skills and reminding me about things I was forgetting.

He suggested I buy a stopwatch because he was beginning to suspect I wasn't being rigorous enough about my time keeping. He was correct in this assumption. Bogged down with everything else, working out an ETA in the air seemed less important than knowing where I was. I told him I'd get hold of one soon.

Overhead Pateley Bridge I turned for the final waypoint of the journey, the giant golf balls of Menwith. A few minutes later, James spoke up. "Forget Menwith. Plan a diversion to Harrogate. And I want an ETA."

I looked at my chart, while continuing to fly the aircraft, and worked out a rough heading. I also measured an approximate distance to Harrogate and from that worked out my ETA. I told James of my plans. Nodding, he told me to get on with it.

Flying my amended heading, Harrogate soon loomed up in the distance. It was gratifying to see it. Overhead the town, I checked my watch and found I was two minutes late with my ETA. James had noticed too. "Not bad though, mate," he said. "At least we're here."

Back in the circuit for landing, I touched down rather heavily. When I asked James what he thought of it, he shrugged, saying, "It was survivable."

In the cabin, James gave me a briefing about my upcoming solo flight.

Lesson 42: *Solo Navigation/Shameful Behaviour*

"Fly the same route," James told me. "Including the Harrogate bit. And when you contact Linton, make sure you give them the correct information. In fact, write this down now."

James dictated a generic message for me, which included all the necessary information to give on a '*pass your message*' request. I wrote it all down on my kneeboard.

"Also," James continued. "Be careful with your timekeeping. And remember to do FREDA checks, especially when you turn towards the next waypoint."

I nodded, rubbing my face, aware of my quickening heart rate. In less than half an hour I'd be in the sky — by myself — leaving the safety net of the Leeds zone.

James paused, looking carefully at me. "I know you're nervous. But you'll be fine. And you know all the emergency stuff. In fact, answer me this, mate. What will you do if you get totally lost?"

Gibber uncontrollably and begin to weep, I thought. Instead I said, "I'll call ATC. Tell them what's what."

James nodded, satisfied. A few minutes later I headed out to the aircraft.

I finished my checks and then climbed inside G-BSDO. As I plugged my headset in, James and another student arrived, heading for a Cessna 152 parked opposite. As I switched on the engine, James turned to face me. After giving him the thumbs up, I was pleased to see him offer his thumb in return. While James and his student watched, I pressed the communication button and contacted Leeds Tower. A minute later I taxied past them on my way to the holding point.

I was quickly in the air, turning towards Eccup Reservoir. Halfway there, I contacted Leeds Approach. It was with this next controller that I suffered shame comparable only to the shame I experienced as a child in Australia.

Aged ten, my mum had caught me holding a Lego aeroplane, already filled to capacity with ladybird passengers and a couple of lizard pilots. I launched it into the air, unable to stop myself. Open-mouthed, we both watched as the insectile airliner arced dreadfully across the garden, heading towards carnage. After a swift whack around the ear lobe, I promised never to try any more cruel aviation experiments.

With Eccup getting nearer, I changed frequency and pressed the button. "Leeds Approach, G-BSDO is heading to Eccup at 1,800 ft."

"Roger G-DO," said the male approach controller. "Basic Service after leaving the zone."

"Copy that, G-DO." I merrily passed over Eccup Reservoir, awaiting the next call, unaware of the shame to follow.

The radio cracked into life. "G-DO," said the Leeds controller. "Squawk 7000 and freecall Church Fenton on frequency 126.5."

"Squawking 7000 and contacting Church Fenton on 126.75. G-DO."

"G-DO, you are barely readable. Confirm changing to Church Fenton on 126.5.

"Affirm, Church Fenton on 126.75."

"G-DO. Say again, 126.5."

What was his problem I thought? I'd said it twice already. Slightly irked, I pressed the button again. "Changing to 126.75. G-DO."

"Negative G-DO, Church Fenton on 126.5." The controller was beginning to sound rather pained. Perhaps he needed a new headset and a cup of tea.

By now, some of you may have spotted my shameful error. Sitting in the cockpit, though, I merely thought the controller couldn't hear me very well. Indeed he'd just told me I was barely readable. Vowing to repeat the message in my clearest voice yet, I pressed the button once more. "126.75. G-DO," I said in a clear and booming voice, for all and sundry to hear. Every pilot on the frequency could hear me.

"G-DO. NEGATIVE! 1-2-6 decimal 5." He sounded highly irritated.

At long last, the truth finally sank in, and I then fully realised the extent of my mistake. "Oh, 126.5... and sorry about that. G-DO." To which I got no reply.

My shame was immense. I could feel not only my ears burning, but also my neck and eyelids. Dialling in the frequency for Church Fenton MATZ, I switched the transponder to 7000, but my mind was in abject turmoil. I couldn't believe what I'd just done. What an idiot!

Trying to get a grip on things, I made contact with Church Fenton.

"Roger G-BSDO," said the military controller. "Pass your message."

I felt like saying, *My message is this: Watch out for the flying fool! I am in your zone and I speak gibberish. Yes indeed. Over and out.*

Luckily, I merely read off my prepared message.

> **"Church Fenton, G-BSDO is a Cessna 152 on a navex out of Leeds. Presently south of Wetherby at 2,000 ft. Routing to Ripon, Pateley Bridge, Harrogate and back to Eccup. Requesting Basic Service."**

Basic Service to pilots consisted of information about the weather and airport info. Air Traffic Controllers may also, if workload permits, offer traffic information if they have you on their radar.

The man in the Church Fenton RAF Tower acknowledged my message, but because I was flying north, he promptly passed me off to Linton MATZ. I carefully made note of Linton's frequency and passed smoothly across the airwaves to another military controller. He also asked me to pass my message, which I did, and then turned towards Ripon.

The next portion of the trip went smoothly and I reached Pateley Bridge right on schedule. On the way to Harrogate, I started to get nervous again. I knew it would soon be time to contact Leeds Approach. I wondered if the controller had calmed down. After telling Linton I was contacting Leeds, I resolutely bit the bullet.

Luckily for me, a different controller was operating the approach frequency. The original one was probably lying down somewhere, perhaps throwing darts at model Cessnas. The new controller granted me permission to enter the zone and I passed over to Leeds Tower and joined the circuit.

After a series of orbits to let commercial traffic come in I landed in the hearty crosswind and parked the aircraft. As I unplugged everything, I felt dejected. Instead of feeling joy at what I'd just accomplished, all I could think about was my stupid error when leaving the zone.

Shame. Shame. Shame.

TOTAL (HOURS) = 43.9

TOTAL SHAME TIME (HOURS) = 10.0+

Day 47. Friday 25 October

Torrential downpours and wild winds added up to no flying. On a more positive note, though, at least it would give the Leeds Approach controller ample time to forget what my voice sounded like. I could abandon my plan of speaking with a Scottish accent had I been flying today.

Instead, let's talk about the psychological fear of learning to fly. As you'll have surmised by now, I was a nervous student, constantly unsure of my own ability especially when talking on the radio. I wondered why this was.

Often I'd meet very young PPL students (in their teens) who didn't have a care in the world. All of them were sailing through the PPL course, many passing within the minimum number of hours. They seemed fearless. And I'd been the same at their age.

In my thirties I was acutely aware of the dangers involved in learning to fly. I knew that *bad things* could happen to me. Back when I was a teenager, I'd been convinced the nasty things could only happen to other people.

I thought back to when I'd first learned to drive. Aged 17, I had very little concept of fear. In fact, when my mother had discovered I'd actually driven on a *real* road on my first lesson she was horrified. She hadn't ventured onto a real road until she had amassed quite a few hours of driving around a large deserted car park. I had no such qualms about driving in traffic, rapidly propelling myself through the course, passing after 17 hours of instruction. My mum took twice that long; my father one hour less.

Let's think back to our first few driving lessons. We've had a few lessons, but are still unsure about things. The instructor reminds us to check the mirrors, to check our speed and even tells us where to go. At busy roundabouts, our brains work overtime to keep ahead of the game.

Imagine then, if at this busy roundabout, your instructor suddenly jumped out, slammed the door and walked off. What would you do? How would you cope? Before you can do anything constructive, the radio suddenly crackles into life, giving instructions in another language and expecting you to reply. Then you hear a horn blasting you from behind and in front a gigantic juggernaut speeds past. Then the engine stalls and a red light starts flashing on the dashboard. This is what flying is like at the beginning.

TOTAL (HOURS) = 43.9

Day 48. Saturday 2 November

The forecast was horrendous so I wasn't expecting to fly. However Kate (who did Dylan's job on a weekend) told me the weather seemed okay where she was. Twenty minutes later I arrived and James told me the weather had taken a turn for the worse. "We'll do some ground school instead. Just give me a minute."

While waiting, I got chatting to Kate and asked her about the Night Rating.

Kate, aged 19, had already done her PPL and Night Rating, and was now studying for her degree before starting on the ATPL exams. "The Night Rating was quite easy," she told me.

I laughed. "Easy? I find navigating during the day hard enough. At night, I'd be well and truly done for."

"No, it's actually easier. All the lights make the towns and roads stand out. And it looks really pretty. You should do it."

I smiled and told her I'd think about it. I went in search of James Jarvis. He was in one of the back rooms with a young man of perhaps 20. Seeing me enter both men turned around.

"Jason, this is Carl," said James. "He passed his PPL a couple of days ago. I'm giving him a lecture about weight and balance. You might as

145

well listen."

For the next 10 minutes James went through the method for calculating the fuel required for a flight and how to not exceed the maximum take-off/landing weight. There was a handy little graph to help with this. Carl and I nodded, listening attentively.

"For a student," James said, regarding me. "It's the flying school's responsibility to calculate weight and balance. But once you've passed, it's down to you. It must be part of your pre-flight planning. It'll cover your back if the CAA come knocking after an accident."

A few minutes later Carl left, leaving me with James. I told him about my shameful incident with Leeds Approach. He surprised me by laughing aloud.

"Don't worry about it," he said, grinning. "Those controllers have heard far worse. In fact, a couple of months ago I made the biggest error ever. I'd just joined the circuit when—" James suddenly stopped speaking.

He shook his head, a wry smile on his face. "I'm not saying anything else, mate. You'll write it in your damned book of yours."

TOTAL (HOURS) = 43.9

Day 49. Sunday 3 November

Lesson 43: *Circuit Checkride/Solo Navigation*

With only a single lesson booked on a cold November morning I was pleased when the weather turned out to be okay. When I arrived, I found John Denson (the instructor I'd met back on day one) waiting for me. He told me James was having a day off.

"But I've spoken to him," John told me. "And after a couple of circuits with me, you'll be doing a solo nav trip." He gave me the route to plan.

In the flight planning room, I worked out my speeds, times and headings for a flight to Market Weighton, via Menwith, before coming back to land via Eccup. The trip would take an hour in total and would be my longest solo trip so far. Strangely, I felt quite good about it.

Ten minutes later I was outside of the aircraft checking the fuel. It was there that I found something peculiar — large globules of brownish stuff lurking towards the bottom of my fuel sample. When John arrived I asked him about it.

Peering carefully at the sample, John swirled it around. "It's just a bit of dirty water," he said eventually. "Keep draining fuel until there's no more."

I did as instructed, and about three samples later the fuel turned clear once more. John nodded, telling me to climb inside. We were soon in the air.

After just one circuit, John deemed me competent enough to go off by myself. After collecting his things, he wished me good luck and headed off towards his car.

At the hold, the controller gave me a strange clearance. It was exactly the same one I'd received when I'd been with John's Dad, Tony on a previous lesson.

"Golf-Delta Oscar," said ATC. "After the landing 737, cleared to enter and cross runway three-two. Hold short Alpha-Two for further instructions."

Unlike the previous time, I knew exactly what to do. After the Jet2 737 had landed, I merrily crossed over runway 32 and followed it towards the hold. Back in August, that request had caused me to panic. This time I was fine. I was quickly given permission to enter the runway. After I took off (in a hearty crosswind) I headed for Menwith.

Staying in contact with Leeds Approach, I turned onto the heading for Market Weighton, 37 nm away. According to my plan it would take 20.5 minutes to get there. I flew onwards, marvelling at the view 2,000 ft below me. Less than six months previously, I'd stared up in envy whenever a light aircraft had flown above me, and now here I was, flying solo in one.

I ended up overhead Market Weighton after 21 minutes of flight. I was pleased because I was only 30 seconds out. I then turned back towards Eccup in a happy mood.

It was then I realised something important. This trip was proving how far I'd come in overcoming the psychological barrier present on my earlier solo trips. I'd been constantly worried about either getting lost or actually *being* lost. If I hadn't been able to immediately recognise something outside then feelings of angst had followed closely. But today, this had happened a few times already and I'd kept calm. I knew that if I kept on the correct heading then I'd eventually see something recognisable.

This was a major breakthrough. It meant I could relax and really enjoy the view. I also began harbouring thoughts of actually being able to do longer cross-country trips, which was a good thing because my qualifying cross-country flight would involve flying to and landing at three different airports, all over a distance of 150 nm.

After 30 minutes I was overhead Eccup and ATC gave their landing instructions. With a crosswind of about 14 knots I still got down in one piece and parked the aircraft. It had been one of my most successful flights ever. Nothing had gone wrong and everything had gone right. Even better was that I'd completed 6.7 hours of solo flying in total. The only downside was that I'd passed the 45-hour mark, meaning I'd used up all of my available pre-paid flying time. From now on I would have to pay as I flew.

TOTAL (HOURS) = 45.4

Day 50. Saturday 16 November

A thick and lingering patch of fog, which lasted throughout the whole day, scuppered any chance of flying. Instead, I powered up the PC, loading up some add-on new software I'd purchased for my flight simulator.

A few weeks previously I'd spotted an advertisement for the add-on, which claimed that its satellite imagery of the UK provided the most lifelike graphics in any home simulator. From the pictures on the advert, it certainly looked like the real thing. Every town, village, hamlet, road, lake, river and railway seemed to be included. I ordered a copy immediately.

Much to my delight, after installing it, I took off over southern England, discovering a very realistic view on the screen. At 2,500 ft, the scenery on my computer screen actually looked very much like what I'd see in a real aircraft. Consulting my Southern Aeronautical Chart, I saw everything was where it was supposed to be. Motorways and lakes, towns and airfields, all depicted in their pixelated glory. It was almost unbelievable.

However the main drawback (or perhaps bonus) of these virtual flights was that I didn't have to speak to ATC. But being able to fly simulated navigation trips in the comfort of my own home meant only one thing to me: my skills simply *had* to improve. At least that's what I hoped.

TOTAL (HOURS) = 45.4

Day 51. Saturday 23 November

Another damp and dreary day with absolutely no chance of flying.

Incidentally, I was reading something the other day that struck a chord. The article said that it was very easy to spot someone who was a pilot because as soon as they step out of the door, they'll immediately look at the sky to assess the weather. I do this all the time. The clouds usually drip on me.

TOTAL (HOURS) = 45.4

Day 52. Saturday 30 November

Mist, fog and a healthy downpour of rain cancelled my four-hour slot. With awful weather all week, my friends think I'm obsessed. But they are wrong. Dead wrong. What do they know anyway? It's only me who knows the clouds don't like me. I hear them whispering at night, you see.

TOTAL (HOURS) = 45.4

Day 53. Sunday 1 December

For the first time in absolutely ages, I awoke to sunlight seeping through the curtains. Eagerly looking outside, I saw a beautiful sunny day with only a few wispy clouds in the sky. Unfortunately horrendous winds were propelling these lonesome clouds across the sky at a manic pace.

When I rang Kate, she told me the winds were gusting up to 35 knots.

No chance of flying.
Damn the wind.

TOTAL (HOURS) = 45.4

Day 54. Saturday 7 December

The fifth consecutive cancellation in a row. This time because the cloud base was at only 300 ft. Winter has truly set in and there is talk of snow. Usually at night.

TOTAL (HOURS) = 45.4

Day 55. Saturday 21 December

Just a few days short of Christmas James Jarvis told me that my lesson would have to be cancelled because of low visibility. Before I put the phone down though, he told me that he and his girlfriend were going to New Zealand for a three-week Christmas family reunion. He wanted to wish me luck in my quest for my PPL.

"I probably won't get any lessons in anyway," I said. "At this rate, I'll still be doing this when I'm 50."

James laughed. "Well why don't you book a plane for a whole day?"

"What do you mean?"

"We've moved a couple of planes over to Full Sutton Airfield near York. You can book one for the whole day with an instructor."

I told him I'd do just that.

TOTAL (HOURS) = 45.4

Day 56. Sunday 29 December

Another lesson cancelled due to poor weather. Nonetheless, to look on the brighter side of things, I'd taken James's advice and had booked an aeroplane for the whole of the next day. I just hoped the weather would break.

TOTAL (HOURS) = 45.4

Day 57. Monday 30 December

Not entirely unexpected, but annoying all the same, my lesson was cancelled due to rain and more rain.

Over the phone, Dylan Dowd sympathised with my sorry plight but offered some encouragement. He told me that because I'd gained all the basic training in a few concentrated weeks; he thought I'd still be able to get in an aircraft and 'do okay'.

I hoped he was correct. After almost two months away from the cockpit, I felt that not only did some of the hinges need oiling, but rust had begun to settle. I would need restoration work soon or everything might fall to bits.

TOTAL (HOURS) = 45.4

Winter Sets in — Will I Fly?

'Me knackers are frozen solid!'

–Geoff McPhail (Flying Instructor)

Day 58. Saturday 4 January

Lesson 44: *Circuit Checkride/Solo Circuits*

A new year rolled around and remarkably, bearing in mind the time of year, the weather was good. Although there was snow on the ground, it was sunny with light wind.

My instructor was a middle-aged lady called Claire. She told me she was a part-time instructor who'd been flying for seven years.

"I'm only filling in here for the Christmas period, though," she said. "Once the normal crew returns, I'm back off to Humberside Airport."

Claire told me we'd be flying a different aircraft I was used to, a Cessna 152 with the registration G-EU. This worried me. Virtually all my training had been in G-DO and I was used to listening out for that particular call sign. When ATC addressed me as Golf–Echo Uniform, I just hoped I'd recognise it as being me.

After preflighting the aircraft, I got in and waited for Claire to arrive. Plugging in my headset, I switched on the radios and checked ATIS for the weather. The wind was 11 knots, blowing almost straight down the runway. Perfect for circuits. Peering at the clear skies above, I couldn't wait to go up. The white, snow-topped fields around the airport were something I'd never seen before.

When Claire arrived, I soon got permission to taxi. After lining up on the runway I did my first take-off in eight weeks. After finishing the circuit, I came in for final approach, and Claire told me she wanted to see the flaps deployed in stages, rather than in one go. This threw my concentration a little and by the time we were on short final my speed was excessively high. Pulling the power to idle we came gliding in, still high and fast.

Somehow though I managed to stabilise the approach and we settled down onto the runway for a relatively smooth landing. Pleased with my effort, I realised my training had not completely eroded. True, it was a bit sloppy in sections of the circuit, and yes, my speed had been a touch high during the approach, but overall I'd done it. I still knew how to land an aeroplane! And the brand new call sign had not been a problem at all.

After two more circuits, Claire got out and left me to it. I listened out for my call sign and clearance.

"Golf-Echo Uniform," said the controller. "Backtrack, line up and wait, runway three-two."

I read back the instruction and moved off. As I was trundling down the runway, ATC spoke again. "Golf-Echo Uniform, vacate runway three-two. Taxi next right off the runway and hold at Lima One."

I did as requested, wondering what was going on. A minute later, the reason became clear. ATC were allowing a business jet to take off before me. Cheeky bastards.

Soon enough, though, I was in the air and loving every second of it. On my second circuit, however, things turned a bit awry. I was downwind at 1,000 ft and had just told ATC I was ready for base.

"Golf-Echo Uniform," replied the female controller. "You are number two to a Robin turning onto a short one-mile final."

Digesting this juicy morsel of information, I said, "Number two to a Robin. Looking for traffic. Golf-Echo Uniform."

However, I was in some confusion. Had I received clearance to turn onto my base turn or did she want me to extend downwind? I wasn't sure. Every other circuit had always included the message "report final". But this time, unless I hadn't heard the controller correctly, I had received no such instruction.

I pondered on what to do. With the clock ticking I had to act fast. The runway was already disappearing over my shoulder so finally I decided to extend downwind until I had the other aircraft in sight. I soon spotted him and so made my delayed turn onto base.

Fully expecting ATC to admonish me for this unapproved turn, I dropped some flaps, and began my descent. The controller said nothing.

A minute later I turned onto the runway heading and pressed the button, at the same time bracing myself for a telling off. "Gold-Echo Uniform is final for three-two," I said. No reprimand came my way. ATC simply gave me the normal landing instructions. I landed and taxied off the runway as usual.

Climbing in my car, I thought over what had happened. I soon concluded that *I* was in error. I had been confused so should have asked ATC to clarify their instructions. This would have erased all doubts in my mind. I should have done this straight away and not delayed in the slightest.

TOTAL (HOURS) = 46.4

Day 59. Sunday 12 January

I'd booked a three-hour slot, but alas, it wasn't to be. The weather was up to its old tricks, with perhaps the wind gaining the upper hand against a backdrop of poor visibility and low-lying clouds.

To console my weary spirit, I read some aviation magazines, coming across something very interesting. It was an article about the safety of general aviation flying. I read it with interest.

The author quoted many facts, but the one that jumped out almost immediately quoted the relative chance of dying behind the wheel of a car compared to behind the yoke of a light aircraft.

Now we all talk about the fact we're more likely to perish on the drive over to the airport as opposed to flying on the plane, and of course statistically this was quite true — but only for commercial air travel. For light aircraft, it was quite a different story.

In the article, mile for mile, a person flying in a single-engined plane was *eight times* more likely to suffer a fatal accident than someone in a car. Gulp and double gulp!

Let's think about that. I myself do a fair amount of driving, probably about 9,000 miles per annum. This is slightly below average. In my trusty Cessna, I do perhaps 85 miles in an average flight but for the sake of simplicity let's assume I fly 100 miles. When I pass my PPL, let's also assume I fly every fortnight. This equates to approximately 200 miles per month or 2,400 miles a year — about a third of what I will travel in my car. Which means I'm only 2.7 times more likely to die in an aeroplane than in my car? Safe as hell then.

TOTAL (HOURS) = 46.4

Day 60. Saturday 18 January

The weather was glorious all day long but my lesson was booked in for late afternoon. All day I sat brooding, watching as the clouds thickened and the winds picked up. At 3 pm I went over for my lesson with Geoff McPhail and when I arrived he gave me a dose of bad news.

"Somehow you've been double-booked, Jason," he said, shaking his head apologetically. "Someone's booked in a trial flight at the same time as you. And there's only one instructor available. Me."

As I digested this, I could see the three recipients of the trial flight waiting in the back of the cabin. An excited boy of about eight was among them.

"So what I'll do," continued Geoff. "Is I'll take them out first, then give you a call to meet me over at the airport when we land. Does that sound okay?"

Obviously not wanting to kick up a fuss in front of these people, I gritted my teeth and nodded. Geoff smiled, giving me a route to plan in the meantime.

Heading to the planning room, I wondered what time Geoff would get back. Dusk came early in January.

Half an hour later I looked outside at the darkening sky. What was Geoff playing at? He should have phoned by now. I tried to concentrate on my flight planning.

Twenty minutes later the door opened. It was Geoff McPhail. He held his palms up in appeasement. "Sorry, lad. ATC kept us at the hold for ages."

I looked outside feeling bitter and resentful. It was more or less dark.

Geoff continued. "As you can see, it's too late for us now. Besides, the visibility's rubbish anyway."

I was heartily disappointed and so packed my things to go home. But in reality, I couldn't complain too much because I myself had caused delays for other students in the past. When James thought I was doing particularly well he'd lengthen my lessons to keep the momentum going. It was all part of learning to fly.

On the topic of time keeping, I think it's pertinent to dispel a few myths related to lesson bookings.

In virtually all flying schools a booking system will be in operation. When you arrange a lesson, the person on the other side of the desk, or the other end of the phone, will give you a precise time slot. Say you want an afternoon lesson? They might offer a slot beginning at 2pm and ending at 4pm. Great, you think.

Turning up at ten to two — just to give yourself some leeway — you enter the training organisation. Nine times out of ten your instructor will not be there. They'll be in the air with somebody else. So you sit down and read a magazine, and if you're lucky, the instructor might turn up relatively quickly, after perhaps 15 minutes. If you're unlucky, it might be an hour. But even when they do arrive, don't expect to go flying straight away.

First the instructor will have to fill in some paperwork about the flight they've just flown. Then they'll have to give their student some sort of lesson debriefing. And maybe the instructor will be hungry or thirsty and will want some sustenance to keep them going through the hours ahead. At the very least, expect the instructor to need a toilet/bathroom break. And all of this is the norm. It happens every day.

But woe betide the student who takes it upon *themself* to turn up late. Almost certainly in this instance, the instructor will have been waiting ages for them to arrive.

TOTAL (HOURS) = 46.4

Day 61. Sunday 19 January

Another cancelled lesson. The weather was dreadful. And now my friends have finally worked out what PPL stands for. Permanently grounded Pilot's Licence.

TOTAL (HOURS) = 46.4

Day 62. Saturday 1 February

Yesterday I found out all the flying school's Cessna 152s had moved to Full Sutton Airfield. If I wanted to carry on training, I'd have to fly from there.

This was good news for me, I realised. Full Sutton Airfield was a quiet aerodrome with no commercial airliners anywhere. Additionally, it had no ATC to bother a pilot at every juncture. No hanging about at the hold at Full Sutton. In the end, though, it didn't matter. Snow and fog meant my four-hour slot was cancelled.

TOTAL (HOURS) = 46.4

Day 63. Sunday 2 February

Rain, rain and rain.
Wind, wind and wind.
Bugger, bugger and bugger.

TOTAL (HOURS) = 46.4

Day 64. Saturday 15 February

More bad weather. Instead, I busied myself with another voodoo doll. A bigger one.

TOTAL (HOURS) = 46.4

Day 65. Sunday 16 February

"Sorry, Jason," said Kate. "It's the visibility this time. It's down to 300 m. No one's flying today."

I groaned deeply.

Luckily Kate knew I wasn't a pervert.

TOTAL (HOURS) = 46.4

Day 66. Monday 17 February

Lesson 45: *Dual Navigation/Short-Field Operations /Soft-Field Operations*

Over the phone, Dylan told me Geoff McPhail was already waiting for me over at Full Sutton Airfield. Located just east of York, near the village of Stamford Bridge (the site of a historical English battle), I set off on a cold and wintry morning.

All along the journey I kept glancing at the sky. Although sunny, it was rather hazy and I wondered if I'd actually get into the air. One and a half hours later, I finally located the airfield. It seemed to be at the edge of a large industrial estate.

Driving across a pot-holed road (which I later learned was a taxiway) I tried to spot any signs of life but could discern none. There was a large hangar at the end of the road and a bit further along an orange windsock flapping about in the cold wind. It was the only thing moving.

And then I spotted the grass runway. It was tiny. It was more of a field than a runway. I turned away wondering what it would be like to land on. No room for errors there, I thought. Then I spotted a building. It looked like the best candidate for a clubhouse. I drove towards it, parking near another car, presumably Geoff's, and took stock of my new surroundings.

There wasn't a single aircraft anywhere. Not even an old one. There were plenty of sheep, though. Did these beasts graze on the runway? It certainly seemed likely because the grass was very short. Full Sutton Airfield was basically a field in the middle of nowhere. Flocking hell.

Pondering this, I walked over to the building and gingerly knocked on the frosty door. There was no answer. I knocked again. Still nothing. Tentatively, I tried the handle and found the door unlocked. I entered a large room.

There was no sign of Geoff but there was a large table in the centre of the darkened room. A tea-stained mug was the only thing in it. I turned my attention to the walls. Various maps, charts and old photos of Halifax bombers adorned it. There were also a few notices that warned against flying over nearby villages. I was about to open the curtains when I heard the door open behind me.

"What're you doing standing in the dark?" Geoff McPhail said.

"I couldn't find the switch," I replied, turning around to face him. "Anyway, where've you been?"

Geoff walked past me heading for a switch on the wall. With an audible buzz, the overhead striplights flickered into life. "I've been down at the hangar fuelling up the plane." He sat down, rubbing his hands together. "Make us a brew, will you. It's freezing out there. Me knackers are frozen solid."

I ventured into the kitchen and plugged in an ancient kettle. After I'd made the teas I noticed a strange contraption I'd not seen until then. It was an electronic drinks dispenser. After I'd handed Geoff his cup I wandered over to examine its wares.

"Whatever you do, mate," Geoff warned. "Don't try the chicken soup. It's lethal. You wouldn't want to be going to the outhouse on a day like today."

Outhouse? What sort of modern airfield still utilised an outhouse? Where the hell was I? I felt like a character in a Dickens novel. I was used to certain luxuries when flying, and toilet paper was one of them. I sat down, warming my fingers on the hot cup.

While Geoff and I deliberated on the route for my navigation lesson,

I took the opportunity to ask him about James Jarvis. I'd not seen him since before Christmas.

"Have you not heard?" Geoff said. "He's left us. He got a job with BMI flying jets. Lucky bastard."

I was taken aback. James? An airline pilot? "When did he leave?"

"About two weeks ago. It all happened quickly. He's in Aberdeen now for two months doing a training course on the Embraer 145."

I was pleased for James because I knew he'd make an excellent airline pilot. I also knew he'd been getting demoralised with the lack of job opportunities. But he'd finally done it. He'd reached his goal. Good luck to him.

Geoff gave me the route to plan. Full Sutton to Sherburn-in-Elmet Airfield, where we'd get something to eat. Then south to Retford Gamston Airport. After that, we'd fly to Beverley Airfield, before heading home. Quite a long trip.

Just before we left the clubhouse, a Cessna 172 pulled up outside. It belonged to a different flying school. Out of it stepped two people — a young woman of perhaps 20 and a grizzled-looking gentleman in his late 50s. As they entered the building, Geoff asked the man about the visibility in the air. He shrugged, saying it was quite murky. We thanked them and headed outside to the hangar. It was bloody bitter.

Opening the main hangar doors we soon located our aircraft for the day — my much beloved G-DO. After pulling it out and doing a thorough walkaround, we both climbed inside, strapping ourselves in.

And then it wouldn't start. It just turned over like a battered old Ford Escort on a winter's morning. It sounded pathetic.

"Give it a couple of pumps of primer," suggested Geoff, breathing hard over his fingers to keep them warm. I did as he suggested and pumped a little knob over on the left, which was used to inject some fuel into the engine. I'd never used it before. That done, I tried the key again. Nothing happened.

Geoff told me that on a freezing day this was normal. "Just give it a bit of time to rest and we'll try it again." And he was right. After 15 minutes or so of careful cajoling, the engine finally spluttered into life. We were in business.

Making sure the engine had plenty of time to heat up before we set off, Geoff and I simply sat awhile trying to keep ourselves warm. A few minutes later the Cessna 172 from earlier taxied past. The man Geoff had spoken to in the clubhouse turned out to be the student. The young woman sitting in the right-hand seat was quite clearly the instructor. Geoff looked at me. "Did you think the same as me?"

I nodded.

"Who'd have thought it, eh?"

After watching the Cessna depart for pastures new, I released the brake and moved off to an area set aside for power checks. As we did so, Geoff pressed the communications button.

"Full Sutton Radio," he said. "Taxiing to runway 22 for a departure to the east."

There was no reply.

Geoff didn't seem bothered. "There's no one there," he said. "But we still make calls to let other aircraft know what we're up to. Someone might be coming in to land. Or that Cessna might be doing circuits."

After lining up on the grass runway, I held the brakes and pushed the throttle to maximum. Five seconds later, we were off. The soft-field take-off was the same as on a hard runway, only slightly bumpier. We were soon in the air with the sky to ourselves. The Cessna 172 was long gone.

At 500 ft, it became obvious the visibility was not at its best. With no horizon to speak of, everything beyond 5 nm was just haze. Still, we headed for the M62 motorway and when we reached it we followed its route until we were between two sets of power stations.

Geoff told me to turn north and pointed at my chart. His finger rested in the military zone of Church Fenton. "Sherburn is inside Church Fenton's MATZ," he said.

I looked and saw that Sherburn and Church Fenton's control zones actually merged into one.

"So we'll need to call Church Fenton and ask for a MATZ penetration," added Geoff.

I shrugged, having no clue what he wanted. I looked at the chart again.

Geoff told me to watch and learn.

After changing frequency to Church Fenton ATC, he pressed the button. "Fenton Radar. This is Golf-Bravo Sierra Delta Oscar."

The reply came back almost immediately. "Golf-Delta Oscar. Pass your message."

"Golf-Delta Oscar is a Cessna 152 out of Full Sutton to Sherburn," said Geoff smoothly. "10 miles south-west of Sherburn at 2,000 ft. QNH 1023. Request MATZ penetration."

The military controller gave us permission to enter his military air traffic zone and then handed us over to Sherburn Radio, who, unlike Full Sutton, had somebody staffing the radio.

As we flew towards Sherburn, I started to get quite excited. This was going to be a first for me. I was actually going to land at a different airfield other than Leeds Bradford Airport! With Geoff fine-tuning my flight path we soon joined the circuit, eventually ending up on final. Following a surprisingly hard landing, we parked up for some refreshments.

After buying Geoff and myself a hearty chip sandwich and cup of coffee each, we pondered on the trip so far. Between mouthfuls, Geoff told me I hadn't been consistent enough with the trim wheel. "You need to let it work for you. It's there to help not hinder."

I took a slurp of coffee, lambasting the creators of such a fiendish contraption. The trim wheel had been the bane of my life all through my training. I told Geoff I'd do better on the next leg. Tony Denson, boss of the flying school at Leeds suddenly arrived. He informed us he was at Sherburn because his twin-engined Beech Duchess was having an engine overhaul.

"When it's done," Tony said, "I'll fly it back to Leeds."

Tony sat down to join us and I took the opportunity to ask him a question that had been on my mind. "How many flights are flown as trial flights compared to PPL lessons?"

Tony thought for a moment before answering. "Probably about a third. But do you know something? About three-quarters of trial flighters never actually turn up. It's quite lucrative for us because most of them pay up front. If they don't turn up after six months, then it's their loss. We keep the money."

I asked him why people didn't turn up.

Geoff answered for him. "Most trial flights are booked as a surprise gift for someone. When this person gets their voucher maybe they don't fancy it. Or maybe they just forget. Lots of reasons."

Tony nodded, drinking his tea. Five minutes later he bid us farewell.

Geoff and I talked about the next leg of our journey: Sherburn to

Gamston, which was located about 32 miles to the south. En route we'd pass over the M62 again, then head to the eastern side of Sheffield until we could see the M1 and the city's old airport. Finally we would head east onto Gamston. It all looked straightforward and after planning it with my trusty whiz wheel we went out to the aircraft.

After taking off, I was again dismayed by just how poor the visibility was; all murk and greyness. I wouldn't have relished flying in the same conditions by myself.

Sherburn Radio quickly passed us to Church Fenton MATZ, who in turn passed us off to Doncaster Approach a few minutes later.

Throughout the journey, Geoff made me work hard at navigating. He was constantly asking me where I thought we were and how I'd deduced this. Sometimes I got it right and other times I got it wrong. When the latter happened, Geoff would make me look outside for obvious landmarks (such as kinks in rivers, large power stations or obvious settlements) and then relate them to the chart. He also warned me against using small villages as potential landmarks because they were useless unless I could identify them with absolute certainty.

Photo © Dave Horrigan

After nearly 37 minutes of flying we could make out Gamston Airport in the listless distance. Like Sherburn, the person manning the airwaves wasn't an air traffic controller, but instead a radio operator. After asking her for the airfield information (i.e. runway in use and wind data) we told her of our intentions to land. Eventually, I landed on the tarmac runway and began taxiing towards the parking areas. My landing was not great.

We were asked to bring the aircraft to a stop at *Parking Bay 5* and this simple request made me realise how potentially difficult it could be for a pilot visiting a new airfield for the first time. Where the hell was Parking Bay number 5?

After turning off the runway I scanned the area ahead. My eyes soon located a large number 5 painted on the side of a large building. I taxied towards it, pleased I'd spotted it so quickly.

"Where are you going?" asked Geoff.

I gestured to the large number five on the building but Geoff shook his head. "That's *hangar* 5. We want parking 5. Look."

He pointed over to our right where someone had painted another number 5 on the ground. I'd not even noticed it. Embarrassed, I turned towards it.

"Bloody hell," laughed Geoff. "I've got to keep my eye on you!"

We decided to have a coffee, but before that we went to visit the Tower to pay for the landing. This was another first for me — actually meeting people who talked to pilots over the radio.

After climbing a small set of stairs we entered a room that offered a grand view of the whole airfield. There were two people present, a lady and a man, both middle-aged. The woman was wearing a headset and holding a microphone in her hand. Her pal was sitting next to her doing nothing in particular.

The whole set-up of equipment looked old. After speaking to another pilot about to land, the woman replaced the microphone, turned around and faced us.

"Hello," I said. "We're here to pay for the landing."

"Yeah," she answered. "We watched it. We only laughed a bit."

Her colleague laughed and so did Geoff. Then I did, because I knew they were all secretly envious of my superior skills. I handed over the money and after chatting for a couple more minutes, Geoff and I turned tails, heading for the cafe.

As Geoff ordered the beverages, I sat down, immediately noticing some geeky T-shirts hanging up in the adjoining shop. They showed a cockpit attitude indicator (sometimes referred to as the artificial horizon) with an inverted gyroscope. In other words, they depicted what it would have looked like if a plane were upside down. Underneath this graphic was a slogan that read: *Bad Attitude!* Suffice to say I purchased two dozen. Hopefully they'll last me a long time.

After we'd finished our coffees, Geoff sent me out to the aircraft while he visited the pit stop. As soon as I stepped outside, my ears heard the unmistakable roar of a jet engine. Looking into the sky, I caught sight of a Cessna Citation business jet landing on the runway. As I began checking Golf-Delta Oscar, it taxied past and parked at the spot next to me. A couple of minutes later, two pilots climbed out and nodded at me. Then they wandered over to the main building. I watched them enviously.

Our next port of call was Beverley Airfield, located 44 nm to the north-east. I took off and after some time could see a town appearing like a mirage on the nose. I hoped it was Gainsborough. I picked up my map to have a good look because I wasn't really sure.

"You are fixated on your bloody map," Geoff said. "Or else you're fixated on the instruments. You should be concentrating on looking outside more. There's nothing in this cockpit that'll kill you but there's plenty of stuff out there that will."

I nodded in agreement, peering outside, wondering where the hell we were. After a moment of silence, I addressed Geoff. "Where are we?"

He said, "Where do you think we are?"

"Gainsborough?"

"Why do think that?"

"Because I checked on the map and the only town it can be is Gainsborough."

Geoff nodded and stared at the town that was now underneath the nose. "You're right. But you've also proved my point. Gainsborough was the only town it could have been and yet you still felt the need to check."

He was right.

About halfway to Beverley Airfield, Geoff told me to plan a diversion back to Sherburn-in-Elmet. "Look at the chart and work out a rough heading and ETA."

After doing this, I turned onto my new heading and tried to forget about the map. Very soon we passed over a town that I knew was Goole. We were heading in the correct direction. And then I could make out

165

the power stations of Ferrybridge and Eggborough. They were like two goal posts leading to Sherburn. I altered my heading slightly, aiming for the centre of them. Then I requested and received another MATZ penetration from Church Fenton. Sherburn was dead ahead. An almost perfect diversion.

Except it was no such thing. Geoff had corrected me numerous times. He'd told me what to say on the radio and had pointed out key features on the ground. He'd even done all my FREDA checks and some trimming too. I was under no illusion that had I been by myself, I would not have made it to Sherburn.

After another hard and fast landing we began moving to the fuel pumps. It was during this taxi that Geoff began to tell me a sorry tale of woe.

The story begins with an eager young man getting the job of his dreams. He toils hard at his chosen duty, often working into the dead of night. Through wind and hail, snow and fog, our mighty worker tries to fulfil his mission, basking in the knowledge that people are depending on him. And eventually the Golden Path is complete and our hero can finally rest.

But our Hero has a Nemesis. This evil enemy laughs in the face of his labours. The scoundrel ignores his diligent work. The Nemesis cares not a jot about what our Hero has done. In fact, he goes out of his way to avoid the Golden Path.

And what is the hero's job I hear you hark? He, of course, paints the yellow lines along the centre of taxiways at most airports. And I was the Nemesis. Geoff told me to follow the lines not ignore them.

After we'd parked at the fuel pumps, I asked Geoff what he had thought of my navigation skills.

He paused, searching for the right words. "They're…okay. Not great though. You really need to work on your timings, especially when working out estimates for diversions. You also need to adjust for errors en route. At the moment I think you're flying by the seat of your pants a lot of the time."

I nodded. He was right. In the air I found it hard to do even the simplest of mental arithmetic. Working out problems such as adding 18 minutes onto the time of 13:45 became a task that could overload me. My brain simply couldn't cope with flying and doing everything else.

Perhaps I'd reached the peak of my flying career, I thought dejectedly.

After we'd refuelled, we both climbed back in for the final jaunt back to Full Sutton. As we taxied to the runway, a drama quickly unfolded before our very eyes. It involved Tony Denson, owner of the flying school.

Moments earlier Tony had taken off in the twin-engined Duchess. As we trundled along, we heard him make a *Pan-Pan* call over the radio. In an aircraft emergency, a pilot can make a *Mayday-Mayday-Mayday* call if the situation is extremely serious — such as an engine fire, or a *Pan-Pan, Pan-Pan, Pan-Pan* call for other less serious situations.

"Sherburn Radio," Tony said. "Pan-Pan Pan-Pan Pan-Pan. There's a problem with one of the engines. I'm returning to land."

While we waited on the ground we could see the Duchess flying downwind. The man on the radio told other aircraft coming in to land to either stay away for the moment, or to continue in the circuit until the Pan-Pan situation had been resolved. Everyone except Tony then maintained radio silence. Sounding impressively calm and collected, Tony Denson brought the aircraft in for final approach.

Electing to land on the grass runway parallel to the tarmac one, Geoff explained this was because Tony was probably worried about an undercarriage collapse upon landing. "With one engine out he'll be better off on softer ground because of the potential hard landing."

As Tony got closer to the ground, fire trucks and assorted emergency vehicles rushed past us towards his landing site. People came out of the clubhouse to watch.

To me, the Duchess seemed to be coming in at a markedly banked angle. I pointed this out to Geoff who nodded; informing me it was the effect of flying on only one engine. "Look. He's coming in now."

I watched as Tony flared the Duchess, and then brought it down softly on the grass. He'd done it. He was down safely. A few seconds later, Tony announced he'd be able to taxi the aircraft back to the hangar unassisted and thanked everyone for their help. The assorted emergency vehicles returned to their posts and very quickly, the airfield returned to normal.

After taking off Geoff told me he'd fly the short 15-minute leg back to Full Sutton so I could relax and watch 'the Master' at work. After we'd landed, we put the aircraft back in the hangar and had a chat about how things had gone.

Geoff told me to concentrate on my own safety first and foremost in the air. "When we were landing at Sherburn for the second time," said Geoff. "Remember that other aircraft in the circuit behind us?"

I nodded. I'd heard the plane making its radio calls.

Geoff continued. "Yeah. He was downwind behind us. But when we were on final, I caught you looking over your shoulder to see where he was. We were almost down on the runway for God's sake! Imagine losing control then? We'd have been dead meat!"

Ten minutes later I was in my car driving home in the dark. I thought back over the lesson, pleased that I'd landed at two different airfields. I'd also managed to negotiate my way inside a military zone, which was something I'd never done before. I'd also spoken to numerous people on the radio *and* flown a diversion. But I still felt downhearted. I was playing catch-up in the air; it was as simple as that. There were so many things to do while navigating that I was worried I'd never have enough mental agility to juggle them all. I arrived at home well and truly knackered.

TOTAL (HOURS) = 49.6

Day 67. Tuesday 18 February

The weather was no good. Limited visibility ruled the day.

TOTAL (HOURS) = 49.6

Day 68. Wednesday 19 February

Marginal visibility weather continued throughout the whole morning and so the flying school put me on permanent standby for my lesson.

By early afternoon, it was a no go. I did some schoolwork instead.

TOTAL (HOURS) = 49.6

Day 69. Thursday 20 February

Fog, frost and freezing cold. Lovely.

TOTAL (HOURS) = 49.6

Day 70. Friday 21 February

The last day of my half-term break. Yet again, the weather conspired against me. It would end up scuppering my lessons for the next six weeks.

TOTAL (HOURS) = 49.6

Where Am I?

'Jason, do you actually know where we are?'

-John Reynolds (Flying Instructor)

Day 71. Saturday 7 March

Low visibility, howling gales and torrential rain added up to a typical spring day in the United Kingdom. Who would want to live in Spain with weather like this?

TOTAL (HOURS) = 49.6

Day 72. Saturday 8 March

Too windy to fly. Instead, I cursed the British weather.

TOTAL (HOURS) = 49.6

Day 73. Saturday 15 March

It's been nine months since I started on the long road to getting my Private Pilot's Licence. When I'd first started back in July, I really thought I'd be done and dusted by September. How wrong I had been! And so, after a week of excellent weather, where I was stuck at work, I woke up to find a dense and lingering layer of fog. Great.

Imagine my surprise when Geoff McPhail phoned me. "Get yourself over to Full Sutton, lad. An instructor called John Reynolds will meet you there."

"What about this fog?" I asked. "And who's John Reynolds?"

"The fog's forecast to lift by mid-morning. And John's just joined the flying school. He's an experienced instructor, though. He used to be based on the Isle of Man."

I gathered my things and set off straight away.

After almost one and a half hours I reached Full Sutton and entered the clubhouse. John Reynolds hadn't yet arrived but there was someone else waiting inside. His name was Richard Cooper, another student from the school. He was studying his charts and weather briefings while sipping a cup of tea. He told me he was hopefully going to complete his qualifying cross-country once the mist had cleared.

"It's already been cancelled six times," he told me. "But hopefully today will be the day."

"You're joking?" I said. "Cancelled six times?"

"Yeah. Every time I book it, the weather's shit. Today's the latest in the long sorry saga. I just hope this bloody weather lifts."

The radio suddenly crackled into life asking if anyone was home. Richard looked at me for a moment and then shrugged. He got up to answer the pilot. "Aircraft calling. Full Sutton Radio speaking." I was impressed; I didn't think I'd have had the nerve to speak over the radio to address another pilot.

After a brief pause, the unknown pilot spoke again. "Oh Good. Full Sutton Radio, I'm overhead your airfield but can't seem to locate it. Can someone look outside to see if they can see me? I've never been here before."

I rushed outside and after glancing upwards and around, I could see neither hide nor hair of him but I could hear the hum of an aircraft somewhere in the distance. He was obviously nearby but it was impossible to tell just where with the dismal visibility. I went in and told Richard.

Richard gave the pilot the news and a reply came quickly back.

"Alright, thanks," the pilot said. "I'll head back towards Ottringham and fly a radial to get back here. Should take me about 20 minutes. See you all later. Golf-Hotel Zulu."

Eventually he did find the airfield and managed to get down in one piece, even though a nasty gust of wind caught his right wing just before touchdown. Richard Cooper went out to speak him. The pilot, a young man in his twenties, told him the visibility had been extremely poor. He added that without his IMC, he'd have got into major difficulties.

An IMC (Instrument Meteorological Conditions) rating is like a mini-Instrument Rating. It gives a pilot specific training on instruments, allowing him or her to fly in conditions that a basic PPL pilot couldn't. However, it is only valid in the UK as no other country recognises it. Richard came back to the clubhouse while the pilot refuelled.

Meanwhile, another member of Full Sutton's flying club arrived, an elderly gentleman in his late sixties. His name was Bill and he told us only a foolhardy pilot who would choose to fly in weather as poor as it was. We all agreed.

"It's ironic, though," he continued. "This morning, the weatherman said it would be a glorious day over the whole region, except for the Vale of York."

"Right where we are," commented Richard. "Sod's law."

Bill then talked about the idiocy of printed aviation weather reports. Pointing at one pinned to the wall, he said he'd never been able to decipher them. Furthermore, he had no inclination to try. "Just look at this gobbledegook!"

EGNU 0750 13012KT 2500 OVC008 09/08

Bizarrely, although agreeing with Bill, I actually understood it. The four letters at the beginning refer to the unique four-letter code of the aerodrome, in this case, Full Sutton. The next four digits are the observation time — 7:50 am. Next is the wind information: 12 knots at 130°. Visibility was 2,500 m with overcast cloud at 800 ft. Finally it gives the air and dew point temperature. Easy.

Just then, the visiting pilot took off again, quickly disappearing north into the gloom.

Bill asked Richard where he was planning to fly to on his cross-country route. When he found out one of the places was Nottingham Airport (a large general aviation airport) he decided to offer some advice.

"Watch out for East Midland's Class D Airspace. You'll want to avoid it like the plague." He paused, grimacing slightly. "A friend of mine got lost near Nottingham and breached their airspace. He got into serious trouble from the CAA. And watch out for Syerston Airfield. It's near Nottingham, and looks very similar. Don't land there by mistake. I did once. Never again."

Richard and I chuckled. "Why?" I asked. What happened?"

Bill looked sheepish. "I was on my way to Nottingham but got totally lost. Eventually though, thanks to some hasty map reading and good luck, I found the airfield and landed, When I went to pay for my landing I got a shock because I got told off for not asking for permission to be there. I told them I'd rung earlier but the man said no one had rung. And then we worked out I had landed at the wrong airport. I felt like an idiot. A total bloody idiot."

As Richard and I mulled these warnings over, John Reynolds finally arrived.

John was a well-built man in his early forties with a shock of black hair on his head. "Sorry for being late, guys," he said. "I had to sort out something at Leeds first. But it doesn't matter anyway. The weather's no good. Not even for circuits."

Richard Cooper nodded, starting to pack his things away. Bloody weather.

TOTAL (HOURS) = 49.6

Day 74. Sunday 16 March

The weather was warm with hazy sunshine. My lesson (and Richard Cooper's) was cancelled due to poor visibility. My tally of 44 cancellations out of 73 bookings, equated to 60% of lessons down the drain. A high, but quite normal statistic for the UK.

On a more positive note, though, I finally got a chance to try out my new software, the *VFR Photographic Scenery of Northern England,* which had arrived through the post. As previously written, these add-ons depict the true scenery of the UK via my flight simulator software. It was actually possible to fly navigation trips using the program. I booted up the PC.

Upon loading, I immediately located my hometown of Bradford, flying over it, hoping to spot some obvious landmarks. They were all there, including my house. Next I found my parents' house up in Middlesbrough, and then found the school where I worked in Keighley. Finally I flew around Leeds Bradford Airport, easily recognising Eccup Reservoir and Harrogate. Pleased, I decided to fly a route John Reynolds had asked me to plan. Adding some sharp winds and low visibility to increase the realism, I took off from the virtual Full Sutton.

With the help of a VOR, I flew to Gamston and then on to Nottingham. I didn't get lost once. Next, I flew north to Sheffield and Barnsley and then entered the Leeds zone at Dewsbury. After landing at Leeds, I took off again, this time heading back to Full Sutton. And this was where the problems started. I couldn't find it. The grass runway was obviously blending in with the multitude of fields surrounding it.

And so I did something *not* possible to do in real life. I simply paused the program so I could look at the ground from every conceivable angle. I eventually spotted the tiny airfield some distance away, lurking among some fields. But I couldn't pause a real flight if I was lost. What would I do then?

I decided to get my *Road Atlas of the UK* out. Flying over the virtual city of York, I saw a dual carriageway on the eastern boundary. The atlas confirmed this. From this dual carriageway, two roads lead east. From my car journeys to Full Sutton, I knew one of these roads went past the Village of Stamford Bridge and that Full Sutton was very close by. Flying along this road until I was overhead Stamford Bridge, I turned slightly south, and hallelujah, there was Full Sutton!

Photo © Victor Carter

TOTAL (HOURS) = 49.6

Day 75. Saturday 5 April

Lesson 46: *Dual Cross-Country*

The weather was okay with only a low cloud base and some blustery winds trying to spoil things. Arriving at Full Sutton, John Reynolds told me to plan my headings and speeds for a flight to Nottingham based on the forecast winds at 2,000 ft.

"I've only got the ground winds," I admitted.

John smiled. "Well, let me teach you this neat little trick. Just double the ground wind and veer its direction by 20°."

I looked at him blankly. "Veer?" Was that clockwise or the other way round? I could never remember.

John said, "So if the ground wind is 8 knots, at 2,000 ft it's 16 knots. And if the ground direction is 130°, at 2,000 ft assume it's 150°."

After I'd worked out the headings and timings I wrote all the radio frequencies I might have to use en route. Additionally, I wrote a script of things likely to come up with the various ATC units I might encounter. These included the *pass your message* instructions I'd receive whenever I changed frequency. I reasoned the script would come to my aid when operating at full-whack during the flight.

Meeting John at the hangar, I took the opportunity to ask him whether he enjoyed instructing.

"It's the best job in the world," he beamed. "Actually flying *and* getting paid for it!"

"But what about the airlines? Don't you fancy that?"

He thought for a few moments. "Maybe. But I'd only want a regional airline job. I don't want to spend nights away from home."

Fair enough, I thought. I could understand that. "What about James Jarvis getting a job? How did everyone feel?"

"We thought he was a jammy bastard! But he deserved it," laughed John. "Plus, when one of us does get an airline job, it gives the rest hope."

On the subject of James, I recently received an email from him:

Gidday mate, The waiting game paid off. I can assure you it was worth it! I'm still marvelling at the Embraer. I spent an hour doing touch & goes this weekend at a height of 1000 ft-ish. (Cloudbase was +/- 1000 ft). Circuits at 220 kts in a 20-ton aeroplane. Ye Ha! James The cowboy reference at the end of his message perturbed me. It threw a completely new light on the *whippings* he'd received when learning to fly in New Zealand. His email went on to say that his first day with passengers would be later that week. He'd fly from Aberdeen to Manchester, then head off to Copenhagen for a Danish pastry or two, before finally finishing in Aberdeen.

After a thorough walkaround Golf-Delta Oscar, John Reynolds and I climbed inside and became reacquainted with the familiar aroma. It was a mixture of oil and gasoline, with a healthy sprinkling of body odour from the hundreds of students who had sweated their way through a demanding lesson.

We took off for the first leg of the journey: Full Sutton to Nottingham via Gamston Airfield. Overhead Full Sutton, I started my stopwatch and turned onto a southerly heading that would take me to my first checkpoint — the town of Goole.

Where Am I?

A few minutes into the flight I realised the visibility was indeed poor. Also, low-lying clouds were only a few hundred feet above us, meaning we couldn't climb above about 1,500 ft. Despite this we were soon overhead Goole. The way the River Humber curved around the town made it an easy landmark. I turned onto a south-easterly heading to avoid Doncaster Airport's Class D airspace. Beside me, John said nothing.

A few minutes later, skimming under the underside of the low-level cloud, we were flying close to small airfield with a grass runway. I had no idea which one it was and so John told me it was North Moor. With this reference point now identified, I decided to do something clever. I dialled in the frequency of the Gamston VOR and rotated the knob to intercept the 210° radial. I'd done similar things on my flight simulator and it had always worked a treat. Watching me closely, John seemed slightly more impressed. We flew on.

Eventually the small town of Retford appeared in the hazy distance. Because Gamston Airport was about 3 miles south of Retford, I switched over to Gamston Radio, who gave us permission to transit their zone.

Overhead Gamston and finally back on track, I began to feel better about things. My VOR trick had been perfect, especially in the poor weather. To get to Nottingham Airport, which was about 13 minutes away, all I had to do was fly on a heading of 190°. It should have been a simple flight, but it soon turned to disaster.

After turning left by 20°, I decided to really concentrate on getting things right. I scanned my map and kept my eye on the heading indicator. After approximately nine minutes of flying (which should have been a big clue) I spotted an airfield 3 miles in front. Consulting my airport diagram for Nottingham (which showed the runway alignments) I could see the airport in front more or less matched up. Slightly perturbed by how quickly we'd reached Nottingham, I reasoned the winds had probably been wrong.

I then remembered something John had told me before we'd taken off. "When you see the lakes," he'd told me. "You'll know Nottingham airport's nearby."

Peering out into the gloom, I scanned for the lakes, and there they were. Seeing them made up my mind. I was the Master of the Skies! Somehow I'd found my way to Nottingham Airport. I started descending.

Quickly dialling in the frequency for Nottingham Radio, they swiftly gave me the airfield information. While pondering on how to join the circuit, John, who'd been quiet for a few moments, suddenly grabbed the yoke. "My control," he said, pushing the throttle in for a climbing turn to the right. "I don't believe it!" he said through gritted teeth.

Wondered what was going on, I sat stunned. Climbing inside the clouds, John dialled a radio frequency I didn't know, giving our call sign and position. There was no reply. There didn't seem to be anyone there. John tried again. "Syerston Radio. Sorry for being so close. We're now out of your zone, heading south-west to Nottingham."

And then I realised what I'd done. Somehow, I'd wrongly identified Syerston Airfield as Nottingham Airport — precisely the same mistake the pilot back at Full Sutton had warned me about a month ago. I'd convinced myself that the airfield had to be Nottingham, even though I'd arrived four minutes early *and* couldn't see any sign of a large built-up area. It had been those damn lakes that had sealed the deal for me. If I'd checked beforehand, I would have noticed that Syerston had lakes too.

As I sat shame-faced, John tapped instrument panel. "There's your mistake. You were concentrating on this weren't you? You were ignoring the clues outside."

I nodded, keeping mute. I felt pitiful.

In silence, John descended through the clouds and handed control back to me. I had absolutely no idea of our position. We could have been flying over the dark side of the moon as far as I was concerned. I told John this and he gave me a heading to steer. A couple of minutes later, I made out a large housing estate, as well as the River Trent beneath us. And then some more lakes.

Very quickly, Nottingham Airport came into view, and I began a standard overhead join for runway 03, feeling rotten.

A standard overhead join is the approved way of joining the circuit at less busy airports. The method is as follows. First a pilot will fly towards the airport at a height greater than the circuit height (2,000 ft is normal for this.) Then he'll fly across the numbers of the runway intended for landing, starting a descent to circuit height (usually 1,000 ft). Then he'll fly along the 'dead side' of the runway (i.e. opposite to downwind) before crossing the runway at its opposite end. Then the pilot will enter the normal circuit.

I managed to do all this and land successfully but still felt pathetic. On a journey of only 64 miles, which should have taken 37 minutes, I'd succeeded in getting lost on numerous occasions and, worst of all, had almost landed at the wrong airport.

After entering the clubhouse, John turned to me. "I'll get the teas. You pay the landing fee. Then we'll talk about the fiasco."

After taking a sip of his drink John regarded me.

"Your general flying ability is no problem. A bit rusty in certain areas but no permanent damage. Also, your radio work is fine. Quite good, actually." He paused, absently stroking his chin. "But your navigation skills are dismal. And I'm not just talking about Syerston here. I'm talking across the board. For starters, I don't think you know how to deal with unexpected diversions. And then there's your fixation with your maps."

After picking up his cup again, John told me an adult human could, at a push, cope with seven things at once. "And it's possible to juggle the seven things, both mental and physical, and keep going. But if an eighth ball is thrown into the mix, then everything starts unravelling."

He told me that when a student first learns to fly, they usually spread the seven things as follows:

Flying the aeroplane	4
Navigating	0 (because at first, there isn't any)
Communicating	3

He told me mine were now like this:

Flying the aeroplane	2
Navigating	4
Communicating	2

Which was one too many. My juggling act was coming apart at the seams. I shook my head. I didn't know what to say.

It was soon time to depart on the second leg of the day, Nottingham to Leeds Bradford Airport. It was to be the longest of the legs, and would, according to my calculations, take 48 minutes to complete.

I was actually quite worried about this leg because of the high terrain to the left of my proposed route. Also, I was concerned about navigating over so many large built-up areas. Mansfield, Chesterfield, Sheffield and Barnsley were just some of the towns along my route. I wondered which one I'd get lost over.

I taxied to the holding point to carry out the power checks. While I busied myself with this, John checked my flight plan. Power checks were carried just prior to take-off. You hold the brakes and increase the throttle, and then check the magnetos and carb heat. Next you check the oil temperature and pressure are within limits. Then check the ammeter's charging, as it should be, before finally pulling the throttle back to idle. If it doesn't conk out or blow up, you're all set to go.

After a minute's perusal of my plan, John said it looked fine. We took off, heading north-west to Mansfield.

It should have taken eight minutes to reach Mansfield, but when I looked at the approaching town, I wasn't sure if it was Mansfield or somewhere else. I'd been planning to triangulate my position by using the M1 motorway, which by now should have been clearly visible on my left, but in the murk I couldn't see it. Deciding it *probably* was Mansfield, I elected to press on regardless, heading for my second checkpoint — the M1 near Chesterfield.

After flying for a while longer, I could see neither Chesterfield *nor* the M1. My spirits were dropping quickly. I began to get annoyed with myself. I was once again utterly lost.

I was reading an aviation article recently that went through the thought processes of a pilot getting lost in the air. First is denial. The pilot will believe he cannot be lost. They'll press on, hoping to come across a checkpoint further down the line. When this checkpoint doesn't materialise, the next stage in the process is anger. *How could it have happened?* And finally comes acceptance. The hapless pilot will have to accept the fact they are indeed lost and must do something about it.

Flying above South Yorkshire, I began to think that if *I* ever became well and truly lost, and was flying solo, then there'd be a fourth stage in the psychological drama: *panic*.

Carrying on flying the heading I'd planned, even though none of the checkpoints had shown up, I considered asking John for help. Back on the ground at Nottingham, he'd told me he would be keeping quiet, giving me chance to sort things out myself. If I wanted help, I was to ask, otherwise he'd say nothing. I decided to fly on for the time being, remaining silent.

Suddenly, the radio cracked into life. It was Doncaster ATC.

"Golf-Delta Oscar," the controller said. "You're very close to Netherthorpe's zone. I'd suggest contacting them if you want to transit. Alternatively, turn left now to avoid their airspace."

I told them I'd turn left. After changing course I looked at my chart. Netherthorpe airfield was to the right of my planned route. I had drifted off course.

Very quickly I spotted the M1 motorway, and because I knew it ran past my next checkpoint, the old Sheffield airport, I felt like clinging to it like a leech. I couldn't do that though; John had already warned me about using roads as a primary means of navigation. Reluctantly I turned, leaving behind the relative security of the northbound M1. Very quickly, a massive conurbation appeared through the haze.

Sheffield was a large city, but it actually adjoined another city: Rotherham. From edge to edge, they covered a distance of about 14 miles. Scanning from left to right, all I could see was built-up area. It was an endless expanse of town and city. Which particular bit of Sheffield I was over, I had no idea, and with the M1 no longer in sight, I quickly became unsure of my position again. I felt about as useless as a totally useless thing. Peering randomly outside, I tried to spot anything I could use, but it was hopeless: I didn't know where I was or where I was going. I flew on, in a seemingly aimless path.

"Jason, do you know where we are?" asked John pointedly. It was the first time he'd said anything since we'd taken off.

"I think so," I answered. "We're over Sheffield... or maybe Rotherham."

John didn't answer. Instead, he nodded and looked outside the cockpit. I wondered if *he* knew where we were.

I looked at my chart. It offered no salvation. In fact, it made things worse. Doncaster suddenly jumped out at me which made me panic slightly. If I was over Doncaster then I was close to Class D airspace. Mind you, Doncaster ATC hadn't said anything so perhaps I was wrong about that. I decided to make a left turn anyway, hopefully I'd spot something I recognised over there.

"Why are you turning?" asked John.

"To get back over Sheffield."

John shook his head. "And where do you think we are now?"

"Over Doncaster?"

"We're over Sheffield, Jason." He sounded exasperated.

Feeling my throat dry up, I turned back onto a northerly heading. How was I supposed to know we were over Sheffield? Everything looked the bloody same. I didn't even know if we were left or right of track. In fact, I was beginning to give up all hope. Perhaps navigation would be the aspect of flying to finally finish me off. I'd managed to fly solo. I'd even done a few short navigation trips by myself. But a big cross-country trip was proving to be well beyond my skills.

A while later we approached some more large built-up areas. As far as I was concerned they could have been Wakefield, Dewsbury or Castleford, or indeed, none of them. Trying in vain to spot some obvious landmarks, I felt a pitying wave of despair wash over me. All hope was gone. It was time to end the misery. I turned to face John, but he was staring out of his window, portable GPS in hand. I decided to postpone my confession for the time being.

Doncaster ATC passed me over to Leeds Approach. The controller told me to inform him when I was over Dewsbury. I told them I would. *If we ever get there.*

A minute later, John obviously decided enough was enough. "Do you want to know where we are?"

I nodded.

Pointing to my chart, he told me we were over Pontefract, some 12 miles right of track.

I was shocked. How could I have gone so wrong? And from Pontefract, how was I supposed to get to Dewsbury? I decided not to think about it. I had no spare capacity to do so even if I wished. I turned the nose slightly.

John pressed the communication button. He told Leeds he was cancelling our landing clearance. He told the controller we'd be heading to Full Sutton instead.

I couldn't believe I'd performed so badly that John didn't think it was even worth bothering going to Leeds. "That bad, huh?" I said.

"No. I had no intention of going to Leeds. There's no point. You know what goes on there. It was always the plan to finish at Full Sutton."

I said nothing. I didn't know whether to believe him.

Because I now knew where we were, John asked me to plan a diversion back to Full Sutton.

By looking at the chart, two options immediately sprang to mind. The first option, a direct route, would take us into the military zone of Church Fenton. I discounted this option immediately. I couldn't face speaking to another controller, so instead, I told John we'd skirt around the edge of the Church Fenton zone by doing a zigzag to the town of Selby and then go on to Full Sutton.

John nodded, telling me it was a good plan. So with my chinagraph pencil, I drew my diversion route and estimated the headings. Amazingly, a few minutes later, Selby appeared in view. Feeling some measure of satisfaction, I waited until we were overhead the small town and turned north-east for Full Sutton.

About seven minutes later I could see an airfield on the nose. By consulting the chart, I identified it as Pocklington, a popular gliding site. Full Sutton was nearby. I turned left, quickly making out the industrial estate as well as Full Sutton Prison. Moments later, I spotted the grass strip. I'd found my way home.

After doing a standard overhead join, I came in for final approach on the grass runway ahead. As I did this, John gave me a top tip. He told me that instead of landing, I was to fly low along the length of the runway for as long as possible. "It'll make it a really soft landing."

Doing as instructed, I flared, keeping the nose up for longer than usual. We were only about a foot off the ground. Because the airspeed was bleeding off and we were ever so slightly settling downwards, a couple of seconds later our main wheels touched down with the gentlest of movements. It was one of my finest landings ever.

"Thanks," I said.

"That's what I'm here for."

Inside the clubhouse was a man about the same age as me. His name was Amer Manzoor and he was also a student of John Reynolds.

"Where's John?" Amer asked.

"Outside," I answered. "Probably making a phone call to the CAA to get me banned from flying lessons."

I told Amer all about my lesson from hell, and he laughed. Then I questioned him about his flying experiences so far.

"Well, I'm a doctor by trade," he told me. "But about six months ago I thought I'd learn to fly. I did my first solo last week. Unbelievable."

I smiled, also remembering my first solo flight. "And a bit terrifying as well," I added.

Amer laughed. "I couldn't agree more. And you're the first person who's said that. Not that I get to speak to many other students. In fact, I sometimes wish I'd learned at a flying club rather than a flying school."

I nodded.

In the UK there are two types of training establishments: flying schools and flying clubs. Flying schools train pilots how to fly aeroplanes and that is that. Their students hardly ever meet up because when one student finishes their lesson they simply go home to make way for the next one. Once the student has passed their PPL, it is thank you and goodbye.

Flying clubs, on the other hand, offer training on a more personal level. A student joins a club and becomes part of a social gathering. Members often hang around the clubhouse, many becoming good friends. After passing the PPL, they often stay on as members, offering advice to others.

There are pros and cons with both. Flying schools are excellent for commercial pilot training because they are usually located at larger airports where a student can get talking to ATC from the start. Flying schools usually have more aircraft and instructors available, and are usually highly organised so they can optimise flight time. Sometimes, they even have a resident examiner. So for an aspiring airline pilot, flying schools offer continuity in training that most flying clubs cannot compete with. And on a purely financial level, flying schools don't charge a membership fee like flying clubs often do, which could run into hundreds of pounds.

After talking to Amer for a while, I realised I had missed the social aspect of learning to fly. Perhaps I should have learned at a flying club because as I regaled my woeful navigation trip to Amer, my mood actually began to lift. Speaking to a fellow student was making me see the funny side of things.

"Sometimes," said Amer. "I wish I'd never started flying lessons. If I'd known how demoralising it was going to be, and how hard, I'd have saved my cash and done something else. Like bashing my head against a concrete block."

I chuckled. Similar thoughts had entered my head, over Pontefract to be exact.

"But when I think of my first solo," continued Amer, a smile forming on his face. "Knowing I was in charge of a plane by myself. No one can take that away."

I nodded in agreement.

Just then, John Reynolds entered the clubhouse. He gave Amer the bad news he was expecting. The weather had dropped and there would be no chance of flying. He then turned to me. "Out of interest," he asked. "How long did it take you to go solo?"

I told him about 22 hours.

"You should pass at 66 hours then."

Amer and I looked at each other. How could he possibly know that?

John explained a simple rule of thumb. Tripling the time it took to go solo was a good indication of the total hours needed to pass the flight test.

"What's your total time now," he asked me.

I told him the low fifties. John nodded thoughtfully. "Sixty-six sounds about right then."

My eyes widened in shock. He thought I'd actually pass! "Hang on though, I thought the average was about 55 hours?"

"Rubbish! Where've you heard that? The average is 65." He grinned. "But it took me 90!"

Five minutes later I got up to leave. On the way out, John stopped me. "About today, Jason," he said. "It didn't go as badly as you think it did. I saw some good navigation in places. You only struggled because you haven't flown recently. Next time, I'll give you a thorough briefing. You'll be fine."

I said goodbye to him and Amer.

TOTAL (HOURS) = 52.0

Honing the Skills

'Thank God for potatoes!'

–Steve Gilmour (Full Sutton PPL Student)

Day 76. Sunday 13 April

I got a phone call from John Reynolds asking if I wanted to sit in the back of an aircraft while he and another student flew a navigation trip. It would give me a chance to get things right in my head, he said, without having to worry about actually flying or speaking on the radio.

"I'd love to," I said. It sounded like an excellent idea, especially when John pointed out I wouldn't have to pay for a thing. "But who's the student?"

"Someone you don't know. He's called Steve Gilmour. He's actually part of Full Sutton's flying club. I'm taking him out as a favour to Richard (Watson — resident instructor of Full Sutton)."

I put the phone down, setting off straight away on a sunny, but hazy April day.

When I arrived at the airfield, Steve hadn't arrived so John and I began chatting. I mentioned my poor radio skills.

"Why? What's wrong with them?"

I told him of my early phobia of pressing the button. "Even now," I said, "I feel my pulse quicken when I know I've got to make a call."

John told me most students he'd taught had also experienced problems when speaking on the radio. "It's just something you get used to eventually. It takes time."

The door opened. It was Richard Watson, resident flying instructor.

Richard was aged 40, with short brown hair. He had one of those faces with a permanent grin etched upon it. Later I found out even when he was angry, he still looked amiable. It made him very approachable.

"Hello Richard," I said. "I'm Jason. I was just telling John about my poor radio skills. Tell me about any embarrassing conversations you've had with ATC."

Richard shook my hand and sat down, smiling as usual. "I'll tell you about a chat I heard a couple of weeks back. It really made me laugh." Settling back in his chair, he chuckled at the memory, beginning to tell his tale.

"I was flying in the Midlands with a student. We'd just changed frequency to a military controller. On the same frequency was a microlight pilot. What a total idiot."

Richard orally transcribed the exchange.

Pilot: Military Radar. This is G-ABCD.

ATC: G-ABCD, this is Military Approach. Have I spoken to you before?

Pilot: Err… Yes, I think so. But it was about a month ago…and it might not have been you personally. I can't remember. G-ABCD.

John and I laughed. Even I was not *that* bad. Suddenly the door opened again. A couple of young women entered the clubhouse. Looking nervous and confused, one of them said they had booked a trial flight or something.

Richard stood up, smiling. "Then I'm the man you want. I'm Richard."

After sitting both women down at a nearby table, Richard began to describe the ins and outs of a trial flight. He told them it would be in a four-seater aircraft. "So one of you will have to sit in the back."

One of the women shook her head. "Oh no," she said. "*I'm* not going up. I'm just here to hold my friend's hand before *she* goes up."

Her friend nodded. "Yeah. Debbie won't go up with me. I just asked her to come with me to the airport."

"Why don't you want to go up?" inquired Richard.

The girl looked nervously around the room. "They're just so little. I wouldn't feel safe."

"Oh come on," cajoled Richard. "Be brave. Plus, if you sit in the back, I'll sit next you and hold your hand. We'll let your friend fly the plane."

Both girls laughed. A couple of minutes later, Richard led them outside. In the end he got both of them up. Later I told him it had probably been down to his winning smile.

Steve Gilmour was in his mid-thirties and told me he was a prison officer at Full Sutton Prison. "I kept on seeing planes take off and land, so one day, I thought, why not?"

John left us alone, going off to make a phone call, so Steve and I sat down. We began talking about our experiences in doing the Private Pilot's Licence. Steve told me he was up to the cross-country stage of his training and had logged 41 hours of training so far.

"At the start, Richard told me I was a natural pilot, especially with my landings. In fact I used to tell my wife I was the King of Landings. How sad is that? But I did go solo after just eight hours. But then I had a crash."

Whoah! Hold on just second! "A crash?"

"Yeah. A crash. I've been involved in a plane crash!"

While notching up his required four hours of solo circuit practice, Steve had been coming in to land. "The approach was looking spot on," Steve told me. "The previous landing had been a bit heavy so I thought I'd try to improve this one."

With the grass-strip under the nose, Steve began to flare and simultaneously reduced power, awaiting his first *greaser*. As he reduced the power even more the stall warner suddenly began blazing away.

"It panicked me. I was still too high to stall. So I put full power back on and pulled up for a go-around."

Unfortunately for Steve though, he pulled back on the yoke too much. Even with full power, he'd increased the stall, resulting in a downwards sink, tail hanging low.

"I knew things had gone wrong. And then when I felt the aircraft roll rapidly to the right as I lost control, I thought that was it; I'm going to die."

Listening to Steve's account, I could feel my own heart beat quicken. I couldn't imagine being in the same situation. It must have been truly terrifying.

"I can't remember much about the actual crash. All I can recall is the plane swinging sharply across the grass strip with me holding on for dear life. I ended up in a potato field next to the runway."

Next, Steve remembered feeling severe jolts as the aircraft careered along its path of potato punishment. Then the plane came to an abrupt halt as the nose and propeller dug into the ground. The rear of the aircraft immediately vaulted upwards into a vertical position before slamming back down with a bang. Luckily, Steve's shoulder and waist harnesses had kept his body relatively safe from the potential damage of the impact.

"Everything went quiet. I remember that vividly. And then the thought of fire suddenly struck me. I unbuckled everything and climbed out. I couldn't believe I was still alive. I jumped off the wing and ran. I've never legged it so fast in all my life."

Sufficiently amazed to find he'd not suffered any injuries, Steve stopped after a discreet distance and turned back to look at the abandoned aircraft. It wasn't on fire and so after a prudent wait he cautiously returned to it. "I remembered I hadn't switched everything off."

"You went back to switch off the radios and stuff?"

"Yeah. How mad is that!"

After turning off the electrics and master switch, Steve inspected the general damage. It wasn't as bad as he'd first thought. Yes there was a bent propeller, and the nose wheel looked a bit worse for wear, but apart from that, it didn't look too bad at all. In fact, the aircraft in question was later repaired.

As Steve walked to the clubhouse to report the accident, he feared the worst. He thought Richard Watson would be furious. But he was wrong. Everyone at Full-Sutton was supportive. They were only thankful that Steve was okay.

And even though it had shaken Steve, he was eternally grateful to the Potato Gods for allowing him to crash-land safely. Still, he considered giving up his dream of becoming a pilot. "I cancelled all my lessons so I could think about things."

I told him I wasn't surprised.

After a few weeks of mulling things over, he decided to carry on.

When I asked him how he'd felt when he'd got back into an aircraft again, Steve admitted he'd been extremely apprehensive. "I remember my legs were shaking. They were like jelly."

I could only shake my head in wonderment.

In the Clubhouse, Steve Gilmour and I both independently planned the same navigation trip John Reynolds had set us. It involved taking off and heading to a large lake called Malham Tarn, then going to the small town of Masham, before finally returning to Full Sutton — a round trip of 96 nm. Afterwards, we compared our times and headings and found they closely matched. We went out to find John.

He was waiting by an aircraft. It wasn't a Cessna 152, but a Piper PA-28 Warrior, a low-winged four-seater aircraft capable of a cruise speed of around 100 knots, 10 knots quicker than the C-152. While John and I fuelled up Steve did a thorough walkaround.

Fuelling up wasn't as easy as it was at Leeds Bradford Airport. Firstly, John and I had to drag a large wheeled cylinder full of fuel (known as a bowser) from the hangar all the way to the aircraft. Then we had to faff around with a lock and handle release in order to free up the hose and nozzle. Finally, John fed the nozzle gun into the wing fuel tanks while I hand-cranked a large wooden handle to pump fuel. It was hard work and took ages. After we'd filled one side, John made me do the other as well. I was knackered.

After clambering aboard, I managed to squeeze into the tiny rear seat. I couldn't believe how cramped it was. When John sat in front of me, I was pinned in place, no doubt risking deep vein thrombosis. I said nothing. It was a free flight after all.

With Steve busy carrying out the internal checks, I examined the cockpit. It was very similar to that of the Cessna 152. The only difference was that some of the controls were in different positions. For instance, the trim wheel was between the front seats as opposed to being on the panel. A few minutes later, Steve started the engine and taxied us to the runway for a quick take-off.

At around 1,000 ft, it became evident the visibility was quite poor. John asked Steve whether he wanted to carry on in such dismal conditions. Steve thought a while before finally nodding. We flew westwards towards the rising terrain of the Pennine Mountains.

Ten minutes later I came to a fundamental realisation. It involved Steve and John. John was constantly nagging Steve Gilmour to check his speed, heading and much more besides. Everything John was reminding Steve about, I'd heard myself, repeatedly. Steve and I were in the same boat.

The fact he forgot to do FREDA checks, or sometimes got tongue-tied when speaking on the radio, made me happy in a way that was astonishing. He was the same as me! To get nagged was normal! The flight, for me, was turning out to be a pivotal moment in my training.

Overhead the golf balls of Menwith, John told Steve he was slightly left of track. After a small correction, Steve soon put that right and not long afterwards, we flew over Malham Tarn, and then turned onto a north-easterly heading towards Masham.

With both my hands free, I decided to sharpen up my map-reading skills. Looking out of the window I saw we were over high terrain, with the odd lake and reservoir glinting in the far horizon. After a few minutes I spotted a long, narrow stretch of water on our right.

Grabbing my chart, I tried to find a lake with the same shape and orientation. There were a few possible candidates, the most likely of which showed a small village at its far end. Squinting into the haze outside, I spotted a village. So that meant I knew precisely where we were.

John also knew where we were but Steve wasn't so sure so John told him, pointing at his chart. Then he asked him whether we were on or off course.

"Erm... we're right of track," said Steve eventually. "By about 10°, I think."

John nodded in agreement. "So what are you going to do?"

Steve said he'd put us back on track by using the *Double Track Error* method. I wondered what he was on about. Seemingly reading my mind, John turned around. "Have you heard of that, Jason?"

I shook my head.

"I'll let Steve explain."

Steve told me that because he'd been flying on a heading of 085° and was 10° right of track by the halfway stage, he could simply double the error to get 20°. "All I do is turn left by that amount. That should get us to Masham." He turned onto a new heading of 065°.

His method turned out to be correct. We ended up overhead Masham about five minutes later.

At Masham, we turned roughly south-east. As this route was going to take us through the military zone of RAF Dishforth, Leeds Approach told us to switch to their frequency because of slow moving aircraft operating there, most probably gliders. After dialling in the correct frequency for Dishforth, Steve tried to make contact but there was no answer. He tried again with the same result.

"You'll have to do a dogleg around their zone," informed John. "We can't go through it with a load of gliders about."

Steve turned right by 30° with Dishforth eventually appearing on our left in the distance. After holding this heading for four minutes he then turned left by 60°, flying for a further four minutes. After that, we were back on track, having avoided some unwanted airspace. Doglegs made sense! They were actually quite straightforward. 30° one way. 60° the other. Four minutes each.

We were soon approaching Full Sutton and because the crosswind was particularly fearsome, John decided to land the aircraft himself. After taxiing back, the three of us vacated the aircraft, with John telling Steve he'd done very well. After putting the aircraft away we began heading for our respective cars.

But destruction and mayhem was just on the horizon. Across the other side of the industrial estate, barely within eyeshot, a car was doing handbrake turns and bashing into barriers. Joyriders we reckoned. As we watched, the car came to a sudden screeching halt and four young men climbed out. Two of them started bashing the windscreen with some bricks while the other two tried to set the inside of the car alight. Twenty seconds later all of them jumped into another car and sped off.

Without pausing to don his leotard or cape, John scrambled into his car and disappeared in hot pursuit. "I'll ring you later," he shouted from the window as he passed us by. The dust hadn't settled by the time I'd got in my car.

TOTAL (HOURS) = 52.0

Day 77. Monday 14 April

The first day of my two-week Easter break brought hazy conditions over at Full Sutton. My lesson was cancelled. John did tell me though that he'd followed the louts to a petrol station and then called the police. They arrived and apprehended the joyriders.

TOTAL (HOURS) = 52.0

Day 78. Tuesday 15 April

Lesson 47: *Dual Navigation (Short)*

The continuing high-pressure system had created a *temperature inversion*. Even though the forecasters were saying there was a mini-heat wave over the UK — with Mediterranean type temperatures — the haze caused by the inversion meant visibility was rather poor.

At the risk of sounding like a textbook, a temperature inversion is when the air temperature at altitude exceeds the air temperature at the surface. On a clear night, the air in contact with the cool ground will cool down. And because this cold air is denser than the warmer air above, it will not rise up — effectively becoming trapped. With a prolonged high-pressure system in place, the temperature inversion can last for days, resulting in smoke particles, dust and all sorts of other bits of pollution becoming embroiled into the trapped, cooler air. And for each extra day the inversion lasts, the soup gets thicker. Okay, you may leave the classroom now.

Even so, John Reynolds said I should head over to the airfield because we might get the chance to do some revision work in preparation for my skills test. I gathered my things.

When I arrived, mid-morning, John told me the visibility was between 6 and 7 km, which although sounding a lot, wasn't. It would be difficult to spot checkpoints in the air. Instead we waited for the weather to improve, which the forecast said it would.

Half an hour later, the haze cleared to about 10 km. We went off to open the hangar. After pulling G-DO from its parking spot, John told me to do a walkaround.

"When you've finished it," he said, "taxi to the clubhouse and park up. I'll see you there."

After doing my checks, I jumped in, cranked the engine, and then started heading towards where John would be waiting. Taxiing along, I noticed three spectators sitting on the grass verge in front of the clubhouse. They were all watching me. As I got nearer, I saw it was a woman and two young children. They all waved.

Waving back, I turned the aircraft into its parking spot with my audience looking on appreciatively. As I climbed out I heard the woman say, "Look, Josh, there's a pilot. That's what you want to be when you grow up, isn't it?"

I had difficulty getting my head through the clubhouse door.

Half an hour later, John and I took off; heading towards Kirkbymoorside, a small town nestled at the foot of the North York Moors. Climbing to 2,000 ft, I made a comment to John about our slow rate of climb. He turned to look at me. "You know why that is, don't you?"

I thought for a while. Was it something to do with the denser air? Or maybe extra fuel? I wasn't sure. I shook my head.

"It's cos you've got a fat bastard sitting next to you," he said, guffawing.

Halfway along our journey, I spotted the first of my checkpoints, the historic estate of Castle Howard. Overhead, I did a FREDA check, actually beginning to enjoy myself.

As we passed over more countryside, I began studying my chart, hoping to see what would be coming up next. Suddenly, without any warning, John reached over and flung it in the back.

"You're becoming too preoccupied with it again," he told me. "You're trying to match every little feature you can see. You should be paying more attention to flying the bloody plane. We've been through this before. And look at your altitude!"

I did. It read 200 ft below what it should have been. Apologising, I added a touch of power to regain the lost height.

"Also," he added. "I've noticed something when you speak on the radio. You're too polite."

"Polite?"

"Yeah." John gave me an example of what he meant.

When I'd taken off from Full Sutton earlier, the conversation had gone something like this:

"Full Sutton Radio," I'd said. "G-DO is changing to Linton on frequency 129.15. Thanks for your help and goodbye!"

John said this sort of language simply wasn't needed. "It's also unprofessional. It could clog up the airwaves with unnecessary chatter." He also mentioned how I'd made contact with RAF Linton:

"Linton Zone," I'd said. "Hello this is G-BSDO requesting Basic Service *please!*"

John shook his head and smiled. "So stop saying shit like that please!"

I nodded and pressed the button. "Right Linton," I snarled down the radio. "Listen to me, you set of bastards. Give me Basic Service, you bunch of ugly gits! G-DO."

Because I had no map, I tried to recall what should be ahead. If a couple of small airfields on my left-hand side appeared, then I knew I'd be nearing Kirkbymoorside. Peering through the window into the soupy conditions I soon had them in sight. And then, as if by magic, a settlement appeared in front. It was Kirkbymoorside. Empowered by this success, I turned west towards the disused airfield of East Moor.

After 10 minutes of flying the new heading, I managed to make out the old RAF Bomber airfield on our left-hand side, so I turned onto the final leg of the epic sortie, back to Full Sutton. All without a map!

Soon after, we landed, with me doing my first *bouncer* in a long time. John laughed, telling me I was lucky because at the point where I'd done my bounce the large hangar had blocked the view from the clubhouse.

When I asked John how far we'd bounced off the ground, he informed me it had only been about a foot or so.

"Really? Is that all?" If I'd been required to give evidence in a court of law, I would have testified it had been at least 50 ft.

"That's what all students think."

Waiting inside the clubhouse was Amer Manzoor. I sat down with him while John went to find Richard Watson.

Amer told me about his lesson the previous week.

"I was up doing circuits with John but felt things were getting a bit too much. I couldn't concentrate. I felt uncomfortable." Amer paused. "And when we landed and John asked if I wanted to do some solo circuits, I said no."

"What did he say?"

"He said it was my call. And if I had any doubts, then I wasn't to fly. So I went home."

I asked him what had caused his stress.

Amer shrugged. "Don't really know. Maybe my job. Endless patients. Endless targets. Endless hassle. Who knows? I feel okay today though."

Just then, John Reynolds returned with Richard Watson close behind. John told me he'd be flying with Amer for a while, but would come back for me later on. After waving them goodbye, I turned to Richard, who was smiling as usual. I asked him about his flying career so far.

He told me that about four years ago, in his mid-thirties, he'd decided to do a PPL. "When I passed, I loved it, so about 18 months ago I decided, with my wife's approval, to give up my job and use our life savings to train for my Frozen ATPL (Frozen Airline Transport Pilot's Licence). When I passed all that, I became a flying instructor. Here I am."

Now, with about 900 flying hours in his logbook, Richard was about 100 hours too short to apply to the airlines. "Every letter I've sent out has come back telling me to get more hours."

When I asked him if he'd ever regretted his decision to become a commercial pilot, he said no. "It's been financially difficult," he admitted. "But I hated working behind a desk. This is tons better. I'm happy, for one thing."

Half an hour later John Reynolds returned to the clubhouse. "Amer's doing some solo circuits," he told me. "So let's talk about any problems you've got. Tell me anything that's bothering you, Jason."

I told John that it was basic things that were getting on top of me, things such as the correct use of the transponder. For instance, I knew that when an Air Traffic Controller told me to *squawk* a four-digit number I had to dial it in using some little knobs on the transponder bit of the radio, but what I was less sure about were the various modes that could be used, and in particular when to use them.

John nodded and told me that once the radios were on, then the *squawk* number should be set to 7000. When taxiing, the mode should be set to SBY (standby). When lining up for take-off, the ALT mode should be set. Then in the air, when ATC gave a new *squawk* code, I should change the mode back to SBY until I'd put the correct numbers in. Only then, John explained, should the ALT mode be put back on.

"Why?"

Richard Watson answered the query. "To make sure you don't dial in one of the emergency squawks by mistake when you're in ALT mode. If you do, ATC might get a warning signal on their radar screen."

The three emergency squawk codes were 7500 (hijack), 7600 (loss of communications) and 7700 (other major problems such as engine failure). In certain books, you'll find a handy way of remembering these: 'Seven-Five, I've been taken alive!' 'Seven-Six, I'm all in a fix.' 'Seven-Seven, I'm going to heaven!'

John added, "But if the mode's set to SBY then this can't happen. In SBY, the transponder isn't actually transmitting anything."

I nodded, thanking them both. The short lecture had clarified things a little bit more. More of the pieces were beginning to fit together.

John asked if anything else was bothering me. After thinking for a while, I came up with flapless landings.

"Why? What's wrong with them?"

"I've never done one."

John's expression turned to horror. "*What?*"

"Well I might have done a couple before I went solo. But that's—"

"Shut up and get in that circuit! You're doing some flapless landings right now!"

Lesson 48: *Flapless Landings/Solo Circuits*

Richard, smirking in the background, told me I could go up with him if I wanted. I looked at John, who nodded. Fifteen minutes later we were in the spare Cessna, taxiing to the runway.

After taking off, we spotted Amer down on the ground, taxiing in after completing his solo circuits. We had the sky to ourselves. Downwind, I asked Richard to give me the flapless landing briefing. In a deadpan voice, he said, "For a flapless landing, do not lower the flaps. Briefing over."

I laughed. He'd been like that throughout the flight.

On the base leg of the circuit, Richard finally gave me more information. He told me to treat the approach as a normal one at first. I nodded, pulling out the carb heat knob and reducing the power. I then trimmed for a 70-knot approach.

"Good," said Richard. "Except because we're not lowering the flaps, we need a bit more speed. Trim for 75 knots."

I did as instructed, turning final.

"You'll notice we're approaching at a much lower angle than usual. It's normal. Don't worry."

Down we went, and even with the altered perspective, I made a fine flapless landing. Richard said well done as we took off for another go. After two more goes, Richard jumped out, telling me to do three of my own.

"But just do normal landings, Jason. I don't want you doing any flapless ones by yourself."

I nodded, latching the door shut after him.

Up I went solo for the first time in four months. It was quite nerve-wracking, especially when I noticed some potato fields near the runway. After one circuit without incident, however, I calmed down significantly. In fact I calmed down so much I actually began to enjoy myself.

This was the reason *why* I'd been learning to fly. This was *why* I'd put myself through so much mental anguish over the past few months. Here I was, up in the sky, flying an aircraft by myself. It was sheer exhilaration. How many people on the ground could say they could fly an aeroplane? And because I wasn't worrying about navigating; or receiving confusing messages from ATC, it was all so leisurely.

After my second circuit, I decided to finish off with a flapless one, even though Richard Watson had told me not to.

On base I did everything correctly and eventually lined up with runway 04. With the airspeed nailed at 75 knots, I crabbed the aircraft to cater for the crosswind approach and flew lower. I reduced the power as I neared the threshold and ever so slightly raised the nose. A few seconds later I made another perfect landing and came to a stop. I'd proved to myself I could carry out a landing if ever the flaps failed on me. Another rung up the ladder of success.

After entering the clubhouse, I told John and Richard that everything had gone well, and that by flying three solo circuits, my confidence had improved no end. They were pleased for me, and I headed back home after a productive day of flying.

TOTAL (HOURS) = 54.1

Day 79. Wednesday 16 April

A high-pressure system was in place over much of England. With visibility down to 3-4 km, John told me it would be a waste of time and money going over to Full Sutton for the sake of it.

Instead, he told me I should re-read the chapters on steep turns, stalls and forced landings, and to start mentally preparing myself for the long qualifying cross-country.

"When might I be doing that?" I inquired.

"If the weather's okay, next week."

"*What?!*"

TOTAL (HOURS) = 54.1

Day 80. Thursday 17 April

A gloriously sunny day. Totally useless to me though. Haze, haze, haze.

TOTAL (HOURS) = 54.1

Day 81. Friday 18 April

Although the hazy conditions had persisted, my lesson wasn't actually cancelled because of the weather. It was cancelled because Good Friday meant everyone was enjoying a day off.

On a lighter note, though, I received a new email from James Jarvis. He told me he was enjoying his new job, getting used to the routes he was flying as a first officer for BMI. He added that Leeds Bradford Airport would be his base again soon and he would keep a look out for me.

With his email came a photograph. It showed him and Craig Jennings (the pilot who'd told me about James's whippings) sitting in a cockpit. They looked cool.

TOTAL (HOURS) = 54.1

Day 82. Monday 21 April

The high-pressure system had finally moved on, replaced by rain, low cloud and cold temperatures. Another cancelled lesson. So let's digress…

In the UK, according to official statistics, there are currently about 30,000 people who hold a licence enabling them to fly a fixed-wing aircraft. Every year 2,500 more people qualify as pilots but the overall 30,000 doesn't change that much. Why? One reason is that older pilots may fail their medical. Other people may simply give up. So this figure of 30,000 remains relatively constant.

Of these, about a third will also hold an ATPL (Airline Transport Pilot's Licence), and this is out of a total UK population of 62 million.

The amount of female pilots is shockingly tiny. According to figures published by the CAA, only 6% of PPL pilots are actually women, and for airline pilots, this figure drops even further — with only 2%. Aviation, it would appear, is a male-dominated pastime. But we all knew that anyway.

So now, just for a bit of fun, let's imagine we're inside a very large auditorium. An auditorium so large, it can hold 30,000 people. The individuals inside have come from all occupations.

How many people do you suppose would be pilots then? A hundred? Fifty? The answer is only fifteen. *Fifteen* people among the mass of 30,000. And only five would hold an ATPL.

And how many of the thousands of women assembled would be pilots do you suppose? The answer is only one. *One* woman in the whole place.

Compare this to teachers. In the UK, there are about 430,000 qualified teachers (and I'm one of them) so in our imaginary auditorium, there would be 210 teachers milling about. And what about doctors? There would be 50 of them. And get this, 750 people in our mixed group will be unemployed. And the other 28,974 people — they do everything else!

Overall, I think I've proved pilots are quite a rare breed. And if you're a woman reading this, then congratulations, you're probably the only one who ever will.

TOTAL (HOURS) = 54.1

Day 83. Tuesday 22 April

Lesson 49: *Diversions*

Relatively good weather, with visibility of around 15 km, meant more flying at Full Sutton. John Reynolds told me I'd be doing a short solo navigation exercise after completing a checkride first. The checkride would involve a diversion.

We took off, with me not knowing where we were going. Overhead the airfield, John told me to fly to Pickering.

Nodding, I drew a rough line on my chart then estimated the heading we'd need to get there. I turned onto this new heading and then worked out my estimated time of arrival. John said nothing.

At the halfway stage we were over the town of Malton. From this, I knew we were going in the correct direction and eventually ended up over Pickering within one minute of my ETA. I'd successfully completed a diversion in the air and had managed to fly the aircraft accurately at the same time. So far so good.

But John wanted more. "Now take me to Driffield."

"Where's that?"

John pointed to my chart, and so I repeated what I'd done earlier: 1) I drew a freehand line on my chart with my chinagraph pencil. 2) I estimated the heading. 3) I worked out how far it was in nautical miles. 4) I converted the mileage into an estimated flight time. 5) I corrected the heading — taking into account the forecast winds.

At the halfway point I was about 7° left of track. Remembering Steve Gilmour's double-track error method, I simply turned 14° to the right. Soon we were overhead Driffield, easily recognisable by a disused RAF airfield nearby.

"Take us back to Full Sutton," said John, nodding his head.

Juggling all my seven balls successfully I made it back without mishap. John was impressed and so was I.

Lesson 50: *Solo Navigation (Short)*

"It's time to go off by yourself," stated John. "Do the trip we flew the other day. Go to Kirkbymoorside, East Moor and back here. Do your planning and off you go."

The flight went without a single hitch, except for a gust of wind that caught my wing on short final. But I managed to get the aircraft down in one piece without any serious problems.

I vacated the aircraft after yet another victorious sortie into the untamed lands of North Yorkshire and entered the clubhouse.

"How did it go?" asked John.

"Really well," I admitted. "I can't believe how well I'm doing with navigation now. I honestly thought I'd never be able to do it."

"I knew it would come together," said John. "And it's a good job it has because tomorrow I'm going to send you on your qualifying cross-country. So get planning it tonight. Full Sutton – Gamston – Nottingham and then back to Full Sutton."

I drove home with my thoughts spiralling. A hundred and fifty miles all by myself? Was I capable? I just hoped the weather would be up to it.

TOTAL (HOURS) = 55.9

Day 84. Wednesday 23 April

Another high-pressure weather system made an unwelcome appearance during the night. I awoke to hazy sunshine, which lasted throughout the day. Bugger.

TOTAL (HOURS) = 55.9

Day 85. Thursday 24 April

A low-pressure system brought rain, mist and an abundance of annoyance.

Instead I moped around the house, occasionally listening to the multi-band radio. After half an hour, I heard a pilot addressing Leeds Approach.

PILOT: Leeds Approach, this is Regional Air 345. We've a problem up here.

The male pilot, the captain of a turboprop airliner that had just taken off from Leeds Bradford Airport, sounded very calm.

ATC: Copy that Regional Air 345. What's the nature of your problem?

PILOT: Erm... we're just trying to establish that... but in the meantime we'd like to return to the airport for landing.

In the background of the aircraft I could hear an audible alarm going off: *whoo-whoo-whoo*. I felt my pulse quicken as the drama continued.

ATC: Regional Air 345, are you declaring an emergency?

PILOT: (Sounding impressively calm) **Negative. We just need vectors to get back around.**

ATC: Understood. Turn left heading 230°.

The pilot of the turboprop read back the instructions and ATC gave him vectors onto the downwind leg of the circuit. As he continued his descent, the controller gave him new instructions, which he read back in a calm and collected manner, even with the racket going on in his cockpit.

ATC: Regional Air 345, turn left, heading 290. Intercept localiser from the left.

There was no response from the turboprop so the Leeds Approach controller tried again. There was still only static.

ATC: Regional Air 345, did you copy the last instruction?

PILOT: ... Leeds? Did you just speak to us? It's just that there's a bit of a din in here. You'll have to speak up. Regional Air 345.

A *din*? A bloody din? How cool was that captain? He sounded like James Bond. Not a hint of panic or worry at all. And a few minutes later the aircraft landed safely. Talk about being calm under pressure. I never found out what the problem was.

TOTAL (HOURS) = 55.9

Day 86. Friday 25 April

I've decided to branch out into poetry. See what you think.

Rain

Fog

Wind

Bugger
Lesson
Cancelled
Again

TOTAL (HOURS) = 55.9

Day 87. Saturday 3 May

My lesson was cancelled due to high winds, gusting up to 40 knots. Through the post, however, I received the following letter from the flying school:

Dear JasonI am writing to update you on the status of PPL training. I am sorry to say that with immediate effect we can no longer accept any bookings for PPL training mid-week at Leeds Bradford International Airport. This is due to the impossible operational and financial situation that the airport authority have placed us in, making it no longer possible for us to offer mid-week PPL training.If you wish to undertake some intensive mid-week training to finish your PPL we are able to offer training from Full Sutton seven days a week. However, this training is only available until Sunday 8 June. If your training is not completed by that date we will be able to transfer your training to Full Sutton Flying Centre if you so wish.Again I am sorry that we have been forced into this position. If you have any questions at all please do not hesitate to get in contact with either Dylan or myself.Best RegardsTony Denson*Head of Training*

Well that certainly put the cat among the pigeons. I didn't like the sound of a deadline in which to complete my PPL, and neither did I relish the prospect of changing instructors yet again. I rang John Reynolds who told me not to worry because I'd easily pass before the 8 June deadline. He reminded me that I had a whole week of lessons booked in at Full Sutton just prior to the deadline, and even if I couldn't finish that week, he'd sort something out for me.

TOTAL (HOURS) = 55.9

14

The Weather Gets the Upper Hand
— Again!

'So you want a banjo then?'

–Unnamed Cafe Server (Durham Airport)

Day 88. Sunday 4 May

The weather was almost perfect, sunny visibility in excess of 30 km. Furthermore, the wind was blowing from the south, which bearing in mind my cross-country flight-plan (virtually a north-south route) meant I wouldn't have been pushed off course much. Regardless of that, my lesson was still cancelled. John was ill, deeming himself unfit to fly.

TOTAL (HOURS) = 55.9

Day 89. Saturday 10 May

John regrettably informed me that the Full Sutton Flying Club were having a *fly-in* to the Isle of Man. A fly-in was where a group of like-minded pilots fly en masse to a different airfield for a sort of aviators' knees-up. "No lessons I'm afraid," he told me.

TOTAL (HOURS) = 55.9

Day 90. Sunday 11 May

To be able to undertake my solo cross-country qualifying flight, all three airports needed great weather. Full Sutton was fine. No problem there. Gamston was even better. But that left the spanner in the works called Nottingham. I rang John to seek his opinion.

"Sorry, Jason. I'm not letting you go. It's not worth the risk."

Putting the phone down, I cursed the weather for the millionth time. I regarded the TAF (Terminal Aerodrome Forecast) from East Midlands Airport, the nearest major airport to Nottingham again. Both places would have very similar weather. It read:

EGNX 22010KT 9999 SCT030 PROB40 TEMPO 1116 7000 SHRA SCT002CB

Winds were 220° at 10 knots (no problem). Visibility was in excess of 10 km (it was more like 25 km, so again, no problem there). Scattered cloud was at 3,000 ft, which was no problem as I'd planned to fly at 2,500 ft. But then the crunch. There was a 40% probability of temporary periods (between 11 am and 4 pm) of visibility down to 7,000 m with rain showers. And to top it all, there was a chance of scattered thunderstorms at only 200 ft.

Another wasted day.

TOTAL (HOURS) = 55.9

Day 91. Saturday 17 May

Inclement weather equalled cancelled lesson.

Later that morning, Amer rang me. We soon got chatting about the radiotelephony practical test. Amer told me he'd passed it the day before. He wanted to know how I'd done.

"I haven't done it yet," I admitted. "I thought I'd put it off until the end of my training."

"I thought you were at the end now?"

I reflected on Amer's question for a moment. He was right. I was nearly done and dusted. I'd better get my finger out. I told him I'd ring John Reynolds straight away.

John told me to book it as soon as I could and that I'd pass no problem. After giving me a phone number, I rang Ian White, an approved radiotelephony examiner. Ian told me I could do my test the next day if I wished. After glancing at the forecast, I agreed. The next day was not looking good at all.

"Do people fail?" I asked.

Ian laughed. "Course they do. But it's rare and usually because they haven't read the books properly."

Ian told me to carefully read the CAA publication *CAP 413: Radiotelephony Manual* because it would contain everything I'd need for the test. He also told me that for an extra £20 on top of the basic fee of £50 I could have an hour's tuition. He said it would clarify things in my head. I told him it sounded like a good idea.

TOTAL (HOURS) = 55.9

Day 92. Sunday 18 May

Radiotelephony Practical Test

The weather was windy with intermittent rain showers. There was even the odd rumble of thunder. I did some quick revision for my radiotelephony test then headed over to a hotel in Leeds city centre.

Upon arrival, I ran from my car as quickly as possible, taking refuge from the developing storm under a porch near a large wooden door. When I rang the bell, a stocky man in his forties greeted me just as a burst of thunder roared overhead.

"So you're not flying then?" he quipped, before guffawing with laughter. It was Ian White.

As he led me inside, Ian told me that as well as being a radiotelephony examiner, he was also a flying instructor and skills test examiner.

"And," he added. "I own this hotel." I can give you a good rate if you ever want to stay here. I followed him into an area near the kitchen set aside for doing radio tests.

Because I'd paid for an hour's tuition before the test, Ian gave me some top tips on what to expect.

"Always use standard phraseology when giving your calls and replies. Don't use words like *currently* as in '*currently* 5 miles west of Harrogate'. Just say, '5 miles west of Harrogate.'"

We talked about some more examples at length until I felt I understood what was going to be required. Ian then described some key differences when speaking to ATC and radio operators. He gave me scenarios for both, and examples of what to say to each. Ian explained that I could make a few mistakes, and that he was looking for key terminology in my messages.

Ian then described the format of the test. I would get an imaginary chart showing my route. It would show all the usual features such as airports, danger areas and towns, etc. I'd also get a sheet filled with all the frequencies I'd need, as well as a pre-prepared flight plan.

Ian stopped speaking and got up. He opened a large cabinet and said, "How about I give you your actual route, Jason?"

I nodded, watching as Ian retrieved some items from a cabinet drawer. He passed me them. They contained every piece of information I'd need for my imaginary flight.

I found that I'd be taking off from a major airport located inside Class A airspace. To fly in it, I'd have to request a Special VFR clearance. After that, I'd be flying towards an imaginary town, and somewhere on that leg, I'd have to request a position fix to determine where I was. Overhead the town, I'd be turning north, and would have to make a Pan-Pan (distress) radio call because of engine trouble. Then I'd have to penetrate a MATZ before finally landing at another airport. What a flight!

And then I spotted the special information box. It got worse. In bold type, it told me I'd have to make either a Mayday call, or else relay a Mayday message on behalf of another aircraft. And this could happen at any point.

Ian told me the test had a time limit of one and a half hours. "But most people finish in about 45 minutes. You also get 15 minutes before the test to study everything. You can do that while I go and do a few jobs. The life of a hotelier, eh!"

With Ian gone, I looked at the test materials again. I quickly noticed that the first airport had three different frequencies: *ground, tower and approach.* What was I supposed to say to ground? Leeds Bradford Airport had no such frequency. I made a mental note to ask Ian about that later. The rest of the trip seemed straightforward.

Ten minutes later, Ian returned. I asked him about the ATC ground frequency.

"A ground controller is used at busy airports to relieve the tower controller from dealing with taxiing aircraft. Treat him as you'd treat the tower controller at Leeds. When you get to the runway holding point, you'll be passed over to the Tower frequency anyway."

I thanked Ian. It made sense.

Next, Ian showed me the test area itself. It was a small box room consisting of a single chair and table with a console placed on it. Attached to the console was a headset for me to use.

Entering the room, Ian explained that when I wanted to enter a frequency I was to press a number keypad on the console, which would inform him that I'd changed frequency. There was also a button to press when I'd finished speaking.

"What's *that* button for," I asked. It was on the console, looking ominous and red.

Ian said, "When it flashes, assume you've got an emergency. Make your Mayday call."

I sat down, arranging my things within easy reach. Ian told me he'd be going into an adjoining room to pretend he was the Air Traffic Control Officer(s).

"Good luck," he said as he departed leaving me alone with the red button. Five minutes later, the test began.

It was harrowing from the outset. As I 'took off', a very familiar feeling of angst began building up inside. The only positive aspect I could see was that I wouldn't actually have to fly a real aeroplane at the same time.

Somehow keeping abreast of all the many developments thrown at me, I managed to spot the flashing red light. I had no idea how long it had been blinking though. I made my Mayday call, and flew on, wondering what Ian was going to do next. Everything was coming at me thick and fast. My pencil was a fury of activity.

Just before the imaginary town, I asked for a position fix, and got one. Then the controller spoke again.

"Golf-Hotel Victor, do you wish to cancel your Mayday call?"

Shit! I'd totally forgotten about that. I apologised, and annulled it. The flight continued. I wondered if I'd failed the test.

Trying my best to forget about the Mayday fiasco, I did my Pan-Pan call, which went without mishap. A few minutes later, I successfully penetrated a MATZ en route to my destination airport. While doing an imaginary circuit, I told Ian I was on final for runway one three.

"Golf-Hotel Victor," said Ian, masquerading as a radio operator at the airport. "Go around. I repeat: go around. Runway blocked. Advise diversion."

I looked at the chart and saw a nearby airfield. I told the controller I'd be diverting there. After changing frequency, I made contact with the new airfield and landed. Once I'd vacated the runway, Ian told me the test was over.

Over the intercom, Ian told me to go into the adjoining room to get my debriefing. When I got there, he had a smile on his face. "Well done, Jason. You've passed."

"Really?"

Ian nodded. Even though I'd made countless blunders along the way, I'd somehow still passed.

"And you hold the new record," said Ian, grinning, "for completing the test in the quickest ever time. Thirty minutes!"

Ian told me I'd spoken far too quickly. To prove this, he pressed play on a small recorder on his desk. It was a recording of our entire radio-telephony conversation. As we listened, my voice could be heard going hell bent for leather. To me, I actually sounded like a *real* pilot! I told Ian this.

"Yeah," agreed Ian. "But it was hard to hear what you were saying sometimes. Imagine what it would be like for a real controller with a crackly old headset and static to cope with. They might ask you to repeat the whole lot. Which, obviously, wastes time for everyone."

It was a fair point.

"And," continued Ian, "If you speak quickly ATC might assume you're an experienced pilot. They might give you longer or more complex instructions."

I told him I'd speak slower.

As Ian filled out the forms to send off to the CAA, I received a sting in the tail. He asked what score I'd got in the radiotelephony written test.

"What written test?"

Ian burst out laughing, putting his pen down. "You mean you've not done it?"

I shook my head.

Telling me I was the first student he'd known who'd done the radiotelephony practical before the written test, he laughed again. "You've done it the arse over tit way round. Mind you, if you can pass this, then the written test will be a breeze."

I told Ian I'd get onto Dylan to sort it out.

On the way back home, I was still pleased. Passing the radiotelephony practical test meant that I'd climbed another rung on the ladder towards my ultimate goal. I was on the home stretch now.

TOTAL (HOURS) = 55.9

Day 93. Saturday 24 May

The weather was overcast, with rain and even the chance of thunder. John Reynolds confirmed there wouldn't be any flying that day. My tenth cancellation in a row. He did say something else though.

"I've changed your cross-country route," he told me. "We'll do it from Leeds again. I've arranged for Golf-Delta Oscar to be there on weekends for you. We can both be there much quicker than if it was at Full Sutton"

He told me my route would be Leeds – Gamston – Durham – Leeds. I wrote this down so I could mark it on my chart later.

"On your next lesson," continued John. "We'll do a quick trip to Durham so you can see what it's like there. It's a lot like Leeds actually." Durham Airport, otherwise known as Durham Tees Valley Airport, is located near Middlesbrough, and is a small international airport similar to Leeds Bradford. It is surrounded by controlled airspace (Class D) and therefore has ATC frequencies for both Approach and Tower.

After I'd replaced the receiver, I suddenly had a hundred questions to ask. Instead of bothering John again I powered up the laptop and posted a question on an Internet forum. I channelled my query into the ATC section, wanting to find out exactly what would happen when I arrived near Durham Tees Valley Airport.

Within a few hours I'd received about 10 replies to my posting, with the most informative coming from an air traffic controller based at the airport itself. He told me the arrival procedures were very straightforward, adding that after I'd landed I could visit the Tower for a look at the inner workings if I wished.

He also answered my query about what to do if I made a hash of everything. In all of the years of working at the airport, he said he'd only known one student to fail their qualifying cross-country. The student had ignored repeated instructions and had ended up too close to another aircraft.

He also mentioned something interesting. If I became lost, he said, it would be prudent to request a *QDM*. ATC would regard it as a sign of good airmanship. QDM was what I'd say to a controller if I was uncertain of my position. They'd reply giving me a magnetic heading to their own position. A typical QDM call would be: 'Durham Tower. G-BSDO requests QDM, QDM.' I would repeat the last bit to give the controller sufficient time to locate my position.

A few hours later, while sitting at my computer writing school reports, I decided to power up the multi-band scanner again and tuned it to Leeds Approach. It was broadcasting away in the background as I wrote my cutting comments to parents. Suddenly, a voice came over the radio.

"Yes, we'll take the visual approach for 32. Midland 616."

I stopped typing mid-sentence. I recognised that voice. The pilot had spoken with a New Zealand accent.

"We're visual with the field. Midland 616."

It was James Jarvis. It seemed so strange hearing him speaking as an airline pilot after spending numerous hours with him in the Cessna 152. There he was, coming in to land after a trip to Brussels.

TOTAL (HOURS) = 55.9

Day 94. Sunday 25 May

Lesson 51: *Dual Navigation*

John told me the winds were very light and even better than that, the visibility was superb. Quickly planning some headings and timings for a quick sortie to Durham Airport and back, we both headed out to the aircraft.

Because my proposed route would take us inside three different MATZs, I questioned John about who I should speak to en route.

"It's Sunday, remember," he said. "The military will probably be inactive. We'll just stay with Leeds Approach. They'll tell us if we need to change frequency."

Taking off on my first flight in over a month, I turned north-east towards the town of Harrogate. After that I turned towards my next turning point — the North Yorkshire market town of Northallerton. Things were going very quickly.

Along this section of the journey I somehow managed to drift off course. With the visibility so good though, I wasn't overly concerned about this: I could easily make out distinguishing features all around me. Besides, I had other things to worry about, like speaking on the radio. Everything was suddenly becoming too much for me again and John did not seem impressed.

"You're not flying an accurate heading. And you're feature crawling. You're looking at things outside and trying to place them on your chart. It should be the other way around. You know that, Jason. Plus I can't believe you're not trimming properly. This is basic stuff." He shook his head, staring straight ahead.

Turning back onto the correct heading, I felt deflated again. Learning to fly really was just a series of ups and downs, except with me, it was mainly downs.

Suddenly the radio cracked into life. "Golf-Delta Oscar, contact Durham Approach on frequency 118.85."

I changed the dials and made contact with them. The new controller told me to report overhead Northallerton.

Luckily Northallerton was simple to spot in such good visibility and I was soon overhead, receiving my clearance to enter Durham's airspace.

"Golf-Delta Approach," said the man in the Tower. "Fly straight in. Report when ready for right base, runway zero five."

Peering out into the distance, I could already see the airport in front of me. I read back the clearance and descended to 1,100 ft.

At right base, ATC gave permission to line up for final. With the long runway stretched out in front, something caught my eye to the right. It looked like a group of airliners parked very close together, each one old and battered. Indeed, one had no wings. John told me that they were De Havilland Tridents taken out of service years ago. They used them for emergency training purposes.

A few minutes later, after making a fine landing at a brand new airport, we parked next to a large private jet.

Inside the building, after paying a landing fee, John and I decided to find some refreshments. We soon found the airport cafe and stood at the counter perusing the menu. I immediately spotted the bacon banjos.

"What are banjos?" I said, pointing to the list.

John shook his head. "No idea. But I'm getting one."

"So am I." The concept of bacon and musical instruments intrigued me. Perhaps it was to do with the shape of the bread? We both waited for the waitress to come over.

"Hi," I said. "What's in a bacon banjo?"

She regarded me like an orderly would regard an imbecilic galoot. "You want to know what's in a banjo?"

"Yes." I tried to give her a winning smile.

Shrugging, she said, "Bacon and egg in bread. What else would it be?" She turned away, shaking her head.

After sitting down with our banjos, John began the debrief. He told me I was still far too reliant on my chart. Instead of using it to *verify* my position, I was using it to *locate* my position.

I nodded, swallowing a mouthful of bacon.

"We need to get this sorted out before I'll let you go on your qualifier. So on the way back to Leeds I want you to plan your flight carefully and then fly the correct headings. If your planning is right, waypoints should appear on time. And you should already know what these waypoints are. It's no good seeing a waypoint and then trying to work out what it is by looking at the chart. Waypoints should not be unexpected. Can you see what I mean?"

I nodded again. I knew exactly what he meant.

On the way back out to the aircraft we spotted the security hut. Inside were two security guards. They seemed friendly enough. One told us to empty our pockets and remove any metallic objects so that we could go through the metal detector. Putting my car keys and small change into a conveniently placed bowl, I went through the detector without setting off any alarms. The second guard frisked me and then I waited for John to go through the same process.

Into his bowl, John placed some keys, as well as a newly purchased chocolate bar. As the conveyor belt began to move underneath the scanner, John jokingly remarked to the security officer that he hoped his chocolate would be okay after receiving its unwarranted scan. The security man said there would be only one way to find out.

Looking quizzical, John and I watched as it had passed underneath. When it emerged out the other side, the guard picked it up, turning it around in his hand. He had a wry grin on his face.

John immediately said, "Oh I know your game, mate. The old chocolate x-ray test again. What is it you do? Just take a small bite and then hand it back? Or do you scoff it all and send me on my way?"

"Neither," said the security officer. "I lick it."

After taking off we headed back towards Northallerton. Unlike the inbound trip, the return leg went much better. I kept an accurate heading for a start. I was soon overhead Harrogate for a rejoin at Leeds. It was there that I experienced something brand new: flying in rain.

Forecasters had threatened rain all day. On the way back from Durham Tees Valley Airport we'd seen a few heavy showers in the distance, their clouds looking brooding and dark on the horizon. Entering the Leeds zone, it finally caught up with us. Dark splodges began dropping on the windscreen but I was surprised to see them dissipate quite well without the aid of wipers. However, with the visibility down to a minimum it became difficult to make out the horizon.

"Just fly as you normally would," said John, guessing I was feeling a bit uncomfortable. "You can still make out things on the ground. Everything's fine."

Five minutes later I parked at the airport. The landing had been the same as any other. Just a bit wetter.

After we'd climbed out, I heard John mutter, "Chalk and cheese."

I asked him if he was alright.

John told me the outbound trip to Durham was full of errors and poor navigating. Conversely, I'd flown the return journey extremely well. "It was like chalk and cheese."

I thought about this for a while before offering John an explanation. I told him the main reason for my poor outbound performance was because I hadn't flown in a long time. I'd been concentrating more on flying the aircraft, rather than putting my energy into navigating. On the way back, I'd been comfortable with flying again. I therefore had time to think about flying an accurate heading. John agreed with my reasoning.

Back in the cabin, Richard Cooper walked in. I'd not seen Richard since his cancelled qualifying cross-country at Full Sutton. I asked him if he'd done it yet.

"No," he said. "Weather and work have got in the way." Suddenly a smile crossed his face. "But I've done something about that. I've re-signed from my job. I'm going to become a commercial pilot. I've already sorted out the funds. I'm off to Spain to do the licences as soon as I've passed my PPL."

I was astonished. "You've jacked your job in?"

"Yeah. Best decision of my life."

While we were pondering this, a car pulled up outside. Two people got out: a teenager and an older woman. Virtually as soon as they stepped out from their vehicle the heavens opened with a torrent. They rushed inside the cabin with water dripping everywhere.

After sitting down the woman explained it was her son's 16th birthday and she'd bought him a voucher for a trial flight. The boy nodded enthusiastically, saying nothing.

Just then, the door flew open and in rushed John Reynolds. He told the two newcomers there wouldn't be any flying. "Even ignoring the rain," he explained, "there's a lot of turbulence on final approach. And it's only going to get worse."

The young lad looked dejected. He looked like I'd constantly felt at the beginning of my training. They got up to leave and John told them to ring up to rearrange another slot. The woman nodded, leading her son into the drizzle.

John sat down. He told me that he'd aborted my solo flight too. I nodded in understanding.

"Yours too, Richard," added John with a sigh. Richard Cooper shrugged. It was not unexpected news for him.

At home that evening, John Reynolds rang me. He asked if I'd checked the weather for the following day. I told him I hadn't.

"It's forecast to be good."

"But it's a bank holiday," I reminded him. "The flying school is always closed on a bank holiday."

"I know. But we have to take every opportunity we can. I'll come in if you're up for it?"

"Up for what?"

"Your qualifying cross-country! You can do it tomorrow."

I told him I'd see there first thing in the morning, "And thanks for this, John." I knew he would not be getting paid on his day off.

TOTAL (HOURS) = 57.5

15

The Final Hurdle

'We're either going to stall or we're going to vomit — and I don't know which will come first!'

–John Reynolds (Flying Instructor)

Day 95. Monday 26 May

Lesson 52: *Dual Navigation*

Bank Holiday Monday. Astonishingly, the weather was sunny and calm. Powering up the computer, I went onto the Met Office's aviation section and downloaded the forecast for various airports around the UK. They all seemed fine. I rang John Reynolds who told me that everything was, "*Go! Go! Go!*"

Before I headed to Leeds Bradford Airport, I made myself a couple of sandwiches for later in the day. I knew it might be a long one. Arriving at the cabin, John told me we'd do a quick half-hour checkride and then if the weather kept up its bountiful promise, I'd be on my qualifying cross-country!

We took off and left the zone to the west, via the town of Keighley. As we approached it, I looked for recognisable landmarks. After all, Keighley was where I worked as a teacher. After a few moments of scanning, I located my school but instead of dropping bombs on it, John and I turned north towards a large reservoir. It was our next turning point.

Because the visibility was so good (around 30 km) I could actually see the reservoir just after turning. On a long solo flight I'd be able to see checkpoints easily. The wind was also not a problem, blowing at 15 knots from a south-westerly direction. Almost perfect for a north-south trip. Overhead the reservoir, I turned south-east towards Harrogate.

En route to Harrogate, John pulled the power off. It was my first practice forced landing (PFL) in about six months. Immediately trimming for a glide at 70 knots, I rapidly thought back to all my previous training. As it came quickly back, I spotted a field on my left-hand side. After going through the process of an engine restart and Mayday call, I pointed out my field to John. He shrugged, saying nothing. It was down to me. Managing to stabilise a semi-decent approach, we dropped down past 200 ft. With the field on the nose, John applied full power. We climbed away.

"How was it?" I asked.

"Not bad at all, Jason. Not bad at all. The only thing was your tentativeness during turns."

I nodded. When turning for my field I'd purposely kept them as gentle as possible.

"Even with power off," explained John. "You can easily do 30° turns. Don't be scared of them."

Overhead Harrogate, I received permission for a circuit rejoin for runway one four. Ten minutes later we were on the ground taxiing back to the apron. John told me he was now happy to let me loose on the big one.

Before that though, we returned to the cabin for a briefing.

"You'll be fine," John told me, going over my route on a large wall map. "And you'll enjoy it."

I smiled thinly. My stomach was telling me otherwise. I felt even more nervous than before my first solo. A round trip of over 150 nm would challenge me to the hilt. I wondered if I'd cope.

"Your flying skills are no problem," said John, "Your radiotelephony is fine. Even your navigation is up to scratch. I've every confidence in you, Jason. You'll pass this no problem."

While I sat down to have a calming cup of tea, John rang Gamston Airfield, asking them about any arrival information I should be aware of. Gamston said runway two-one was in use, adding that I had to be careful of Doncaster's controlled airspace just to the north of the airport.

After thanking them, John drew a diagram on a large whiteboard. It showed the runway alignments of Gamston. Together, we went through different scenarios of joining the circuit.

Next, John rang Durham Tower. Though they couldn't give any detailed joining instructions, they did say they would keep them as straightforward as possible, adding that runway two-three would probably be in use. This meant both Gamston and Durham would involve landings more or less into wind. Some nervousness disappeared.

John handed me a sheet filled with tick boxes. John explained that they would prove he'd given me all of the relevant information before I flew off solo. After I'd ticked them, John made me sign it.

He then got up, picking up an envelope from a nearby table. "Whatever you do," he warned. "Don't lose this."

I put it in my flight bag and asked him what was in it.

"The Form." he said solemnly.

John explained *The Form* was what I'd give to the controllers at Gamston and Durham. On it, they'd grade my landing and airmanship. You'll either get a good, a satisfactory or an unsatisfactory."

I nodded. "And what happens if I get an unsatisfactory?"

"You fail the flight. You'll have to repeat it all. Even if you get a 'good' on the other one."

While I went to the toilet to vomit, John got the latest weather for me. It had actually improved. Collecting my things, John told me he'd fuelled the aircraft to maximum. With an endurance of four and a half hours, I wouldn't have to bother with any refuelling on my trip. I bid him farewell, driving to the airport with butterflies flapping gigantic wings against my innards.

Lesson 53: *Qualifying Cross-Country (QXC)*

As I checked out G-DO, I realised it was lunchtime. I'd not eaten anything all day. Locating my sandwiches in my flight bag, I forced one down while watching a Ryanair 737 departing for Dublin. I couldn't face the other, so put it away for later and climbed into the aircraft, preparing myself for the first hop on my epic adventure: Leeds to Gamston Airport, 45 miles to the south-east of Leeds.

After taking off, I headed out of the zone towards Dewsbury. I soon began to feel apprehensive. Virtually everything below me was town and city. And Dewsbury was just a small part of it.

Levelling out at 1,800 ft, I looked ahead for the large red B&Q superstore. Without it, I'd be doomed. As Leeds Tower passed me to Approach, I scanned the buildings coming up. Flying my planned heading, I checked my watch. Dewsbury should be on the nose, I felt my pulse quicken as I peered outside.

And then I spotted it. A large red building with a white roof. Dewsbury B&Q. I relaxed somewhat. I could tick off the first checkpoint.

Overhead Dewsbury, I turned left by 40° watching Wakefield appear on my left. With Gamston Airport 22 minutes away, I sat back, taking stock of the situation. Not bothering with the VOR after the last fiasco, I looked at my flight plan and read my next checkpoint. After eight minutes, I passed over it, an M1 motorway intersection. My timings seemed accurate.

A short while later, abeam Barnsley, I noted down the time and worked out my ETA for my next checkpoint, the M18 motorway. Writing it down on my kneeboard, I settled down again, humming a happy tune to myself.

A short while later, with the M1 veering away to my right, I glanced at my watch. I was only a few minutes away from the M18. Peering ahead to see if I could make it out, I wasn't overly worried when I couldn't. After all, everything had been going smoothly so far, my headings had been perfect.

Quite soon though, I started to feel differently. With my humming on hold, I tried to spot landmarks that should have been coming up. Shaking my head, I wondered what had gone wrong. I focused my brain, thinking of what to do next. The checkpoints were not appearing.

I did a FREDA check; hoping that it would help. If it showed the heading indicator and magnetic compass incorrectly aligned, that would explain a lot. Checking them against each other I found they were fine. So what else could it be? Had I already passed the M18 but not noticed it? Had I veered off course somehow? I was beginning to feel alarmed. I was all alone at 3,000 ft and I had to be careful because a band of Class D airspace was only 1,000 ft above me.

Carrying on regardless, I weighed up my options. Perhaps it was time to face the situation and request a QDM from Doncaster Approach? Or maybe I should return to Barnsley and start again? Suddenly, another thought struck me. Maybe it was something to do with the ETA? Maybe my timing estimate was wrong?

Studying my planning, I recalculated the ETA for the M18 checkpoint. And then the error hit me in the face. The ETA I'd written earlier was wrong. Actually, it wasn't wrong; it was just so unreadable that I'd misread my own writing. That explained why I couldn't see the MI8 — it was still somewhere in the distance. I exhaled loudly, mentally berating myself for such a stupid mistake

A few minutes later, with Rotherham on my right, and the River Don passing below the nose, the M18 appeared like an apparition. I passed over it at precisely the right time. My planning had been right all along!

Nearing my destination airfield, Doncaster Approach passed me over to Gamston Radio and I descended to 1,500 ft. After dialling in the correct frequency, I introduced myself via the 'pass your message' routine.

"Golf-Delta Oscar," said the man at Gamston. "Runway in use is two-one. Left-hand circuit. Winds calm."

Two minutes later I had the airport in sight. Making a left-hand downwind join, I eventually turned final. After an uneventful landing, I taxied in, parking up my much-trusted G-BSDO.

Photo © Richard Collins

After locking the aircraft, I grabbed the envelope and I entered the Tower. In the control room the gentleman who'd been manning the radio met me. Aged about 50, he was the only person there. He came to the counter. "Hello, son," he said smiling. "You've picked a good day for flying."

I nodded, telling him about my adventure so far. He seemed genuinely interested. Then I handed over my landing fee.

After he'd taken a call from another inbound aircraft, the radio operator returned to the counter. I handed him the envelope containing *The Form*. Just as he was about to open it I decided to make a pre-emptive strike. I used the age-old tactic of buttering up the controller.

"Thanks for the help, by the way," I said. "It was nice to hear such a friendly voice up there."

The man looked up, nodding. "We try our best. And it's nice to be thanked."

"You must get lots of students here? I bet you get sick of it?"

The man put the envelope down. "Oh no," he said. "Quite the opposite in fact. Most students we get are great. And it's nice to hear a new voice every now and again." He picked up the envelope and started to fill in both boxes. Twenty seconds later he handed me it back. I looked down, spotting two goods! I nearly whooped for joy.

Putting *The Form* back in its envelope, I thanked the radio operator, leaving his room in jubilant spirits. Outside at the aircraft, I decided to eat my remaining sandwich in celebration and then rang John Reynolds to update him on my progress. He was pleased everything had gone so well. After I put my phone away, I climbed into the aircraft in preparation for the 50-minute jaunt to Durham Tees Valley International Airport.

Ten minutes later, I was in the air, heading north-east towards the town of Gainsborough. After clearing the Gamston zone, I changed frequency to Doncaster Approach, who offered me a Basic Service as I flew towards the small town.

After clearing Doncaster's airspace I climbed to my cruising altitude of 3,000 ft and began to relax. My first checkpoint appeared dead on time. The next one, the River Humber, was right on the nose. Once more, the humming began.

Fifteen minutes later, approaching my third checkpoint (RAF Church Fenton) I asked Doncaster Approach whether the airfield was open.

"Affirm, Golf-Delta Oscar," the controller said. "Church Fenton MATZ is active. Change to frequency 126.5."

I acknowledged this, then changed the dial on the radio stack. But when I called up Church Fenton, there was no answer. Trying again, I was dismayed to find there was still no response. Shaking my head, I changed the dial to the Leeds Approach frequency instead. After establishing contact I asked them to clarify things.

"Church Fenton is inactive today," said the female controller. "But there is a fly-in at Sherburn with multiple contacts in the Fenton zone. Keep a good look out on your left-hand side."

Looking in the far distance to my left, I could see a plume of smoke making pretty patterns in the air, obviously an aerobatic aircraft operating out of Sherburn. The fly-in explained Doncaster's mistake. Sherburn was inside Church Fenton's zone. To them, the RAF airfield was busy and they'd assumed it was open for business. I told Leeds Approach I'd route to the right of the Sherburn.

Passing to the east of the RAF airfield, I pushed the throttle in for a climb to 3,500 ft. With three other MATZs coming up after Church Fenton, I reasoned it would be easier to cruise above them rather than go through the rigmarole of checking whether they were active or not. As a bonus, from the higher altitude, I would be able to see further as well.

My next checkpoint, RAF Linton-on-Ouse, appeared a few minutes later. I was more than halfway to my destination.

"Golf-Delta Oscar," intoned the Leeds controller. "Contact Durham Approach on one-one-eight-decimal-eight-five."

After thanking Leeds for their help, I changed frequencies, and the new controller told me to report overhead Northallerton for an approach to runway 23, the opposite end to the previous day.

With Northallerton only about 10 miles away, I checked my airport diagram for Durham, mentally working out how I'd join the circuit. Below me was countryside but in the far distance I could see the metropolis of Middlesbrough looming up. I smiled to myself as I mentally prepared myself for landing.

Overhead the North Yorkshire town of Northallerton, Durham Approach told me to report left downwind for runway 23. I said I would, marvelling at how far I'd come on in my training. Here I was, approaching a new airport, and I was calm and taking everything in my stride. Over to my right, in the distance, I could see the rising terrain of the Cleveland Hills and, beyond them, the power stations of Middlesbrough. I was loving every minute of it.

Eventually turning final, something caught my eye to the left. Glancing sideways, I saw a massive jet of water arcing into the air towards the battered Tridents. Clearly the emergency services were having a training session. I faced the front again; it was almost time to land.

A minute later, I touched down without incident and parked my aircraft next to an executive jet. Donning my high-visibility vest, I wandered to the security hut, where he frisked me, and then entered the passenger terminal. After paying the landing fee, I asked the lady where I should go to get *The Form* signed.

"You need to get one of the controllers to do it," she said. "Just give them a ring. They'll get someone to meet you. You need to ring them anyway to book yourself out." She proceeded to give me a phone number.

Finding a nearby phone for internal airport calls, I rang Durham Tower. A man answered after the second ring. "Hello," he said with a Scottish twang, "Durham Tower."

I booked my flight out, which involved giving him the aircraft registration and type, my name and where I was going, as well as the VRP I was exiting the zone from (Visual Reporting Point — which existed at Leeds, Eccup, Menwith and Dewsbury). I asked about getting my form signed and explained I was a student on a qualifying cross-country.

"No problem. When you get back to the security hut, just tell the guard to give us a ring. I'll come down and let you in."

Thanking him, I left the terminal and walked outside towards the hut. Once more, the guard checked me over, and then rang ATC for me. Two minutes later, I was standing outside the Tower.

"Hello," said the controller who opened the door. It was the same voice on the phone. "Come in."

Following on his heels, he led me up some stairs into the control room. It was gadget city. Panels, buttons and screens were everywhere. Slaving over them were two female controllers. Both were peering at their screens, talking to pilots over the airwaves. I was *actually* inside a proper control tower. *I was looking at real air traffic controllers!*

Emboldened by my success at Gamston, I used the same tactics at Durham. I told the controller I was very grateful for their help when approaching the airport. He nodded, saying it was their job.

Before handing over the envelope containing *The Form*, I told the Scottish controller I'd never been inside a proper control tower before. He smiled, asking if I wanted a tour. I nodded, handing over the envelope.

He said, "I'll just fill this in, then I'll show you around." After handing it back to me, I spotted two more goods; the best possible grades I could have hoped for.

Wandering over to one of the women, my guide stopped. "These ladies are the Tower controllers. Each one works for two hours," he explained. "And then they get a break of half an hour."

"Is that because the job's so stressful?"

"Yes, it does have its moments. But it's normally okay."

The Scotsman pointed to a large red button located on a console to the right of one of the controllers. He told me it was the emergency button. If pressed, the airport's emergency services would be unleashed.

"Was your hand hovering over it when I landed?"

The controller laughed. "No. But my foot was."

Next he took me downstairs into the radar room — the domain of the Approach Controllers. It was windowless and, like upstairs, two more women manned it. I asked him about this.

"It's just coincidental today. We have male controllers working here. It's just a strange shift pattern."

He showed me a large radar screen that showed lots of yellow contacts. These contacts represented aircraft. As the dial (or hand) swept around the screen every 10 seconds or so, these contacts would develop a tail. My guide explained the tails represented movement. Some contacts had long tails, others short. The contacts with long tails were jet airliners, and the length of the tail indicated the speed of the aircraft in question.

"Look at this one," he said, pointing at a contact with a small tail. "This is a light aircraft. That's how you'll look to us later on."

I nodded, taking it all in. Then I noticed two contacts with virtually no tail at all. I tapped my finger on the screen. "What about these?"

"Gliders. And notice the lack of information above their contacts."

I looked. He was right. All the other contacts had snippets of information about their altitude and speed. The gliders had nothing.

"It's because most gliders don't have transponders," the Scotsman said. "We can't give them a squawk code."

It made sense. Whenever ATC had warned me about gliders in the past, they'd always given me a message like: "Golf-Delta Oscar. Keep good look out on your three o' clock. Multiple slow moving contacts. Possibly gliders. Height unconfirmed."

After the impressive gadgetry of the radar room, he took me downstairs to the exit. After shaking hands with my new pal, I headed out to the aircraft for the final leg back to Leeds. He wished me luck on my final sortie.

Following a quick check of the aircraft I climbed inside, readying myself for the short 35-minute flight back home. Less than five minutes later, I was on the runway, power to the maximum, lifting the nose into the air.

The whole journey from Durham to Leeds went without mishap. And then disaster struck on runway one-four after an impressive crosswind landing. ATC instructed me to vacate the runway to the right via the *Foxtrot Two* hold. I acknowledged this, looking for the hold in question. There was a problem though. The information on the hold was on the other side of it. All I could see was bare wood and I couldn't remember which hold was which. My chart was no help either. It was in my flight bag and I couldn't reach it.

Trundling along the runway, I spotted a helicopter moving up along one of the exits. I headed for the other one, happy that I'd got away with it. As I entered the taxiway ATC spoke again. He was addressing the helicopter pilot.

"Sorry about that, Golf-Alpha Bravo. The Cessna's gone down the wrong taxiway. Carry on your present track. Line up runway one-four."

Inside my aircraft, I immediately went bright red. I pressed the button, apologising to both the helicopter pilot and controller. Preparing to beg for mercy, I wondered if I'd failed my flight because of such a silly error. I released the button.

"Don't worry, Golf-Delta Oscar," came the reply from Leeds Tower. "No problem."

As I parked, John Reynolds approached the aircraft. When I'd shut down everything down, I climbed out to meet him. He congratulated me on passing my qualifying cross-country.

"How do you know I've passed?"

John shrugged. "I just assumed you had. Why? Is there something I should know?"

I told him about the helicopter incident. He surprised me by bursting out laughing. "Forget it. You won't fail because of that. Besides, the controller said it was no problem. So now tell me your grades."

I passed him the envelope.

He opened it and retrieved the piece of paper. Then he grinned a big grin and patted me on the shoulder. "I've never seen four goods before," he said. "You've done really well. And it's a good job you passed this because I've already booked your Skills Test in."

My heart leaped. Skills Test? The end of the road for my training? I asked when.

John beamed like a cat. "This Friday."

I put my flight bag down, suddenly feeling unsteady. Four days time. *Was my licence really that close?*

"So for the next few days," said John. "I'm going to put you through your paces. By the time Friday comes around you'll be more than ready.

I went home half-euphoric, half scared to death.

TOTAL (HOURS) = 61.1

Day 96. Tuesday 27 May

The weather was dull and dreary, with mist and low clouds hanging in the air. With my lesson cancelled, I busied myself with writing more school reports.

TOTAL (HOURS) = 61.1

Day 97. Wednesday 28 May

Lesson 54: *Dual Navigation/Steep Turns/Stalls/Spin Avoidance/PFLs/Recovery from Unusual Attitudes*

The warm and hazy sky was good enough for a flying lesson. Arriving at Full Sutton, John told me I'd be doing a mock skills test with him. It would involve a navigation trip of three legs. Along one of them, I'd have to do a diversion.

"After you've worked your route out," John said. "Calculate how much fuel you'll need. Then tell me the maximum take-off and landing weights. When you've done all that, check that the centre of gravity is within limits."

Nodding, I got busy with my tasks. John went outside to pull the aircraft from the hangar.

As I sat working out my headings, the door opened. Two people entered — a middle-aged woman and a young man of perhaps 19. I did a double take. Pop icon Gareth Gates had just entered the clubhouse. Or else his doppelganger. About to ask for his autograph, he introduced himself as Nathan. "And this is my mum," he added. "I'm taking her flying today."

After they'd sat down, Nathan explained he already had a PPL, and was now biding his time before starting full-time training towards his ATPL (Airline Transport Pilot's Licence). He had already passed the 14 exams and was off to Florida soon for some hour building.

"Mind you," he said. "About a year ago, I almost joined the RAF. I got offered a scholarship to be a fighter pilot."

My eyes opened in surprise. The RAF only offered a handful of people scholarships. He must have had something special. "What happened?"

Nathan shrugged and his mother shook her head. She answered for him. "When he was 15, he was playing rugby at school and got into a bad tackle. Isn't that right, Nathan?"

"Yeah. I ended up on the ground. Absolute agony. I had to be stretchered off. A few days later though I felt fine. I forgot all about it." He paused, shaking his head. "And then, when I was 18, I went for my Class 1 medical. I passed it no problem. But the RAF medical was more stringent. They spotted something wrong with my spine. Nothing major; just enough to give them cause for concern. They withdrew my scholarship."

"Bloody hell," I said, without thinking.

"Yeah," Nathan smiled. "Tell me about it. So I'm going to be an airline pilot instead."

Ten minutes later I was in the air with John sitting beside me acting as examiner. The first port of call was the town of Goole. After 10 minutes I spotted a disused airfield underneath the left wing. Looking at my chart I noticed with growing concern that there should *not* have been any airfield on my left hand. I'd somehow drifted off course.

Keeping calm, I looked at the chart again. I soon worked out where I was. The only other airfield within distance was Breighton. From this, I knew I was about 12° to the right of track. By using the *double track error* method, I waited until half my flight time had elapsed, then turned left by 24°, closely monitoring my progress. A few minutes later, features started appearing that told me I was beginning to come back on track. By my side, John said nothing.

And then, exactly as planned, we were overhead Goole. I turned to John, a smug expression adorning my face. He nodded in acknowledgment, telling me to turn for my next waypoint, Wetherby.

Turning onto a north-westerly heading, I flew onwards, marvelling at my growing navigational awareness. John told me to contact Church Fenton for a MATZ penetration. I dialled in the frequency, passing my message along with the request. The controller gave me permission to enter his airspace.

"Now cancel it," commanded John. "We're doing a diversion to Driffield."

Feeling slightly foolish, I did as asked, telling the military controller I'd be turning to the north-east instead. He accepted the change of plan without comment.

With my diversion destination named, I had to pinpoint my current position. This proved easy. There was a huge power station below the left wing and an east-west motorway just behind me, so I *had* to be overhead Ferrybridge. Drawing a rough line on my chart from Ferrybridge to Driffield, I measured the approximate distance with my pencil. Then I laid my pencil along the line and transferred it to the compass arc sticker I'd stuck on my chart earlier. This gave me the approximate heading because, before my flight, I'd marked 10 nm points along my pencil with permanent ink. With this simple tool, I could easily estimate distances in the air.

Noting down the time, I turned onto my rough heading. Telling John the ETA was 21 minutes away, I looked outside for features indicating I was going in the correct direction. With another power station coming into view, I knew I was, so I settled down. John did too. Slumping down in his seat, he informed me he was going to catch forty winks. "Wake me up when Driffield's in sight."

After 19 minutes of flying, I could see Driffield in the distance. I gave John a shove, telling him RAF jets had been dispatched toward us and I didn't know why.

Ignoring me, he told me to climb to 4,000 ft. "The navigation part of the test is over and you passed. Now it's the general handling section."

At 4,000 ft, John asked me to do the *HASELL* checks. HASELL = Height (sufficient) Airframe (is configured as desired — i.e. flaps and undercarriage), Security (hatches and harnesses are secure and loose articles are stowed), Engine checks, Location (away from airports or built-up areas), Look out! After doing so, he had a quick look around himself. "Right then, Jason," he said. "You're going to do a normal stall for me. Reduce power now, wait for my signal and then recover."

"What will the signal be?"

"You'll know when it happens."

I reduced power to idle, pulling back on the yoke. Very quickly the controls became unresponsive and the stall warner began warbling. I made a move for the throttle.

"Not yet," snapped John. "Keep the yoke pulled right back." A second later we started dropping.

"Recover!"

Pushing the nose forward, I simultaneously pressed the throttle in for full power and in no time at all I'd recovered and was flying straight and level once more.

"Not bad," said John. "Only 150 ft lost. That's good enough for the skills test. Climb back to 4,000 ft."

The next one was a stall with flaps. John explained that it simulated a stall that could occur in the circuit. "It usually happens when turning final. So for this as soon as you hear the stall warner recover. Don't wait for me to say anything."

Nodding, I deployed 20° of flap, then reduced the throttle to idle. When the airspeed had reduced to 60 knots, I waited for the stall warner to begin. A few seconds later, it did. I immediately recovered by dropping the nose, adding full power and then levelled the wings. John said I'd done well.

Next we moved onto stalls carried out in the landing configuration, i.e. with flaps fully down.

"The trick with these," said John as we climbed back up to 4,000 ft. "Is not to lose more than 50 ft of height. In real life, if you stall with full flaps, it will most likely be on final approach. You'll probably be only 50 ft from the ground. So as soon as you suspect a stall, make a recovery."

I was a bit confused as to what he wanted me to do. To remedy this, I asked John to demonstrate one for me. He nodded, taking control of the aircraft.

After doing his HASSELL check, John told me to watch. With the flaps lowered, and power reduced to idle, the symptoms of a stall soon began. Without waiting any further, John pushed the nose down, adding full power. Almost simultaneously, he retracted the flaps by 10° allowing the aircraft to begin a climb. A second later, he retracted another notch of flap, levelling out. Finally he retracted the flaps fully. He'd recovered to straight and level.

Glancing at the altimeter, I noticed he'd lost only 40 ft. I was impressed.

"Now it's your turn," John said.

Regaining the height John had lost; I did a quick HASELL check, before beginning the routine. Ten seconds later, it was all over. We were straight and level again. I'd lost 70 ft. I'd have crashed had the stall occurred at 50 ft. I shook my head in disappointment.

"Don't worry," said John. "70 ft's fine. Just don't lose any more than that on your skills test." I told him I'd try my best.

"And now," continued John. "We can do the meanest of all the stalls. This one's not for the faint-hearted. And it's not actually part of the PPL skills test. But if you're up to it, I can do one for you. It's called a full-power stall." He turned to look at me. He was grinning.

After tightening my harness, I told him to go ahead.

Pushing the throttle to maximum, John explained that a full-power stall could occur on the climb after take-off. With the revs increasing, and the blare of the engine becoming almost deafening, John pushed the nose down a fraction to build up even more power. As the airspeed indicator spun alarmingly towards the red, John finally yanked back on the yoke. My stomach felt a lurch. We were heading upwards at an angle only Space Shuttle pilots should feel familiar with. And then I experienced something brand new. Blood rushing to my feet. I felt faint.

Back pressed into my seat, clinging on in vain, we continued shooting skywards. Between gritted teeth, John said something that did not raise my floundering spirits. "Jason, we're either going to stall! Or we're going to vomit. And I don't know which will come first!"

I closed my eyes and prayed.

Mercifully, a few seconds later, the speed began to bleed away, but then, unfathomably, things got even worse. The dramatic stall that followed was more hellish than anything I'd previously encountered. Facing upwards, but heading downwards with ever-increasing velocity, my stomach reeled like never before. With blood rushing to my head now, my eyes spun in their sockets. I was in some sort of aerobatic nightmare. Knuckles white with clenching, I barely registered John pulling the throttle out and levelling the wings with rudder. With the wind still screaming past the windows, somehow he managed to push the nose down until the stall was broken. And then he turned to me, grinning even more.

"Great isn't it!" John yelled.

Before I had chance to tell him otherwise, he pushed the power in again. With the speed building once more, I grimly prepared myself for another go on the Rollercoaster of Doom.

A second later, shooting upwards, John surprised me by shoving the aircraft back down. Then he banked the wings at a death-defying angle.

"*Your aircraft!*" he screeched above the melee.

Innards floundering, I grabbed the yoke and attempted to level the wings.

"*My control!*" shouted John, immediately reducing the power to idle. After recovering to straight and level, John turned to me. "In a steep dive, with airspeed building rapidly, you *must* close the throttle straight away. If you exceed the maximum speed, it could put the airframe under excessive stress."

Wondering how I would possibly chunder out of the window without John noticing, I watched as he manoeuvred the aircraft into another unusual nose-down attitude.

"Recover!" John instructed.

Once again, I raised the nose and attempted to level the wings.

"*THE POWER IS STILL ON!*" John bellowed in my ear. "My Control."

After he'd recovered it back to normality, he shook his head. I waited for the telling off.

"When you looked out the window just then, did you see any blue?" John asked cryptically.

"No. Only green things like fields and trees."

"Exactly!" said John. "You only saw green because we were pointing at the fucking ground. If all you see is green (which incidentally was the hue of my face) then before you do anything else, pull the power off. Got that?"

"Yes, John."

"Good. Let's move onto steep turns."

After a good look out, I banked the aircraft 45° to the left and eventually turned back to our original heading. Steep turns were a godsend after what I'd just been through. It was positively refreshing to have my stomach merely churned instead of minced. After another steep turn to the right, John told me he was satisfied with my performance on them.

Without any preamble, John closed the throttle. "You've just had an engine failure."

Trimming for a 70-knot glide, I spotted a field on the nose. Pondering on the best method to get to it, I glided downwards, heading more-or-less straight in. A minute later, on final, I found myself too high so reached for the flap switch.

"Full power and climb away," commanded John. "You'd have made that field no problem. Mind you, I'm not sure which method you're using to get down. Tell me."

My method was simple. Get the bloody thing down in a field. I told John this.

He shook his head. "You need a workable method. You were lucky today. We'll practise more tomorrow. Having said that though, you've passed my skills test. Well done."

TOTAL (HOURS) = 63.2

Day 98. Thursday 29 May

Lesson 55: *Instrument Flying/PFLs/Radio Navigation (VORs)/ Circuit Work*

Amer rang and told me about a scary incident that had taken place during his qualifying cross-country flight the week previously. It had occurred on his first leg: Blackpool to Carlisle.

"I'd just taken off. The sky was hazy. At 2,000 ft I couldn't see much at all. Visibility was only 7 km."

I made suitable sounds of acknowledgment down the phone at this. I certainly wouldn't have enjoyed flying in such conditions.

Amer continued. "Anyway, as I started crossing Morecambe Bay I lost sight of land. It was bloody scary."

"What did you do?"

"I just kept on the heading I'd planned. I knew land would eventually appear in front. I just needed to see some islands."

Amer explained that visual contact with these islands was vital. Some tricky airspace was just beyond them: on the left was a large military danger area and on the right the high terrain of the Lake District.

"Luckily," said Amer. "They appeared on the nose. I breathed easily after that. Thank God. Then Blackpool Approach told me to contact Scottish Information on 119.87. That's a frequency I'll never forget."

"Why? What happened?"

Amer told me a tale to remember.

For his qualifying cross-country flight, Amer had a different aircraft to his usual one. Although it was still a Piper PA-28, it had a different radio set up.

"Before I took off," he told me. "I had a fiddle around with the radio. It seemed pretty straightforward and so off I went."

But there *was* a difference with the radio, and it was only after ATC told him to contact Scottish Information that he found this out.

"I dialled in the 119.8 part of the frequency but I couldn't get the seven bit to go in. It kept on switching between zero and five. There was nothing in between. I got myself into a right flap. I was flying over water. I couldn't see much. And I was in radio limboland.

"Finally I noticed a sticker on the radio panel. It saved my bacon. It gave instructions on how to change the last number in smaller increments. I had to pull the knob out first before turning it. I couldn't believe it was so simple."

The rest of Amer's flight ended up being uneventful. He passed his qualifying cross-country after getting to Carlisle and Liverpool without incident. He didn't tell his instructor about the radio problem.

Before heading off to Full Sutton to meet John Reynolds, I stopped off at Leeds because I wanted to get my final exam out of the way, *Radiotelephony*.

Dylan Dowd gave me the paper and I sat down with it in another room. Most of the questions were straightforward and after 15 minutes of the 30 allowed I handed it to Tony Denson, owner of the flying school. I passed no problem.

Half an hour later, I pulled up outside the clubhouse at Full Sutton. I went in and, finding no one else there, sat down and started reading over some of my flight manuals. Ten minutes later the door opened and in walked two men I'd never met. After getting a cup of tea each, we all started chatting.

Both were private pilots, part of a syndicate based at Durham Tees Valley Airport. A syndicate is a group of pilots who each own a share in a plane. Being part of syndicate means the members have much greater access to the aircraft compared to hiring from a flight school, where the aircraft is regularly tied up with lessons. These men were visiting as many grass airfields as they could in one day. Full Sutton was just one of many on their route down south. They asked me what I was doing.

"Some revision for my skills test," I said, gesturing at the books scattered around my seat. "It's booked in for tomorrow."

Both men smiled. "Are you nervous?" one asked.

"No. I'm petrified. I'll probably fail."

"You'll be fine," his friend said. "And it'll be easier than you imagine. Besides, your instructor wouldn't have put you in for it if he didn't think you'd pass. It would look bad on him."

"And remember," added the other pilot. "The examiner's not there to fail you. He's only checking that you can safely operate an aeroplane in decent weather."

I nodded at their logic. But it didn't take away my feeling of profound dread. What if I did fail? Would I want to carry on flying? And what if the examiner told me I was a danger to other aviators? It was always a possibility, wasn't it?

Both wished me luck for my skills test, heading off to Beverley Airfield.

Half an hour later John Reynolds arrived. We were soon in the air for some revision. First up was radio navigation with instrument flying.

Dialling in the frequency for the Ottringham VOR (located 10 miles south-east of Hull) John told me to intercept the 305° radial. "When you're established on it, fly along until I say otherwise."

I asked him about the foggles.

"Don't worry about them. I trust you not to look outside. Besides, the visibility is crap. You wouldn't see much anyway."

He was right. The murky conditions were not very congenial to visual flying. I looked down at the instruments and flew on them alone.

Twenty minutes later we were overhead the VOR. John told me to fly the outbound radial. "It'll take us to Spurn Point."

Looking forward to seeing a geographical feature that I'd once studied at secondary school, I established myself on the radial but suddenly John pulled off the power. He sat back, folding his arms.

While trimming for a 70-knot glide, I tried to locate a suitable field. There were too many to choose from. Dawdling in making my choice the altitude slowly bled away.

"Hurry up," said John. "Make up your bloody mind."

Plumbing for a long field on my left-hand side I was just about to start my turn when John asked me where the wind was coming from. I had no clue at all. "From the west…?" I guessed.

John snorted, "From the west? Didn't you look at the windsock when we took off?"

"Yeah, but I can't remember which way it was pointing."

"It's coming from the south. Give me the controls."

Climbing away, John told me my PFL was dismal. It would have failed in the skills test. He told me to watch his demonstration.

Sitting back, I felt another wave of shame wash over me. My skills test was the next day. I was not even going to come close to passing. What madness had possessed John to book it for me? He would look like a fool and I would become a laughing stock. I rubbed my forehead in frustration.

When John had finished his demonstration of how to do a proper PFL, he told me to have another go. Luckily, my second attempt was marginally better.

"In the test," said John. "The examiner will give you two goes at a PFL. Tonight, when you get home, read up on how to do them properly. Practise on your bloody simulator if you have to. I know you can get them right if you put your mind to it. And make sure you remember about the wind. Always land into it. Always have an arrow on your chart showing the wind direction, and in the test, always keep glancing at it so that when the PFL comes, you won't be faffing about picking fields that are *not* into wind. It makes things easier, Jason."

I nodded, miserable to the extreme.

Back in the circuit at Full Sutton John told me to do a flapless landing. It went without mishap. Next up was a powerless landing. With the throttle pulled out to idle, there was no way I could fly a normal circuit and so I did the natural thing, I turned for *base* earlier than normal.

"Good," said John. "You're using your brain for once. Now let's see if we make the runway."

Like the PFL, I trimmed for a 70-knot glide and began my turn onto final. Once lined up, I took some time to assess the approach. Would I reach the runway? Could I lower some flaps? Beside me, John was saying nothing.

With things looking okay, I elected to lower 10° of flaps. After stabilising the aircraft again, I deployed a further notch of flaps. We were high enough to reach the runway. In fact, as we approached the grass strip, I realised we were far too high. Lowering the final stage of flaps, I pushed down on the yoke to get the nose down causing the airspeed to begin to creep upwards. I began to have serious misgivings about the landing. I voiced these concerns to John.

"No," he said. "Everything's fine. Keep going."

Battling with the yoke as the runway threshold appeared, I raised the nose slightly and at last the speed began to bleed away. Flaring earlier than normal, the aircraft started to settle down and eventually touched down with a small thump. We were back down on terra firma, after quite possibly the scariest landing of my training so far. We taxied to park the aircraft.

Inside the clubhouse, John told me I was ready for the skills test. "Your landings at the end were very good. Impressive, actually. And for the record, my standards are higher than an examiner's will ever be. You'll be fine."

"What about my shite PFLs?"

He paused before answering. "Like I said earlier. Think about the wind. Choose a long field. Go through all the checks and head towards it. Read your books again tonight." He finished by telling me to get a good night's sleep. "I'll see you tomorrow, weather permitting."

I smiled thinly, heading for my car.

At home, I'd received an email from First Officer James Jarvis. He wanted to give me some final tips for the test.

Top tip is to retain your cool no matter how bad (or good) you think it's going. Never throw it away. You can still get a partial pass in the test, even if you get something wrong. Don't forget your engine failure drills. The examiner will give you a good height to start from so don't be rushed. Good luck. You'll be fine. James But would I be fine? Was I good enough to pass the skills test? God only knew. I spent the evening reading up on PFLs, stalls and steep turns. I also rehearsed filling out a weight and balance sheet. Afterwards, I set myself a quick navigation trip on the computer. It went remarkably well.

Turning in for the night, I closed my eyes, hoping for peaceful slumber.

TOTAL (HOURS) = 64.6

The Big Day Arrives!

'Where's the toilet?!'

-Jason Smart (PPL student)

Day 99. Friday 29 May

Lesson 56: *Skills Test*

To say I had a good night's sleep would be a lie. To say I was not nervous would be a bigger lie. To say I was looking forward to my skills test would be the biggest lie of them all.

Getting up at dawn I checked the weather forecast on the Internet. It was forecasting light variable wind, clear skies and high temperatures. However, hazy skies might mean poor visibility.

Tony Denson, the examiner, rang me. He told me to meet him over at Full Sutton at 11 am.

"Your route," he told me, "is Full Sutton – Sandtoft – Ripon and back to Full Sutton. Make sure you have all the planning done by 11. We'll be setting off at noon."

Replacing the receiver, my legs started to wobble. It was worse than before my first solo. I wondered if my nerves would hold out during the trip. The way my heart was thumping, I'd be lucky to last out the day. I wondered where the nearest hospital to Full Sutton was. And Sandtoft I quickly realised would be a bit of a bugger to get to. It was right on the edge of Doncaster's controlled airspace. I'd need to be careful with my planning to get that one right.

Gathering my things, I pondered upon the weather. Looking out the window the visibility did seem rather poor. I didn't relish the prospect of doing a navigation trip in bad visibility. It would be a recipe for disaster, I thought.

Arriving at Full Sutton just after 10 am, I entered the empty club-house. Tony Denson and John Reynolds were not due to arrive for another hour so I sat down to plan my flight. With the wind so light and variable, it turned out to be quite straightforward. It was soon finished and triple checked.

Then, producing a checklist from my flight bag, I spent the next 10 minutes memorising some key speeds of a Cessna 152. The speed never to exceed was 149 knots. The best rate of climb speed was 67 knots. If I ever had to clear a tall hedge, the best angle of climb speed was 55 knots. That was a handy one to know. Hedges surrounded Full Sutton. Turning the page, I looked at the different cruising speeds available but my mind wouldn't focus. I needed to go to the toilet, and not for a quick visit. I put the checklist away, looking at my watch. Ten to eleven.

Returning from the outhouse, I decided to eat one of my sandwiches. It went down like a piece of Lego. As I put the rest away for later the clubhouse door opened and in walked John Reynolds. After making himself a cup of coffee, he drew lots of diagrams on a large whiteboard. It was his last ditch attempt to get me to understand PFLs.

"You can do PFLs, Jason. And today with no wind, you can pick any you like. When Tony pulls the power, trim for best glide. Find your field. Attempt an engine restart. Do the Mayday call. Land. Simple as that."

John's head turned to the left. He was peering through the window. "Tony's here. He's on his phone. I'll go out and speak to him. Stay here and prepare yourself."

My blood pressure rocketed. My throat turned dry. I looked outside and could see John and Tony Denson chatting about something. Then the door opened. In came Richard Watson, Full Sutton's resident flying instructor. He must have arrived with Tony.

"Ah Jason," he said, smiling as usual. "I'm glad I caught you. Good luck for your test. Fly a blinder for me will you?"

I told him I'd try, and then Tony Denson entered the clubhouse. He spotted me quivering in the corner and asked how I was feeling.

"Nervous." I replied. That was an understatement. Tony smiled, asking me if I was ready for the pre-test briefing. Nodding, I followed Tony into a small room.

Question and Answer

Tony sat down behind the desk opposite me. He looked at my flight plan, telling me it was fine. He then had a cursory glance at my weight and balance calculations and deemed them okay as well.

"Now for the skills test briefing," said Tony, crossing his hands in front of him. "So listen carefully."

The briefing covered everything that would happen in the test. First would come the navigation part. I'd fly south to Sandtoft Airfield then, without landing, turn north-west for Ripon. Somewhere on this second leg, I'd fly a diversion.

"And I'll be looking for an approved method of getting to the diversion destination," added Tony.

I nodded, taking everything in. I couldn't actually believe I was sitting in a room with an examiner. There was no joy in this revelation; only dread.

"And I'll expect you to make all the radio calls during the navigation portion of the test. "But after that, I'll take over to let you concentrate on the general handling section. Following general handling, we'll return to Full Sutton for three landings. Any questions so far?"

I thought for a while. Lots of questions, but none seemed relevant. I shook my head, waiting for Tony to continue.

"Good. So now I'll ask *you* some questions to determine your knowledge. Answer them as best you can, Jason."

My left ventricle squeezed and then opened again. The heart attack was getting closer.

The first thing Tony asked me about was the various flying speeds of the C-152. Mercifully, I managed to remember most of them. Thank

God I'd looked in the book earlier. Next, he asked me to explain what regional QNH was.

I wracked my brain. I'd set regional QNH many times in the air. Every time I'd passed over to a different controller they gave me the regional QNH. But what the hell was it? Eventually I said, "Is it a forecast for the average pressure above sea level for an area?"

Tony shook his head.

"...Is it given by controllers so all aircraft flying the regional QNH will be flying at the same altitude?"

"No," replied the examiner, uncrossing his hands.

My right ventricle made a play in the game. I closed my mouth. It seemed the safest bet.

After a pregnant pause, Tony put me out of my misery. "Regional QNH is the *lowest* forecasted pressure for a defined area. With regional QNH set on the altimeter, an aircraft will be flying at a higher altitude than it really is. It's a built-in safety factor."

While I digested this piece of information, I waited fretfully for the next question. Had I failed in the question and answer session already? Or could I make some mistakes? I prayed I could. I looked at Tony hopefully.

"Why are steep turns taught in the PPL?"

The question was an easy one. I felt some colour returning to my cheeks. "They are a collision avoidance technique. If an aircraft was heading straight for me, I'd do a steep turn."

"Good. Now tell me how you'd fly a bad weather circuit."

A *bad weather circuit?* I'd never heard of such a thing. I gathered my thoughts, attempting to answer the question as best I could. "I'd fly it slower than a normal circuit."

Tony didn't say anything. He regarded me, tight-lipped.

I continued. "And I'd also fly the circuit a bit tighter than usual...?"

Tony nodded, remaining mute.

"... and I'd fly it lower than normal..."

"Exactly," said Tony. "Fly a bad weather circuit at 600 ft with two stages of flap. And you'd keep the circuit tight, like you said. Good."

He closed his book and looked outside. I followed his gaze, noticing the bright, but hazy conditions. Tony looked back at me and said, "Do you think the weather's okay for the trip?"

I shrugged. "If I was with an instructor, yes. Flying solo, no. The visibility looks too low for that."

Tony nodded. "I see. But I think the weather's fine."

I sat back and folded my arms. Was this a test? If I said yes, Tony might think I had poor judgement. But if I said no, he might cancel the test. I didn't know what to say.

"Look," said Tony, sensing my indecision. "Why don't we take off, assess the visibility and then decide on what to do. If you don't feel able to do the navigation part, that's fine. We'll do the general handling instead. We don't need great visibility for that. You can do the navigation at a later date. You'll get a partial pass. What do you think?"

It sounded like a good plan. I decided to go for it. The test was on. Tony nodded. "Go out to the aircraft and start your checks. I'll meet you there in five minutes."

Gathering my things, I got up and left the room. Back in the other room, John Reynolds was leafing through a magazine. He looked up when he saw me. "You'll be a qualified pilot in a few hours. I've no doubt about it. And don't forget to treat Tony as a non-flying passenger. Make sure you give him a safety briefing."

Smiling thinly, I stepped outside, coronary thrombosis edging ever closer.

Part One — Navigation

While I was busily checking the exterior of the aircraft, Tony Denson appeared behind me. Instead of looking over my shoulder, assessing my knowledge of the walkaround, he removed his phone from his pocket and dialled in a number. With a wave of his hand, he told me to carry on. Five minutes later I climbed inside the cockpit of G-BSDO. Tony soon followed. As he reached for his seat belt I told him about the emergency equipment carried aboard our craft.

"There's the first aid box," I said, pointing to a green box behind the seat. "And if you feel the urge to vomit, please try not to do it over the controls. Use the bag in the pouch behind your seat."

Tony nodded, thanking me for the information.

After strapping myself in and making sure Tony was secure too, I began the internal checks with my innards churning. Tony said nothing, patiently waiting.

A few minutes later, I switched on the engine and turned on the radio. "Full Sutton Radio," I said into my mouthpiece. "Golf-Bravo Sierra Delta Oscar is taxiing to the hold for runway two-two."

"Copy that, Golf-Delta Oscar," replied John Reynolds, clearly sitting in the radio room.

At the hold, I did the power checks. Everything went according to plan. Releasing the brakes, I informed Full Sutton I was going to enter the runway for a departure to the south.

Just then, a voice came over the airwaves. It wasn't John Reynolds. It was Richard Watson. "Golf-Bravo Whisky on final for two-two," he said.

Looking to my right, I could see the landing lights of an aircraft on short final. I immediately cut the power and stepped on the brakes. Coming to a quick standstill, I told Full Sutton Radio I'd remain at the hold.

But had I done the correct thing? The fact I hadn't even spotted an aircraft on final worried me. I wondered if Tony knew I hadn't spotted it. Had I failed the test before I'd even taken off? I watched as the aircraft made a nice landing, then told Full Sutton Radio I was entering the runway.

As we lined up, Tony turned to face me. "I want you to demonstrate a soft-field take-off for me please."

I nodded and lowered the flaps by 10°. After telling Full Sutton Radio I was about to take off, I pushed the throttle in as far as it would go, holding the brakes with my feet. As the engine spooled up to full power, I released the brakes, soon taking off into the hazy sunshine. When I'd climbed to 800 ft I turned back around to fly overhead the airfield. Only then did I turn onto my first heading and at the same time started the stopwatch.

Sandtoft Airfield, located 25 miles to the south, would take 17 minutes to reach. I continued my climb to 2,000 ft, trying to keep calm. The poor visibility didn't help. Looking outside, I could hardly make out anything; such was the murk in the air. I flew on, hoping that I'd spot my first checkpoint — Breighton Airfield.

After contacting RAF Church Fenton for a Traffic Service, I could just make out a large power station in the far distance on my left. It had to be Ferrybridge. But according to my flight planning, it should have been on my right. Clearly I'd drifted off course somehow.

Not overly worried about this, I waited until the halfway point, then corrected my error by using the *double-track error* method. Except I got it wrong.

Thinking I was only about 2° to the right of track, I turned to the left by 4°. Next to me, Tony didn't say anything. He was simply staring out the front windscreen. But I should have turned left by 10°. But, unfortunately I didn't know that then.

On we flew.

Looking for recognisable ground features outside was proving very difficult. Everything beyond 5 miles was just dull and hazy. I couldn't tell if I was returning onto the correct course or not. A few minutes later over the River Humber, I changed frequency to Sandtoft Radio and descended to 1,800 ft to avoid the Class D airspace that was about to start at 2,000 ft.

"I reckon I'm right of track," I said to Tony a minute later. I had just turned onto a southerly heading and couldn't see any features I'd been hoping to see. Next to me, Tony Denson kept quiet, waiting for me to come up with a strategy of my own. It didn't take long to come up a cunning plan.

"I think I'm going to make a turn to the right," I said.

Tony turned to face me. "Are you sure you mean that?"

I delayed my turn, thinking things through. Tony had offered me a lifeline; one I intended to use. Turning right was evidently a bad idea. But why? And then it came to me. If I were right of track, which I was, then by turning right *even more* I'd be going further off track! Finally I engaged my brain. I needed to do a turn to the left. It was obvious.

Mentally berating myself, I turned left, trying to spot features telling me where I was. A few minutes later, a town appeared indistinctly on my right. But it was no help. Stress rising with every minute, I wondered where I was. Thinking I'd already failed the test, I was beginning to give up hope. At least I hadn't infringed any controlled airspace yet.

Biting the bullet, I spoke over the intercom. "Tony, my ETA's up. Sandtoft should be around here somewhere. But I can't see it and I don't want to go any further and infringe Doncaster's Airspace."

Tony said nothing, staring into the distance.

Resigned to my fate, I lowered the nose and began a turn but still couldn't see the airfield anywhere. I exhaled slowly, wondering what to do. Maybe the game was up.

"Why don't you finish the orbit to establish your position?" offered Tony. "It might help."

Shrugging, I did the orbit, wondering if there was actually any point. And then I spotted it. Sandtoft was just below the wing, its thin runway almost merging in with the surrounding fields. No wonder I'd had such difficulty spotting the damned thing. Instead of feeling elation, though, all I felt was resignation. There was no doubt in my mind that I'd failed the navigation part of the skills test. I turned north-east, heading to Ripon.

As I passed over Selby, a strange thing happened. I calmed down. Knowing I'd already failed the test had caused an inner peace to take hold of my mind. With all the stress gone, I could actually concentrate on navigating now. My checkpoints were coming up as expected and I knew exactly where I was, and 15 minutes later, after successfully completing a MATZ penetration through Church Fenton, I felt strangely happy. Approaching the town of Tadcaster, Tony told me to divert to Brough, a small airfield to the south-east.

I nodded, looking outside to verify my position. With a motorway junction below the left wing, this was quite easy. I quickly worked out some rough calculations for the diversion.

"Brough is about 26 miles away," I said to Tony. "Which should take 18 minutes."

The examiner didn't say anything, his expression neutral. I began my turn onto a new heading of 102°. Tony turned to face me again. "Are you sure you want to be on that heading?"

I rubbed my face, wondering what he was referring to. And then it struck me. I'd misread my compass arc. After drawing my rough line to Brough, I'd placed my pencil along it and had then transferred it to a compass arc. And then I'd only gone and misread the bloody thing! Tony must have spotted me doing this. The correct heading was 112°. What a buffoon. I changed course.

After 10 minutes or so, Tony informed me that the diversion was over. "I'm satisfied you could find your way to Brough. So now I want you to fly to the Ottringham VOR from our present position. Track the radial please."

Nodding, I dialled in the frequency and then checked its Morse code identifier, like James Jarvis had once taught me to do. With that done, I turned the knob on the VOR instrument until the needle centred. I read off the heading, then turned east, tracking the radial directly to the VOR. Things were going well.

A few minutes later, Tony asked me to obtain a position fix. Thankfully, I knew what he meant. I'd practised position fixes with John Reynolds the previous day. Doing one involved verifying our position by using two different VOR stations. Where the radials intersected, I could pinpoint our position.

Since I already knew the Ottringham VOR radial I was on, I dialled in the frequency of the Gamston VOR. Turning the knob until the needle centred again, I read off the radial. Because Gamston was located to the south, I knew the radial would be a northerly one. It turned out to be the 359° radial. I then looked on my chart and worked out where both VOR radials intercepted and, hey presto!, I'd successfully carried out a position fix.

Tony nodded. "Good. That's the navigation part over and done with. Time for general handling. I'll take over the radio for you."

Sitting beside him, I breathed out heavily. What a performance.

Part 2 — General Handling

First came instrument flying.

Tony covered up my side of the windscreen with a large piece of cardboard and asked me to perform a 180° turn, simulating flying into cloud. I proceeded to do this manoeuvre without issue. Next, he asked me to do some turns by just using the instruments. These proved to be no problem either. Then we moved onto slow flight. Tony told me to fly at 60 knots.

Nodding, I told him I'd lower 10° of flap to get the speed down.

"No," said Tony. "I want 60 knots in a clean configuration."

I pulled back the throttle, trimming for slow flight. It took ages, but I managed it in the end.

"Good," said the examiner. "Now climb to 2,000 ft at best angle of climb."

I couldn't remember what the best angle of climb was. My mind was blank. Hoping for the best, I pushed the throttle in for maximum speed and pointed the nose upwards. Watching me carefully, Tony asked a question. "What speed is needed for best angle of climb?"

Not knowing the answer, I made a guess at 65 knots.

"Are you sure?"

"No," I admitted. "I'm a little confused. I think I'll lower some flaps." I moved my hand towards the lever.

"Leave it alone. And stop going on about flaps. You're obsessed with them. If I want you to use flaps I'll tell you. Climb at 55 knots."

Cursing myself, I trimmed the aircraft for a best angle of climb at 55 knots. What a total disaster. Tony must think me some kind of imbecile. Worse was what John Reynolds would think. He'd never had anyone fail a skills test before.

After straightening out at 2,000 ft, Tony told me to climb another 1,000 ft. "You're going to do some steep turns."

At the higher altitude, after completing a clearing turn, I did a 45° turn to the left and then to the right. Both went okay. And then it was time for some stalls. None ended in calamity.

"Okay, Jason," said the examiner, taking hold of the controls. "I'm going to manoeuvre the aircraft into an unusual attitude. When I tell you to, recover to straight and level."

I nodded, preparing myself for what was to come. Almost immediately, Tony banked the aircraft steeply, pushing down on the yoke with both hands. Two seconds later, he yelled "Recover!".

Grabbing the yoke with my left hand, I pulled the power off with my right. After levelling the wings, I gently pulled out of the descent. Once straight and level, Tony thanked me, saying I'd done well. He told me to climb to 3,000 ft.

As we slowly climbed through the air, Tony suddenly pulled off the power.

"You've just had an engine failure."

There it was, the dreaded PFL. Quickly going through the drills, I looked outside. Over to my right was a long runway, which looked ideal. By looking at my chart, I identified it as Elvington, an old RAF base, which was now an air museum. In an emergency, its runway would be perfect. I told the examiner I was going to head right for it. Tony nodded but didn't say anything.

After quickly pretending to do a Mayday call, I turned onto base a touch higher than I would have ordinarily liked, so began a steep descent to lose height. On final, I knew I'd easily make the runway, so I dropped 10° of flaps. At that point, Tony told me to climb away so we could head back to Full Sutton.

I'd done it! I had successfully carried out a PFL! I had overcome a major hurdle. John Reynolds would be proud. I felt good for the first time during the test.

Totally disorientated though, Tony gave me directions to get back home. As we approached the airfield, he told me to carry out a standard overhead join. "And you can have the radio back," added Tony, sitting back in his seat.

After switching frequency, I called up Full Sutton Radio and was surprised when Richard Watson answered. "Golf-Delta Oscar," he said. "Runway two-two is in use. And there is one other aircraft in the circuit. Keep a good look out."

That other pilot turned out to be John Reynolds flying with another student. I could see his aircraft on final approach. As I started descending to circuit height, John told me, via the radio, that there was a bit of a gusty wind on final approach. He told me to be careful. I acknowledged his warning as I descended onto the downwind section of the circuit. John landed and started taxiing in.

Tony said, "This will be the first of three landings. Make this a precision landing."

I told him I'd never heard the term 'precision landing.'"

"It's just a normal landing," he explained.

After making a good approach, I made a very good landing, which received a well done from Tony. Pleased, I added full power, taking off for another circuit.

The next landing was to be the scary one, a powerless landing. After taking the controls from me, Tony said, "When you think you can glide it in, tell me. I'll hand control back to you."

I nodded, looking at the grass strip on my right. I had to judge the distance carefully. Taking it too late could mean I'd miss the end of the runway. Too early, and I'd be too fast and high. After waiting for a few seconds, I told Tony the time was right. Without comment, he pulled the power off, handing control back to me.

On base, I knew I was far too high so to counteract this I dropped some flap and pushed down on the yoke. A few minutes later, approaching the turn for final I was still too high. Dropping all of the flaps I pushed down even further. My heart was beating ten to the dozen as I battled with the yoke and rudder; the landing was going to be a close one.

With the airspeed building up rapidly I turned final, doing a steep descent towards the runway. Then, after passing over the threshold, I began my flare.

"Go around!" Tony commanded. "Go around!"

Panicking slightly, I pushed the throttle in, retracted some flaps, and climbed away. I wondered what I'd done wrong. I asked Tony.

"You didn't do anything wrong," he answered. "It was fine. You'd have easily got it down. I just didn't want to waste any more time, that's all. So now show me a flapless landing. Then we'll call it a day."

Turning downwind, I made my radio call and then did the pre-landing checks. Suddenly, Tony grabbed the yoke. "My control."

I sat back, wondering what was going on. Pitching the nose upwards, Tony removed the power. "Recover," he commanded.

Like the PFL, I dropped the nose and trimmed for a glide. When I'd stabilised the descent, Tony finally explained himself.

"Sorry about that, Jason. I suddenly remembered we hadn't done an engine failure after take-off. So I improvised and you did fine. Continue with your flapless landing."

I laughed, despite myself. Everything was coming in thick and fast.

Because I couldn't use flaps to slow down, I had to pull the power right off. I touched down a few minutes later, taxiing off the runway with the blood returning to my face. The flight from start to finish had lasted 2.1 hours.

After we'd parked and switched off the engine, I waited for the moment of truth. Had I passed or had I failed? Or had I perhaps done well enough for a partial pass? Even though the navigation had been a disaster, I felt the general handling had gone relatively well. As I removed my headset, Tony mumbled something.

"Sorry?" I said. "What did you say?"

"Yes, it was good enough, Jason. You've passed," he repeated.

"*What?* Passed it all? Even the navigation?"

"Yes. Everything."

My brain went numb.

I couldn't comprehend that I'd actually passed my PPL skills test. I'd moved across the line separating a student pilot from a real pilot. A grin began to form on my lips just as Tony started speaking.

"Your landings impressed me the most," he said, smiling. "That was a good thing. After all, getting the aircraft back on the ground is 90% of the battle. And your radiotelephony was good. It was professional and smooth. I also liked the way you handled the sudden arrival of that aircraft at the beginning of the flight. And in case you're wondering, I hadn't spotted it either."

He paused, looking at me for a moment. "Out of interest, what do you think was your weak point?"

"Navigation," I said without pause. "I couldn't even find Sandtoft."

Tony nodded. "True. Your navigation was a tad on the sloppy side. But with the poor visibility it was harder than usual. And like you said before we took off, you wouldn't have normally flown by yourself in conditions like that. So I decided to give you the benefit of the doubt. Plus, after Sandtoft, you were fine. No problems whatsoever."

Tony unplugged his headset and closed his kneeboard. "But do you know what *really* made my mind up? Whenever I fly with a pilot on a skills test, I always ask myself a simple question. Would I let my daughter fly with this person? With you, the answer was yes. So you passed."

I shook his hand, thanking him.

Out of the corner of my eye, I spotted John Reynolds walking towards the plane. As he neared, Tony opened the door. "Bloody instructors," he said in a deadpan voice. "What have you been teaching him?"

John's face momentarily turned bleak before he realised Tony was jesting. Reaching into the cockpit, John shook my hand, offering words of congratulations, before heading back into the clubhouse. Tony and I followed hot on his heels.

Inside the clubhouse, Richard Watson started clapping. "Well done," he beamed. "I told you you'd pass."

I laughed, unable to tell him about how close it had been.

For the next few minutes, Tony Denson signed a few forms, before telling me to ring Dylan Dowd, who would send everything off to the CAA so I could get my licence sorted out.

"Be careful on your drive home," Richard told me. "I know it'll be hard, but please concentrate on your driving. I had a student once who crashed his car after passing his skills test."

"And when you're on your way back, keep an eye out for me," John said. "I'm flying Golf-Delta Oscar to Sherburn. Today was its last day with us. It's being sold."

"Really?" I said shocked. "Sold? And I was its last student?"

"Yeah," John grinned. "That's why I'm glad you passed. I didn't want you to change aircraft."

Sitting in the seat of my car 10 minutes later, I closed my eyes. I'd finally done it; I'd achieved the dream of my childhood. I was a pilot! *A real pilot*! And John had been correct; it had taken me 66 hours to do it. I started the engine, setting off home.

So was it all worth it? Was it worth the pain, misery, torment, self-doubts and feelings of failure I'd felt throughout my training? Was it worth all the money I'd spent on lessons? Was it worth the feelings of anger when yet another rainy and overcast day ruined a lesson? And would I do it all again?

Absolutely. No doubt about it at all.

TOTAL (HOURS) = 66.7

17

Pilot-in-Command

'I love Satan!'

-Jason Smart (Private Pilot)

Conversion to Piper PA-28 Warrior

For three whole weeks I didn't set foot inside an aeroplane. The first week was easy; I actually enjoyed the break. The second week was harder, but I consoled myself by purchasing a headset to call my own. But after the third week, I couldn't wait any longer. I rang Richard Watson at Full Sutton to arrange a conversion lesson in the Piper PA-28 Warrior.

On a hazy summer's day in June, I headed over to the airfield, parking near the new clubhouse. Stepping inside, a man in his mid-twenties greeted me. "Ah, you must be Jason?"

"Yes…" I said, shaking his proffered hand. I wondered who he was.

"I'm Patrick Emmett. I'll be flying with you today." He paused to look outside, obviously assessing the weather.

I asked him where Richard was and Patrick smiled, "He's outside sunbathing. Look."

I walked to the window and saw Richard Watson lying flat on the grass, taking in the rays. A lonesome sheep was nearby, keeping a discreet distance.

Patrick Emmett turned out to be a thoroughly nice chap. He told me he'd only been an instructor for a couple of weeks, working as Richard's assistant. "Hopefully," he said, "I'll build up a few hundred hours over the summer for my logbook. Then I can start looking for a job with the airlines."

He took me out to the aircraft, a four-seater Piper Warrior, the very same aircraft I'd flown in as a passenger with Steve Gilmour. Patrick demonstrated the external checks, which seemed very similar to the Cessna 152 — nothing strange or alien there. Indeed some things were easier. The Warrior had low wings for a start, which meant I didn't have to clamber furtively upwards to check the fuel. Instead, I could merely bend down and look in the tanks.

We climbed inside the cockpit. It was larger than the Cessna 152's. And with two rear seats, items could be stowed in the back within easy reach. I also noticed some differences between the positioning of certain flight controls. And there was a strange handbrake type thing between the seats. I asked Patrick what it was.

"That's the flap lever. If you pull it up like a hand brake, the flaps come up. Lower it, flaps go down. And it's mechanical not electronic like the Cessna's. Even with an electrical fault, the flaps will still operate."

Patrick also pointed out some other differences. The throttle lever looked much more like a 'proper' throttle that airliners had and the carb heat control was a simple on or off switch, as opposed to an in/out knob. The parking brake was also different. It consisted of a hefty handle-type lever, rather than a simple pullout knob. I wondered what it would be like to fly.

Ten minutes later I lined up on the runway. The resulting take-off was relatively simple. The same as a Cessna take-off. Flying the aircraft was also straightforward, except for me reaching instinctively forwards instead of downwards in an attempt to rotate the trim wheel.

Flying east, Patrick made me demonstrate some slow flight, which again turned out to be straightforward. We flew on towards the coast.

Overhead the seaside town of Scarborough, I was told to do some steep turns to the left and right and then to demonstrate some stalls for him. Everything went without mishap and so we headed back towards

Full Sutton.

Approaching the airfield, Patrick said, "So how does the Warrior compare to the Cessna 152, then?"

I thought for a few moments. "It's more stable. It seems to handle a bit more smoothly. I quite like it."

Patrick nodded. "That's what most people say."

At the airfield, Patrick wanted me to do two landings. On the first, I flared a little bit high, coming down with a bit of a thump. But it wasn't bad for a first attempt in a new type of aircraft. We went around again, and the second landing was much better. As we taxied in, Patrick informed me he was confident in my abilities to handle the Warrior. I was now free to hire it for my own purposes.

Circuits

Two weeks later, I was back at Full Sutton for some circuit practice with Patrick. I still wanted to fly with an instructor before going off by myself.

Entering the clubhouse, Patrick greeted me with a smile. "You'll never believe what happened last weekend," he said.

I shook my head. I didn't have a clue.

"A student wrote off one of our aircraft. He flew it into the runway. You should've seen the propeller and nose wheel. Total write-off."

My eyes opened in surprise. "What about the student?"

"Oh, he was fine. Just shell shocked."

Patrick explained that Full Sutton Flying Club had already bought another Piper Warrior, and was now just awaiting its delivery. I asked him whether the crashed aircraft had been insured.

"Yeah. But the student who totalled it had to pay the excess."

"And how much was that?"

Patrick grinned. "£850 quid."

I made suitable sounds of astonishment.

Inside the Warrior I noticed someone had dialled the NDB frequency to the number of the beast — 666! When Patrick climbed inside a few minutes later, I pointed this out to him.

"Oh, you've noticed then?"

I nodded, saying nothing.

Patrick looked mildly embarrassed. "I know we shouldn't, but me and Richard like it. But we only listen to it occasionally."

I shook my head. "Patrick, what are you on about. Are you a devil worshipper?"

"*Devil worshipper?* What are *you* on about? 666 is the frequency of a radio station broadcasting out of York. We can pick it up via the NDB. Listen."

When Patrick pressed a button on the communications panel, I could hear a man talking about dogs. And not Hounds of Hell; the racing variety. I nodded in understanding, relaxing again. Patrick was not a servant of the Dark Lord after all. "And," continued Patrick, "the needle points to York when 666 is dialled in. It's a good navigational tool."

Taking off into the circuit, I was downwind when I asked Patrick a question that had been bothering me. "This hatch," I said, pointing to a little Perspex porthole within my left-hand window. It had a little catch on it, so a pilot could open it from the inside. "What's it for?"

"I think it's called the storm hatch," said Patrick. "In really bad weather, I suppose you could open it and look out. I'm just guessing though." He suddenly laughed. "But I once knew a guy who used it for something else."

Patrick told me that he and this other chap had been in Florida doing some training. At one point in their training, Patrick's pal went off on a long solo cross-country flight and, to cut a long story short, he had used the storm hatch in a novel way.

"He told me his todger was forced backwards by the slipstream," chuckled Patrick. "And it made a right mess!"

We both laughed.

After the fifth landing, Patrick got out, leaving me to it. I was finally going to fly solo as a fully qualified pilot for the first time.

After four circuits, I taxied back to the clubhouse, vacating the aircraft. Things had gone well.

Solo Navigation

On a sunny day in July I was once again at Full Sutton. I was really looking forward to flying somewhere *I* wanted to go to as opposed to somewhere an instructor wanted me to go.

After a thorough external check of G-BTVR I climbed inside, preparing myself for my first solo cross-country trip since passing my PPL.

The trip was to be quite straightforward. Full Sutton – Scarborough – Bridlington – Hornsea – Humber Bridge – Full Sutton, a round trip of 85 nm. After one touch-and-go landing, I left the circuit towards Scarborough. With the visibility in excess of 40 nm, I had an excellent view of all the surrounding countryside. At 2,500 ft I levelled off, beginning to really enjoy myself.

And then I got my GPS out. For the first time in my flying career, I'd brought along a piece of equipment as an aid to my navigation. Although I'd planned my journey the old-fashioned way, i.e. by using the old whiz wheel and everything else, I'd brought along the GPS as a back-up. Its display told me three important things:

1. An arrow pointed towards my chosen waypoint (Scarborough).

2. A numerical display told me the heading I needed to fly to get there.

3. A number told me how long it would take to get there.

Ten miles east of Full Sutton, I contacted Humberside Approach as I traversed towards the coastline of North Yorkshire. Approaching Scarborough, I flew through a small number of slight rain showers and so applied some carb heat because I didn't want any ice to build up. I also switched fuel tanks, remembering to turn the fuel pump on beforehand.

"Golf-Victor Romeo," said the lady on the radio at Humberside. "Are you heading much further to the north?"

"No, I'm heading south shortly. Initially to Bridlington and then Hornsea. Golf-Victor Romeo."

"Roger, Golf-Victor Romeo. Caution: Parachute-dropping zone at Bridlington will be active in the next five minutes. I suggest you turn for Hornsea now."

"Turning for Hornsea. Golf-Victor Romeo," I said, turning right.

And then the GPS really came into its own. Selecting Hornsea from the list of available waypoints, a new arrow appeared telling me where to fly. I changed heading.

After a few minutes, I could make out Hornsea. It was easy to spot because of some nearby lakes. Overhead the small coastal town, I altered course for my next checkpoint: the famous Humber Suspension Bridge.

Photo © John Allan

With the Humber Estuary right in front of me, as well as the large built up area of Hull, I knew I was heading in the correct direction. Just then, the radio crackled into life.

"Golf-Victor Romeo," said the Humberside controller. "Converging traffic to the south of you, three miles. Indicated altitude 3,000 ft."

"Looking for traffic, Golf-Victor Romeo," I said.

The controller gave a similar warning to the other aircraft. The pilot said he was looking for me.

Reading my altitude, I noticed I was 300 ft higher than the other aircraft. Even so, I turned left immediately. And then I spotted the other aircraft, a Cessna 172. The controller had been correct; we *were* on a converging flight path. I increased my turn.

"Golf-Victor Romeo has the traffic in sight," I said. "And climbing to 3,500 ft on 1005." 1005 was the pressure setting I'd set in my altimeter.

"Roger G-VR," said the controller.

"G-XX is maintaining 3,000 ft on 1005," said the other pilot.

I saw him go behind and below me, before reappearing on my right-hand side. It was the closest I'd been to another aeroplane in the sky ever. I'd even seen the pilot's expression. It was similar to mine — total confusion.

So who'd had right of way? I didn't really know and so told myself I'd check when I got home. Coming back on course, I flew overhead the mighty Humber Bridge, before turning back towards Full Sutton.

At home, I discovered that under Air Law, if two aircraft are converging, the aircraft with the other to its right, must give way by turning right. So I'd had the right of way. The other aircraft was on my left. He should have turned right. Oh well, no harm done, mainly because we'd both been speaking to the same Air Traffic Control Unit.

Fun Trip Together: Full Sutton – Gamston – Humberside

Amer had passed his PPL, and so we decided to go flying together. Heading over to Full Sutton on a beautiful summer's day, we were looking forward to our first trip.

We decided upon a straightforward triangular route. We'd leave Full Sutton and head off to Gamston Aerodrome. Once there, we'd have a cup of coffee, then fly to Humberside International Airport. Then fly back. The whole journey was roughly 100 nm and, with breaks in between for refreshments, we reckoned it would take about two and a half hours. But before we could take the plane, Amer had to become a member of the Full Sutton Flying Club. This meant a checkride with Patrick Emmett.

Before they set off, Patrick told us a story about a student who'd got hopelessly lost on his qualifying cross-country trip the previous day.

"The weather was gorgeous," said Patrick. "He set off to Gamston with excellent visibility. It should've taken him 25 minutes. But he got lost. He eventually arrived at Gamston one and a half hours later."

I couldn't help but laugh. Amer did too. "Bloody hell! Where had he been?"

"I don't know," replied Patrick. "And neither does he. We'll probably get a letter from the CAA, saying one of our club aircraft infringed controlled airspace without permission."

Patrick leaned forward. "Anyway, he took off for Durham and got there okay. But on the way back here, he got lost again. I heard him over the radio. I couldn't believe my ears. I was doing a trial flight and he asked me to help him. Can you believe that! Over the radio he asked me to help him. The trial flighters had no idea what was going on. They were oblivious."

Amer and I shook our heads. The story was almost too incredible to believe. We waited for Patrick to continue.

"He told me he didn't recognise anything around him. He kept saying everything looked the same and I could hear panic in his voice. I told him to keep calm and fly the plane safely. Then I made him tune his NDB receiver to 666. I told him the needle would point to York and he had to follow it."

"Did he?" I asked.

Patrick nodded. "He said the needle was pointing in the opposite direction. I told him to turn round to follow it. He eventually did. He seemed to calm down then."

Fifteen nail-biting minutes later, the student pilot informed Patrick he was approaching York, and wanted to know what to do next. Patrick told him to fly overhead the city, and then to track directly east for a few minutes until Full Sutton Aerodrome came into view. The student told him he'd try.

Five minutes later, the jittery student came back over the radio. He'd failed to locate Full Sutton, and was now returning to York.

"I was really worried," admitted Patrick. "He'd obviously lost it. I could hear it in his voice. And he was probably low on fuel. I told him to circle around the edge of York. In the meantime, I tried to raise Richard. He was outside sunbathing again. I started yelling over the radio."

Richard came to the mike allowing Patrick to explain the predicament. Scrambling like a fighter ace, Richard jumped into another aircraft and took off.

As Patrick came in to land with the trial flighters, he could hear Richard speaking to the student over the radio. They'd managed to rendezvous overhead York. Five minutes later both aircraft arrived back over Full Sutton, with Richard leading the formation. On final approach, Richard broke away, allowing the student priority. A minute later, the hapless student touched down without incident. He taxied in slowly.

A short while later, Richard landed himself. As soon as he'd parked, he ran over to the student's aircraft to check the fuel tanks.

"There was nothing in them," Patrick told us. "He landed on vapour."

The student failed his qualifying cross-country.

Amer and Patrick left for some checkride circuits. While I sat reading a magazine, a small, grey-haired gentleman walked into the clubhouse. After saying hello, he asked me whether the black car outside was mine.

"No," I replied. "It's Patrick's."

"Oh," he said, grimacing. "It's just that I've accidentally scraped it. Bugger."

The man sat down. He was called Tom, a new part-time instructor at Full Sutton. He'd only started the previous week.

I regarded him with interest. In his sixties, he seemed a bit old to be starting out on a flying career. He caught me looking.

He smiled, "I can tell you're wondering what I'm doing here, aren't you? Well I used to be in the RAF. Church Fenton was my base. I used to train fighter pilots."

I sucked in air. "Fighter pilots?"

"Yes," he replied, wistfully. "Fast jets. Too old for that lark now though."

Getting up to get myself a drink of water I asked Tom whether he still got nervous when flying.

"How do you mean?"

"Well, whenever I go flying," I said, "I feel a little apprehensive. But you, you've trained fighter pilots. So getting into a small aircraft is probably like going for a walk."

"Oh, I see what you mean. But the answer is yes. I still sometimes get nervous. Things can go wrong in a small light aircraft, and in some ways it's worse. I don't get to wear a parachute. In the military, I always wore one."

Ten minutes later, Tom left the clubhouse with a student. What an interesting man.

By one o'clock, Amer had returned from his checkride. He was now an official club member. We sat down to go through the details of our flight.

Since we'd never actually flown together, we went over a few ground rules. Whoever was in the left-hand seat would be in charge of controlling the aircraft. They'd do the take-offs and landings. The person in the right seat would be navigator and radio operator. But, crucially, both of us would have an equal say in decisions. It was a democratic approach.

With that sorted, we decided Amer would fly the first leg to Gamston, primarily because he'd never been there before. And then we'd swap seats for the trip to Humberside. We gathered our things, heading out to the aircraft.

While Amer fuelled up Golf-Victor Romeo, I rang Gamston, asking for permission to land at their airfield.

At most airfields, prior permission must be obtained before landing. A quick call is all that is required. During my phone call Gamston wanted to know the aircraft's registration and type, how many people were going to arrive, and our approximate arrival time.

The man on the end of the phone told me we we'd be most welcome, but added some bad news. The wind was 15 knots, blowing directly across the runway. I covered the phone with my hand, informing Amer of the wind information. He looked pensive for a moment. "I don't like the sound of that. Fifteen-knot crosswind?"

I nodded, saying nothing.

"What do you reckon?" he said.

I thought for a moment before answering. "I think we should fly to Gamston. Then get in the circuit to assess the wind. If you don't like the feel of it, we don't have to land. We can come back to Full Sutton or even head onto Humberside. The wind might not be too bad there."

Holding the fuel nozzle, Amer nodded.

I uncovered the phone, telling the Gamston radio operator we'd be there in about half an hour. We climbed aboard the aircraft shortly afterwards.

Settling into the right-hand seat for the first time ever, I took stock of the situation. The perspective out of the window was different for a start. But that was to be expected. While Amer busied himself with the pre-start checks, I put my right hand on the yoke. It felt so *wrong*. But if I were to be radio operator, then I'd have to get used to it. I sat back, wondering if I'd be able to land the aircraft from the right-hand side. (Note: I *could* land it from the right-hand side, and so could Amer. Both of us had various goes in the future, but for now, that was something neither of us wanted to toy with.)

Five minutes later, I lined up on runway two-two, ready for departure. The windsock was flapping heartily in the blustery conditions. And then we were off. As we left the ground, the wind blew us around like a cork in a bathtub. Amer climbed the aircraft past 2,000 ft where suddenly the wind calmed down. We headed south.

After contacting Humberside Radar, they gave us a Basic Service as we flew towards Gamston. Surprisingly, there was very little chatter clogging the airwaves. Usually the Humberside frequency was very busy but today there was just us and a KLM passenger jet. I looked out of the window, marvelling at the superb visibility. I could see for miles. Despite the threat of wind at Gamston, I was thoroughly enjoying myself. I couldn't help but smile. "You know what, Amer?" I said.

He turned to face me. "What?"

"*This* is why we became pilots!" I gestured outside.

Amer smiled. "Yeah. I know exactly what you mean."

"We're flying where we want, how we want, and we can even do some sight-seeing if we feel like it,"

He nodded. "Amazing isn't it. We're both bloody *pilots!*"

Although I'd brought along the GPS, with two of us sharing the workload, navigating was very easy. With two pairs of eyes looking outside, spotting checkpoints was straightforward. It was all so leisurely. And 10 minutes away from Gamston, I made contact with the radio operator, informing him we were inbound to land.

"Roger, Golf-Victor Romeo," came back the crackly reply. "Right-hand circuit for runway two-one. Wind 280° at 17 knots. Gusting to 22 knots."

"Right hand for two-one," I replied. "And copy the wind. Golf-Victor Romeo."

I looked at Amer. He was shaking his head. Gusts of 22 knots might take us over the crosswind capabilities of the aircraft. Mind you, it was no longer a 90° crosswind, just a 60° one. Still bad though.

Neither of us spoke, mentally going through our options. I broke the silence. "Right, let's join the circuit and when you turn final, get a feel for the wind and decide from there. How does that sound?"

Amer nodded, saying nothing.

I continued. "And if you don't like the wind, we can go around or head off to Humberside."

Amer nodded again. "Fair enough."

With our plan sorted in our minds, Amer descended the aircraft and because no one else was in the circuit, we asked for permission to fly straight onto final. After being told this was okay, we were descending through 700 ft when the right wing suddenly dropped. With a sickening lurch, we tilted sideways, a massive gust catching us out of the blue. Half a second later, we were back straight and level, adrenalin flowing.

"Bloody hell!" Amer gulped. He was battling with the yoke as we continued our descent.

Breathing heavily, I asked him if he was carrying on.

Amer nodded. "It's calming down now I think."

With the runway less than a minute away, I nodded at Amer's decision. He was the one flying the plane. I trusted his judgment.

Falling through 20 ft, the wind abruptly weakened. A few seconds later, Amer flared, settling down upon the tarmac with a tiny squeak of rubber.

"We made it!" said Amer, grinning.

The relief was palpable.

After paying for our landing, Amer and I decided to have a look inside a nearby hangar. Entering it, we noticed a few Cessna Citation business jets parked together. Peering through the side window of one we looked enviously at the flashy interior inside. Compared to the cockpits we were used to, it was a different world.

Soon it was time for the second leg of the journey, Gamston to Humberside Airport, with me taking the controls this time. While I got myself sorted out for the flight, Amer made a phone call to Humberside, asking for permission to land there.

With this authorisation granted, Amer climbed inside and I started up the engine. Five minutes later, we were airborne, climbing through the turbulent air.

Overhead Gainsborough, Amer made contact with Humberside Approach, who gave him the latest wind information. It was blowing at 16 knots from a direction of 280°. The controller then gave us the choice of two runways: two-one or two-seven. Amer looked at me, passing the decision over. After thinking for a moment, I told him we'd go for runway two-seven. Even though it was much shorter than the other runway, there'd only be a slight 10° crosswind blowing across it. Amer gave the controller our choice.

"Copy that, Golf-Victor Romeo," said the man in the Tower. "You'll join the right-hand circuit for runway two-seven. Report overhead Elsham Wolds."

Amer acknowledged this request, and proceeded to consult his chart.

"Elsham What?" I asked. "Where's that?"

"Dunno. Never heard of it," Amer replied. "But I've found it on the map. I think it's a disused airfield to the north-west of Humberside. I'll direct you."

It was then that I realised something fundamental about flying with Amer. With him sitting beside me, sharing the workload, nothing was fazing me. By myself, I'd probably have been panicking. Flying to an unfamiliar regional airport, battling with gusty winds towards an unknown VRP, I'm sure it would have been too much for me.

A few minutes later the town of Scunthorpe appeared on my left-hand side and Amer informed me that Elsham Wolds was up ahead. By looking over the nose, I could see it was indeed a disused airfield.

With the airport on our right-hand side, we joined the circuit, informing ATC we were downwind.

"Report final for two-seven," came back the response from the controller. "You're number one in traffic."

Descending to 600 ft, I turned onto the last section of the circuit. Even though the wind was blowing virtually straight down the runway, I was still worried. Gusts of wind were trying to lift each wing in turn. Amer called final.

Crossing the piano keys, I pulled back the throttle, flaring the aircraft. A few seconds later, we landed on the runway with a bit of a bang. We had cheated death for the second time in one day. And then the buffoons came to town.

As we slowed down on runway two-seven, ATC said, "Golf-Victor Romeo, enter and backtrack runway 21.Vacate to the left via the alpha taxiway."

Amer read this instruction back, consulting his airport diagram at the same time. By this point, I'd entered runway two-one (the main runway) and began turning right along it. As I approached a taxiway to my left, I asked Amer whether it was the one we were supposed to exit by.

He looked up from his chart, nonplussed. "I'm not sure. Hang on. I'll ask ATC."

I brought the aircraft to a standstill while Amer pressed the communications button.

"Humberside Tower, this is Golf-Victor Romeo. Can you confirm we're exiting the runway via the alpha taxiway?"

"Affirm Golf-Victor Romeo. Vacate runway along the alpha taxiway. From your present position, continue along runway two-one to the next exit on the left. Do *not* turn left where you are."

"Wilco," replied Amer.

Feeling embarrassed to be causing such a scene; I released the foot-brakes, moving onwards. Nearing the correct exit point, the controller came back over the airwaves. He asked us whether we were familiar with the airport.

About to tell him, no, Amer beat me to it. In an act of utter folly, he said, "Golf-Victor Romeo is *vaguely* familiar with the airport."

"Okay…" said the controller. "When you exit the runway, taxi and park to the left of the Swiss-registered aircraft."

Laughing, I turned left along the taxiway, spotting three large airliners to my right and a few light aircraft to my left. I wondered which aircraft the Swiss-registered plane was. Slowing down to a virtual snail's pace we both craned our necks.

"It's not that 737 is it?" I asked Amer, pointing to the right.

"I don't think so," came back his tentative reply. "He wouldn't tell us to park next to a big jet would he? It must be on our left."

Suddenly the controller was back on line. "Golf-Victor Romeo" he said in clipped tones. "Your parking spot is to your left. If you're not sure which aircraft is Swiss-registered, then look for a Swiss flag. It's painted on the tail."

We both looked to our left, immediately spotting the aircraft in question. Amer thanked the controller.

After parking, Amer and I climbed out. As we were walking across the apron towards the security building, I turned to Amer. I said, "Vaguely?"

"What?" he replied, confused.

"Vaguely?" I repeated. "Vaguely familiar with the airport!"

"Oh that." Amer shook his head and sniggered. "It was the only thing I could think of."

I couldn't help but laugh again.

After a quick cup of coffee in the airport cafe, we presented ourselves back at the security building. As well as a woman, an older male security guard was present. He was sitting down studying a black and white monitor.

After the officers frisked and scanned us, we began chatting. While Amer talked to the woman about the pros and cons of mobile phones, I asked her seated colleague a question.

"Do you ever get passengers who try to escape?" He was watching a KLM airliner on his monitor. It had just landed and he was watching people walking down the steps of the aircraft.

"Oh, yes," he solemnly informed me without turning around. "We sometimes get a few stragglers."

I leaned forward. "What do you do to them?"

"Shoot them."

"Sorry?" I said, shocked by the answer.

"We shoot them," he repeated without a trace of humour. He was still staring at the screen.

"You're joking, right?"

"Why would I joke about it?"

I walked away, hoping he *was* joking.

After climbing back inside the aircraft, I started the engine for the third final leg back to Full Sutton. Amer tuned into the approach frequency. The controller, the same one as before, gave us the option of runway two-one or two-seven. With the wind no different from earlier we opted for the latter.

"Copy that," said the controller. "Taxi along the yellow line and wait at the Alpha Hold."

Amer read back the instructions while I pushed the throttle forward a touch and released the brakes. As we started to move off, I asked Amer where the Alpha Hold was.

"I'm just looking for it," he said, peering at his chart. "But I think it's to our left."

I slowed down. I thought it was on our right. Continuing forward, we came to a yellow T-junction. I brought the aircraft to a standstill and studied the chart with Amer.

Just then, the controller came over the headset. He'd probably been watching us for some time. "Golf-Victor Romeo, have you got a problem?"

Startled, Amer pressed the button. "No. We're just a bit unsure where the Alpha Hold is. Can you confirm that it's on our left?"

"No," said the controller icily. "It's to your right. From your present position, turn *right* and follow the yellow line as instructed."

I turned right, eventually finding the Alpha Hold. I was laughing all the way. Twenty minutes later we landed back at Full Sutton.

"Let's do Blackpool next time." I said to Amer as I turned off the runway.

Amer nodded. "Yeah! That will be a great flight!"

Aborted Flight

A week and a half later, Amer and I were going to do just that. We had booked the aircraft for a six-hour block on an almost perfect day for flying.

Because I was flying the first leg, I read each item from my checklist very carefully. I started the engine and held the power at 1200 rpm while I did the three main after-start checks. They were:

(a) Temperature and oil pressure gauges in the green.

(b) Ammeter is charging.

(c) Suction is registering.

All of these were fine, so I did the carb heat check. This involved giving the engine some carburettor heat, and then noting the subsequent drop on the rpm counter. The drop was within allowed limits so I went on to the magneto check.

It was with this next check, that I noticed something amiss. When I turned the key to test the left magneto there was a large drop in rpm, bigger than I'd ever experienced before. I brought it to Amer's attention.

"That *is* a big drop," he said when I did it again. "What's the right magneto like?"

I turned the key to the right magneto setting. The rpm drop was normal.

We both looked at each other. I tried the left one again. The rpm drop was still excessive. The engine didn't sound like it was going to conk out, but it did sound rough. I turned the key back to the normal position, wondering what to do. Eventually I came up with a plan. I told Amer I'd taxi to the hold. "Then I'll do the power checks. After that we can reassess the situation. What do you think?"

Amer nodded. "Good idea."

At the hold, I held brakes and increased the rpm to 2000. The oil temperature and pressure showed up in the green, which was good. The ammeter and suction were fine, and the carb heat drop was still within limits. As I turned the key to the left magneto position, we both watched the rpm counter. We heard the large drop once more.

"It's still there isn't it?" I said to Amer, grimacing.

Amer nodded.

I turned the key back to the normal position, then reduced power to idle. The engine didn't stop. Increasing power back up to 1200 rpm, I sat back in my seat, concerned. "What do you want to do?"

Amer tapped the top of the dashboard absently. He turned to face me. "The fact it didn't stop when we idled it suggests it's alright. Plus, everything else seems okay. I don't know. It's up to you."

After thinking things through, I decided Amer was right. There was no point cancelling the trip just because of a dodgy magneto. It probably needed a good clean, that was all. Maybe the blast of power during take-off would clear it up. Satisfied, I entered the runway.

Lining up on the grass strip, I pushed the throttle in for full power. With everything looking fine, I released the brakes. As the speed gathered pace, I kept one eye on the rpm counter and the other on the temperature gauge. Both were functioning, as they should have been. A few seconds later we lifted off, gently easing into the air. With everything operating as normal, we breathed a collective sigh of relief. We climbed and turned west towards York.

While Amer busied himself talking to Leeds Approach, I flew overhead York, marvelling at the view below the wing. It really was a fine day for flying. I could already make out Harrogate in the distance. At this rate, flying across the Pennines would be a cinch. I stared out my side window, looking at York Race Course.

Ten minutes later, approaching Wetherby, Amer tapped me on the shoulder. "Look," he said pointing to the oil pressure gauge. When I looked my heart almost stopped. The needle was completely over to the right, hovering in the red danger area.

"Shit!" I said, tapping it. "How long has it been like that?"

"About 30 seconds. It just kept going up and up."

My stomach knotted. "Do you think it's related to the magneto drop?"

"I don't know. But look at this." Amer pointed to the temperature gauge. It was also moving into the red. Things were happening very quickly.

I turned the aircraft around immediately. I wanted to get back to

Full Sutton as soon as possible. Pulling back some throttle, I prayed the engine would last the 15-minute journey back home.

With an edge of urgency filling the cockpit, Amer and I kept conversation to a minimum. I alternated my gaze between the gauges and the ground outside. I wanted to spot suitable emergency landing sites should the need arise. Beside me, Amer was doing the same. He'd already told Leeds we were returning to Full Sutton.

Scanning the mixture control, carb heat lever, fuses and primer, I was hoping to spot something amiss but saw nothing. We flew on with the needles hovering in the red.

Routing around the edge of York, every noise seemed to be a signal for imminent engine failure. I had visions of the cylinder head cracking, spraying plumes of black oil over the windscreen. What would we do then? It didn't bear thinking about.

Amer leaned forward, trying to spot Full Sutton. "We're doing fine," he said. "We're going to make it. I can see Elvington."

Pulling the throttle back as far as I dared, Amer's news gave me heart. Elvington Aerodrome was close to Full Sutton. And if push came to shove, we could always land there instead. It was where I had done my PFL during my Skills Test. I breathed out. I'd been holding my breath.

With Full Sutton sighted in the distance, I reduced the throttle even further, beginning a descent. Even with power reduced to idle, the needles remained in the red.

Joining the circuit, I flew downwind and base, and was soon on final approach for runway two-two. With the engine still running we crossed the threshold and touched down gently. With sweat dripping from my face, I taxied back to park the aircraft. Amer pointed at the two gauges. Both were now in the green portion of the scale.

"Well we're down," I said. "Let's find Patrick or Richard to talk about this mess."

We found the instructors in the hangar checking out a twin-engined aircraft parked there.

"You two are back early," said Richard. "I thought you were going to Blackpool?"

"Yeah we were," I said, "But we had a bit of a problem."

"Oh?" said Patrick, turning to face us.

We explained what had happened.

Patrick and Richard gave each other a knowing look. Then Richard climbed down from the stepladders he'd been perched upon. "Good call, lads. You did the right thing. We'll get the engineers to check it out." He stopped speaking, wiping his hands on his overalls. "But this has actually happened before. The gauges are just faulty. And we replaced the magnetos recently. I should've mentioned it. But the log mentions it. You would have been fine to carry on."

Afterwards, Amer and I discussed what had happened. Even though the engine had probably been fine, we still agreed we'd done the right thing. As far as we were concerned, the engine had been about to seize up and we'd taken the only sensible course of action.

And one other thing we'd proved was that neither of us had panicked. Even though tensions had been hellishly high, we'd remained calm and collected throughout. We'd even had the presence of mind to look out for potential landing sites. Flirting with death had been a good learning experience even if it was one we had no wish to repeat.

First Non-Flying Passengers

A week later, I decided to go flying again. It was going to be a milestone because I intended to take my first ever passengers up with me. My friends Jon Brough and Michael Spiller were my chosen victims. Both had expressed a keen interest to go up in a small aircraft. So on a glorious summer's afternoon the three of us headed over to Full Sutton.

Before we got there, I told my pals I'd be flying a couple of solo circuits initially, just to get back into the rhythm of things. Then I'd take them up, one at a time, for a trip to Castle Howard and York.

Once I'd landed after doing two solo circuits, I parked the aircraft and switched everything off. I then beckoned Michael to approach. After getting him all strapped in, I explained about the emergency equipment and how to adjust the seat. I passed him a headset (kindly loaned from Patrick Emmett) and switched everything on. I was actually quite nervous. I didn't want anything to go wrong, especially seeing as Michael had never been up in a light aircraft before.

After lining up on the runway we eventually departed to the north, towards Castle Howard. As we approached the historic estate, I asked Michael if he'd like to have a go at flying the aircraft. He nodded enthusiastically. I told him to put his hand on the yoke.

Instructing him to maintain straight and level flight at 2,000 ft, I kept control of the rudder pedals and throttle. Staring fixedly out the front windscreen, Michael pushed the yoke downwards, then overcorrected by pulling it back up. I wondered if I'd been the same on my first few lessons.

With Michael enjoying himself immensely, I told him to do a gentle turn to the left, and soon we were overhead Castle Howard. After flying around it a couple of times I took control back, heading for York. Eventually we arrived back in the circuit at Full Sutton and as I turned onto base I began to explain to exactly what I was doing. Staring enthusiastically out of the window, Michael nodded, smiling. Not long afterwards, we were back down on terra firma. The landing had been one of my best.

Next I took up Jon Brough. I repeated exactly the same flight, also letting Jon have a go at flying the aircraft. After yet another good landing, I parked the aircraft and we both climbed out. Both friends told me they'd loved the flight. They told me that they had been particularly impressed with my landing abilities. Jon added that I'd exuded an air of quiet confidence throughout the flight.

We drove home, buzzing from the whole experience. I had climbed another notch of the ladder.

Flight to Sleap, along the Manchester Low-Level Route

Almost a year after passing my skills test, Amer and I drove over to Blackpool Airport. We thought the change of scenery would be good for us. We'd more or less exhausted the possibilities around Full Sutton.

We'd decided to fly to Sleap, a little airfield near Shrewsbury. To get there, we'd have to fly down the notorious Manchester low-level corridor, a long, narrow cube of airspace over 20 miles long and 5 miles wide. It sliced its way through Manchester's busy Class A airspace like a tunnel through a huge mountain. To get through it in one piece, Amer would navigate (because he'd done it before) and I would sit in the left-hand seat flying as accurately as I could.

The weather was fine, if perhaps a little hazy. After booking the aircraft out, we strapped ourselves down and started the engine. We were soon in the air, heading south-east.

Before the flight, Amer and I had decided not to bring the GPS along. We felt we were becoming too reliant on it. Getting to Sleap by traditional navigational methods would be more satisfying, we thought. We passed Southport and Amer switched frequency to Manchester Approach. Almost immediately, a surge of radio chatter began. My headset filled with the voices of airline pilots negotiating their way to and from Manchester Airport.

"Lufthansa 234, turn heading two-five-zero and descend to altitude 3,000 ft. QNH 1019." It was the Manchester controller. We could only wait for them to finish. After getting the correct response from the German pilot, the controller immediately started talking to another pilot. "Speedbird 535, climb to flight level seven-zero."

"Climb flight level seven-zero. Speedbird 535." The chatter was non-stop.

The low-level corridor was actually a superb piece of work. Without it, a pilot wishing to traverse a north-south route would have to take an almighty detour around the huge expanse of Class A airspace surrounding Manchester and Liverpool. Even so, there were still pitfalls in using the corridor. Not least the actual narrowness of the passageway. Margin for error was small within its 5-mile width. Furthermore, just above the corridor's altitude restriction of 1,250 ft, airliners flew in abundance. A pilot had to be on the ball when flying the corridor.

Approaching the northern edge of the low-level corridor, I descended to 1,100 ft on the Manchester QNH. I could feel my stress levels rising. Amer turned to me. "You ready?" I nodded, checking the altimeter. A few minutes later, we entered the corridor over the M6/M58 motorway junction.

With built-up areas on our left and right, the corridor looked no different from anywhere else. Amer pressed the button to tell Manchester we'd arrived but received a burst of static. He'd tried to make the call at the same time as someone else. He released the button, shaking his head. He had no option but to wait for a gap.

Flying overhead Haydock racecourse, Amer finally got through. The controller's next response was rather strange.

"Golf-November Tango in approximately five minutes' time a parachute drop has been approved south of your position. I'd appreciate it if you could tell me when you have the aircraft in sight."

I turned to Amer, shaking my head. That's all we needed. Parachutists plummeting in our path. I flew south over Warrington, passing underneath large airliners climbing away from Manchester Airport.

Suddenly Amer raised his arm, pointing at something out the windscreen. "There they are. Look!"

I looked. A fair distance above us, four or five parachutists were lazily floating downwards. The aircraft dropping them, a large twin-engined turboprop, was depositing more as we watched. Thankfully we were nowhere near them. Amer told Manchester we had them visual.

"Copy that, Golf-November Tango. Thanks for your help."

Ten minutes later, we emerged at the southern end of the corridor without having violated any of the controlled airspace around us. I breathed a hearty sigh of relief as we climbed back up to 3,000 ft.

"I felt like a student again." I said to Amer as I wiped the sweat from my brow.

Photo © Steve Ball

Half an hour later, we landed at Sleap, an airfield neither of us had been to before. As we were slowing down on the runway, I asked the radio operator if she could give us taxi instructions to the parking area. There was no response. I tried again, wondering where she'd gone, but again there was no reply.

Still on the runway, I slowed down. Beside me Amer started studying his airport diagram. On our right-hand-side there were some light aircraft already parked up. But a Cessna 172 waiting to enter the runway blocked the only taxiway to them. I trundled along the ever-shortening runway.

Eventually we turned off the end of the runway onto a taxiway we hoped would lead us to the parking area. And then we noticed the man running towards us, arms flapping above his head.

After holding the brakes, the man in question came around to my side of the aircraft. Utilising the storm hatch, I said hello.

"You can't come down here!" he shouted, gesturing behind him. "It's a bloody road! You'll have to turn around! You'll have to go back down the runway!"

I looked at the runway. The Cessna 172 had already taken off. I turned back to face the man. "This is a road?"

"Yes. A road. And you're blocking it!"

I closed the hatch, muttering something along the lines of *well if they'd told us where to go in the first place* and released the brakes. Then I noticed the man's car waiting some distance from us, obviously waiting for us to get out of the road. Sighing, I turned around, avoiding bushes and potholes, and paused only to wave at the man. A minute later, we re-entered the runway and managed to park without further disaster.

A Trip to Remember: the Isle of Man

Getting to the Isle of Man would be a brand new challenge. Neither of us had ever flown over such a large expanse of water before. After some rough calculations, we worked out that we'd be over water for about 45 minutes. Forty of those minutes would be so far away from land that in the event of an engine failure, we'd have no option but to ditch in the open sea. This stark fact did not fill me with merriment.

A couple of days before the trip I read up on the correct procedure for ditching, which basically involves landing on the crest of a wave, unlatching the doors just before the 'landing' and then swimming away as quickly as humanely possible from the sinking aircraft.

Merely reading about it made me feel nervous. I began to question my motives for undertaking a flight over water for so-called enjoyment. What if we got lost? What if we couldn't sight the horizon and had to fly on just instruments? What if the engine blew up? What about the cold temperatures of the sea? Did sharks prowl the Irish Sea? What if…?

Amer, of course, had been feeling exactly the same. Ringing me up the day before our journey, he had some good news. He'd managed to get us a couple of life jackets to borrow. Hearing this made me feel a little better. At least we'd float towards the sharks.

The weather could not have been any better. No clouds in the sky, virtually nil wind, and even better than that, visibility of 50 km, the highest either of us had ever experienced.

After arriving at Blackpool Airport, Amer and I planned our trip meticulously. We didn't want to end up flying in the wrong direction over water. However, just in case this event did happen, we made sure we filled the fuel tanks to maximum. The amount of fuel we had would easily get us to Ireland if things went pear shaped. And just in case, we had the GPS in my flight bag.

Deciding to fly along the Class F Advisory Route, which ran along a westerly radial from Pole Hill VOR to the Isle of Man VOR, we would intercept the route just north of Blackpool and then follow it all the way in.

Grabbing the life jackets Amer had managed to procure from the flying club, we donned them un-inflated as we walked out to our aircraft for the day, a PA-28 with the memorable registration of G-UANT.

"Are you nervous?" Amer asked me as we climbed aboard.

I told him I wasn't so much nervous as filled with trepidation. "But I'm really looking forward to it."

Amer nodded, climbing into the left-hand seat. For the outbound trip, he would be pilot-in-command while I would be chief navigator and radio operator.

While Amer got busy with the cockpit checks, I tuned in the radios. After turning the dial for Blackpool Tower, I made sure I had the correct VOR frequency dialled in and then I tuned the VOR receiver to the correct radial, 285°. Afterwards, I made Amer double-check my handiwork. He deemed it fine and so a few minutes later we took off into the blue sky.

Instead of heading straight out to sea, we flew north for a few minutes, flying along the seafront at Blackpool. Five miles north of the airport, the needle on the VOR instrument began moving towards the centre. We were intercepting the radial that would take us to the Isle of Man. Turning right into the open sea, Amer whistled. "Here we go."

In front of us was a sea of blue and more blue. There wasn't a drop of land in sight. With 45 minutes of flight time ahead of us we had no choice but to settle down for the trip.

Climbing past an altitude 3,000 ft on the QNH of 1031 mb we

switched the altimeter pressure to the standard atmospheric pressure of 1013 mb and continued our climb until we reached Flight Level 55, the base level of the advisory route.

Above 3,000 ft QNH, pilots should change the pressure setting on their altimeter to the standard of 1013 mb. This makes it safer for all aircraft flying above 3,000 ft. All airliners cruising above this transition altitude will have 1013 mb set in their cockpits. They will report their altitude as Flight Level. For example, Flight Level 260 was about 26,000 ft). When they descend below the transition altitude, they'll revert to the QNH pressure.

"Good afternoon, Blackpool Radar," I said through the headset. I was doing my best impression of an airline pilot. "This is Golf-Uniform Alpha November Tango, a PA-28, climbing to flight level 55 on a westerly track. Currently 5 miles out of Blackpool flying direct to the Isle of Man along the Class F advisory route."

"Copy that Golf-November Tango. Report when crossing the rigs," replied the controller.

The rigs were a set of five or six gas and oil rigs at about the half-way stage of our journey. They were on our chart and even though we couldn't see them, we knew they'd eventually appear at some point in the journey. Unless, of course, we got lost.

"How are you feeling?" I asked Amer as we settled into the cruise at Flight Level 55 across an unbroken sea.

"Fine," he said, nodding. "How about you?"

I told him I was glad there were two of us flying this trip. Even though everything had so far been straightforward and relatively easy, it was still a good feeling to know there were two pilots on board should anything go wrong. It also meant I could sacrifice Amer to the sharks if need be.

Because there was little in the way of a horizon, or any other distinguishable landmarks for that matter, Amer decided to fly on instruments while I kept a good lookout for the rigs. As we flew along, the radio was silent, except for the odd transmission between Blackpool Approach and a few locally bound aircraft. The only things worth looking at were the vapour trails of airliners flying above us, or occasionally a tiny boat below, but apart from that, there was nothing to see.

A few minutes later, I could make out some blurred dark specks in the distance. I pointed them out to Amer. We both surmised they had to be the rigs we were looking for. As the only landmark between the UK coast and the Isle of Man, we certainly hoped they were the rigs.

With something to head for, Amer turned right a touch, pointing straight at them. Soon afterwards, we saw that they were indeed the rigs, and so flew onwards. Still keeping on the 285 radial, we swapped VOR frequencies to Isle of Man. The needle quickly centred once more.

After telling Blackpool Radar we were over the rigs, the controller told us to contact Ronaldsway Approach, the radar controller based on the Isle of Man.

"Ronaldsway Approach," I said. "This is Golf-Uniform Alpha November Tango. Over the rigs at flight level 55. Inbound for landing."

Very quickly, a man, whose voice was very reminiscent of a black and white newsreel broadcaster, answered me. "Roger Golf-November Tango. Expect a straight in approach for runway two-six on arrival. Report when visual with the field."

"Wilco. Golf-November Tango."

Fifteen minutes later, Amer tapped the windscreen. "Land ahoy!" he said. "Isle of Man in sight!"

And it was, even if it was just the faintest blur of land in the far distance. I began to feel excited. We were nearly there. We had done it. We'd flown across the sea.

But on we went, until the coastline became more distinct. Then we turned right slightly, veering off the VOR radial. We wanted to fly to Douglas, the capital of the Isle of Man. We told the controller of our intentions. He was fine about it. As well as seeing Douglas from above, we reasoned a straight in approach to runway two-six would be easier from overhead the town.

Douglas, nestled within an attractive bay, looked beautiful from above. To our left, we could see Ronaldsway Airport. I pressed the button, telling ATC we had the field in sight.

"Roger, Golf-November Tango. Cleared for a straight in approach to runway two-six. Number one in traffic. Report final."

A few minutes later, Amer touched down on the Isle of Man. It had all been so easy! I checked the time and noticed that it had taken us 44 minutes to reach our destination. Only three quarters of an hour to get to somewhere neither of us had ever been to before. Absolutely amazing!

ATC instructed us to park over at the south-western end of the airport, where the local flying club — Manx Flyers — was located. After climbing out of our trusty aircraft, we immediately wandered over to a beautifully restored US Air Force World War II aircraft, complete with silver paintwork and American insignia. It looked to be in mint condition. While Amer inspected the engine, I inspected the lady painted on the side.

After an hour-and-a-half of sightseeing in Douglas, we returned to the airport for the flight back to Blackpool.

Strapped back inside the aircraft, I did the pre-flight checks while Amer tuned in the radios. Then we dialled in the ATIS frequency to get the latest weather. When the recorded voice started speaking, Amer glanced over at me. He raised his eyebrows. It was a different voice from all of the other ATIS reports we'd heard. Tuning into the message, I thought the voice sounded just like Harry Hill, the comedian. I wondered who it really was.

Ten minutes later, after waiting for a turboprop to depart for Dublin, we were airborne. We headed towards the western side of the island until we reached the small coastal town of Peel. After circling around for a while, I turned back east, heading towards the open sea and then Blackpool.

If anything, the visibility had improved since our inbound flight. At the halfway stage, we could actually see the Isle of Man behind us, and the long coastline of England to the front. Later, we found out this was a very rare sight indeed. There are not many days of the year when both are visible at the same time. The rigs appeared on time, and everything went according to plan. Amer soon changed frequencies to Blackpool Approach.

Twenty-five minutes later we parked up at Blackpool. After handing in our life jackets, we paid our aircraft hire fee. Neither of us minded paying the hefty charge. After all, we'd just had one of the best days' flying since beginning our PPLs two years previously.

Filling in another 0.9 hours of command time for my logbook (the same as Amer) I worked out my total number of hours flown since passing my PPL. I'd managed to accumulate almost 20 hours. When I asked Amer, he told me he'd done a similar amount.

On the drive home, I looked outside at the glorious sunshine. It really was an immaculate afternoon for flying. I smiled to myself, thinking back to the days when I had fought with the weather, believing the cloud and wind were conspiring against me, rejoicing whenever I gnashed my teeth due to a cancelled lesson. But in the end I had won that battle, though it *had* been a close one.

In the sky up to my right, I noticed a light aircraft. It looked like a Cessna 152. For a minute I wondered whether it might be G-DO till I saw that it wasn't. As it disappeared from sight, I thought about my trusty little Cessna. Together we had formed a strong bond. That tiny aircraft had seen me progress from a bewildered novice to a qualified pilot and, apart from its dubious fuel gauges, it had never let me down once.

Completing the Private Pilot's Licence had been a challenge, probably one of the most difficult things I'd done in my life. Indeed I had almost given up at one point. Yet despite this I could only look back on my training with good feelings. The rush of pure adrenalin as I took off on my first solo could still give me a thrill, as could thinking about the moment when I knew I'd passed my qualifying cross country. I could vividly recall the tremble in my stomach as I gave my first radio message and the apprehension I'd felt when I'd taking off on my first solo navigation exercise. But I'd come through the training with a real licence in my hand: a Private Pilot's Licence, no less! When it had plopped through the letterbox, my euphoria had been the same as if it had been a cheque for a million pounds.

If the version of me aged 9 could meet the version of me aged 32, he would stare in wonder at the adult, wondering how it was possible for him to be a pilot. And the adult version of me would look down at the youngster and say something like this: *You can do it. And you will do it one day. But please don't build a Lego airliner and fill it with ants. Your mother won't like it and neither will the ants. Now go and finish your model Messerschmitt, and tonight, dream of flight.*

My 8-Point Plan of Action for a Pre-PPL Pilot

Have a trial flight

There is absolutely no point in doing any of the things listed below if you've not experienced what it's actually like inside a small aircraft. Flying in a general aviation training aircraft is a completely different proposition to flying inside a commercial airliner.

To see if you can handle training in a small aircraft, book yourself in for a trial flight. Ring up the nearest airfield to your house, and ask about any trial flights they have on offer. They'll usually offer you a flight for 20, 30 or 60 minutes. Prices will vary, but expect to pay around £130 for a one-hour flight. I personally would advise going for the full hour because you'll get more time in the air to experience what everything's about. Also be prepared to have a go at flying the aircraft by yourself at some point. Trust me, you'll have great fun!

Once the trial flight is over, you'll have a good idea about whether you can handle being cooped up inside a small aircraft for long periods.

Get a medical

When I was learning to fly, I heard about a student who'd started his training before actually going for his medical. When it was time for him to go solo, his instructor asked to see his medical certificate. Because he didn't possess one, he had to quickly organise one. He ended up failing it. There was some problem with his hearing he didn't know about. With over £1,000 already spent on lessons, he had to give up flying.

If you are harbouring any desire to become a commercial pilot, then go for the Class 1 medical straight away. It will save a lot of potential heartache later on. Ask any flying school about where to go for your medical or alternatively, do a search on the Internet. If you're happy to stick with private flying, the Class 2 will suffice.

Look for a flying school/club

Do you want to get your licence quickly, with an intensive 3- or 4-week course? Or do you want to complete it at a more leisurely pace? For intensive training, look on the Internet for approved JAA PPL courses in the USA, South Africa or Australia. You'll fly in a highly intensive block period and when you return home you'll have your licence all done and dusted. However, you'll still need to do some training back home, in order for you to get used to the peculiarities of UK airspace — not to mention the hassles of coping with the good old British weather.

If this intensive style tickles your fancy, then be prepared to work hard. You'll be flying every day and will not get weekends off. Though flying every day sounds attractive to the novice, it is bloody hard work. The instructors will push you to the maximum throughout, and at night you'll have to study the books.

Alternatively, you may decide to do your training in the UK. You'll end up paying more for your training, but you can do it at your own pace. Training in the UK, however, does mean you'll become a slave to the weather.

Talk to other students of your chosen school/club

If you can, ask your potential school/club whether you can have any email addresses of other students who have trained or are currently training at their establishment. Other students will tell you what the school/club is really like and what certain instructors are like. But you must bear in mind that these comments will be personal opinions. Visit the school and chat to students in person. Chat to the instructors. Do they seem friendly? Are they welcoming? What are the training aircraft like? What about the airfield itself?

Buy the study books

You will need to get your hands on the study books so you can pass the exams. However, if you really want to learn to fly, studying from them will not be as tedious as you might imagine.

Your instructor will also expect you to have read various chapters before each flight. By doing so, you will be mentally prepared for the lesson. In the UK, there are currently two different approved sets of study books, and both cost about the same amount of money. Buy them, read them, make notes and read them again.

Buy some equipment

At some point in your training you'll need to purchase some equipment. Many pilot shops offer a package whereby you can buy all the equipment in a bundle, thereby saving yourself some valuable cash. I can't see anything wrong with doing this, but if you're short of money, then shelling out over £300 in one go can be a bit hard on the wallet, especially if you haven't actually started lessons.

I'd personally advise buying the equipment in stages, and then buying it as you need it. Things to save until later include the kneeboard, aircraft checklist, logbook, and headset. In fact, I didn't buy a headset until I'd actually passed my PPL.

If you cannot wait to buy some of the goodies on offer, then I'd suggest starting with a 1:500000 chart covering the area you'll be training in (note: there are three areas to choose from). Study everything on the chart. Examine the airspace around your chosen training establishment. Look for any nearby controlled airspace, and attempt to fathom out how it all works. What altitude does that Class B Airspace start from? How high up does it go? What does that Danger Area mean?

Buy some chinagraph pencils or marker pens so you can write on your chart. You'll need to draw lines on your chart when you begin your navigation studying, and if you've already bought the books as a precursor to flight training then you can get on with this straight away.

At first, non-permanent pens will suffice, but later, when doing navigation trips for real, a black permanent marker pen will be vital. If you're worried about making a mess of your lovely new chart, then don't worry. A splash of nail-varnish remover will remove permanent ink.

If you really want to have fun before you begin your training, then buy a whiz wheel. Shops sell these complicated inventions at varying prices, ranging from around £20 to £80, and buying a mid-priced aluminium one would be your best bet. Learning to use your whiz wheel is a nuisance. Luckily, though, they come with a manual, and your study books will cover their use in detail. Also buy a square protractor and a navigation ruler (which will measure distances on your newly purchased aviation chart). Both are cheap and look good in your flight bag.

And speaking of flight bags, buy one. The glossy magazines sell them at extortionate prices. Don't bother with them. A common-or-garden holdall will do the job just fine. Mine cost less than a tenner.

Visit www.pprune.org/forums or similar websites

This discussion website will answer most of the queries you'll ever have. Registering with them is easy and free, and will allow you to post questions to the many thousands of pilots/air traffic controllers/students, etc. who browse their site. Even if you don't register, you can still look at the daily postings.

Make sure you have the funds available to pay for the

course

Accept the fact that you will, in all probability, not complete the course in the minimum hours required. You'll need some extra funds available to pay for this contingency. Also be aware of hidden extras! These might include landing fees (especially on away landings), travel expenses to the airport and paying for the licence fee itself. All of these things can add up considerably.

Mentally prepare yourself!

Expect jubilation during your training. Expect feelings of absolute amazement. But also be prepared for misery, anxiety and feelings of extreme despondency. You'll experience them all at some time. Sometimes on the same day.

Buy flight simulator software

This will give you situational awareness of airports. If you can get hold of the VFR scenery available then you'll get a good idea of what the British landscape actually looks like from above.

Get hold of a handheld receiver

They pick up ATC frequencies (if you live near enough) and you can listen in to pilots and controllers speaking in their peculiar language. They can be quite costly — usually between £200-£300. Be warned though, it is actually illegal to listen in to these conversations, though no one has ever been prosecuted.

Buy some sunglasses

To look super cool to the guys and chicks!

Glossary of Some Aviation Acronyms

ADF - Automatic Direction Finder (linked to the NDB)
ALT - The altitude mode of a transponder
ATC - Air Traffic Control
ATIS - Automated Terminal Information Service (current weather report)
ATPL - Airline Transport Pilot's Licence
ATZ - Air Traffic Zone (the airspace around an airport)
CAA - Civil Aviation Authority
CPL - Commercial Pilot's Licence
DME - Distance Measuring Equipment (linked to the VOR and ILS)
ETA - Estimated time of arrival
GPS - Global Positioning Satellite (a simple way of navigating!)
FBO - Fixed Base Operations (usually your flying school's HQ)
IFR - Instrument Flight Rules
ILS - Instrument Landing System
IMC - Instrument Meteorological Conditions (not suitable for a PPL)
JAA - Joint Aviation Authority
MATZ- Military Air Traffic Zone
NDB - Non-Directional Beacon (a navigation beacon)
OBS - The knob thing on the VOR instrument!
PFL - Practice Forced Landing
PPL - Private Pilot's Licence
POB - Persons on board
QDM - What to ask ATC if you're lost. They will give you a bearing.
QFE - Pressure setting for airfield elevation
QNH - Pressure setting for regional mean sea level
SBY - Standby mode of a transponder
VFR - Visual Flight Rules
VMC - Visual Meteorological Conditions
VOR - Very High-Frequency Omni-directional Radio Range

Thanks

There are a number of people I'd like to thank and perhaps it is only fair I start with James Jarvis. He had to put up with my constant worrying. He had to endure my pathetic attempts to speak on the radio. But James was the man who taught me to fly an aeroplane, something I'd dreamed of doing since I was a child.

Similarly, I must also give a huge measure of thanks to John Reynolds. If James Jarvis taught me to fly, then John Reynolds taught me to navigate. In fact I'd like to thank all of the instructors and staff I met, including Geoff, John, Dylan, Kate, Stuart, Tony, Claire, Clive, Ian and Kevin. Richard Watson and Patrick

James Jarvis the airline pilot

Emmett at Full Sutton Aero Club also get a message of appreciation. Each one taught me something in my quest to become a pilot.

Roy Barber, microlight pilot extraordinaire, receives a round of applause. Following miserable lessons when I felt like giving up, Roy would methodically and calmly go through what had happened, pulling out positive things for me to grasp onto. Roy also provided a lot of the initial momentum I needed to take up lessons in the first place.

Some of my friends and family deserve a mention of credit. Before I even considered learning to fly, a friend of mine called Phil Jones had become so sick of my endless conversations about aeroplanes that one day he snapped. "For pity's sake, why don't you just save up and become a bloody pilot? Anything just to get you to shut up!"

I'm a pilot now, Phil. I'll try to shut up.

Michael Spiller checked my book for consistency. He'd also ask questions such as: "What does QNH mean?" "Does runway 32 mean there are 32 runways?" His comments made me add many of the explanations found in this book. Therefore, he can take some blame for my ramblings.

My father, together with another friend of mine called Simon Stuart, worked diligently and tirelessly poring over my manuscript for any errors or 'boring bits' as one of them succinctly put it. They found many.

Andrew Sinclair needs a hearty mention of thanks. Being a private pilot himself meant he could offer many helpful insights into my training. He also checked my writing for technical errors. Kelvin Denize checked my manuscript towards the latter stages. Being a student pilot himself, he offered tips on things he felt should be included and things to remove. My monologue about the stall characteristics of a Cessna 152 will just have to wait for another time.

A hearty thank you goes to my friend and fellow pilot, Amer Manzoor. We were students together and now we fly together. Chocks away, mate.

Now to a long list of individuals who all know how they played their part: Rob Sawyer, Dean Dashwood, Jonathan Fox, Nick Axeworthy, Neil White, Michael Cross, Mike Freeman, Pete Lodge, Andy Dyson, Julian Bunkerhill, Jack Welsh, Ian Simpson, Tom Kirkland and of course Matt Falcus. Thanks to each and all.

Finally, to my good friend Jon Brough. He was my guinea pig, though he didn't know that then. Jon was the first person to read *anything* of my fledgling book. As he started reading it, I'd watch for any reactions, listening for yawns or for laughs and I'd carefully watch his eyes in case they started to glaze over. Jon's positive comments about my musings were one of the main reasons I carried on writing beyond the first few chapters. Blame him.